Vocational Aspirations for Future Career

Vocational Aspirations for Future Career

Etash Ranjan

RANDOM

RANDOM PUBLICATIONS

NEW DELHI - 110 002 (INDIA)

Vocational Aspirations for Future Career

ISBN 978-93-51112-93-8

Published in 2014 in India by

RANDOM PUBLICATIONS

4376-A/4B, Gali Murari Lal, Ansari Road
New Delhi-110 002
Phone: +9111-43580356, 23289044
E-mail: randomexports@gmail.com; sales@randompublications.com; info@randompublications.com

Reprinted 2026

Type Setting by: Friends Media, Delhi-110089

Preface

In its most usual use, the word "vocation" refers to a strong feeling within an individual that they are meant to do a certain job. Sometimes people feel that they are "called" to a particular kind of life or work, such as nursing or a religious life. The word "vocation" can also be used to refer to a trade or profession. Vocational guidance is the process through which an individual is helped to choose a suitable occupation, make the necessary preparations for it (such as enrolling in a training programme), enter into it, and develop in it. This is a continuous process since an individual is likely to re-evaluate the career choice at various points in his/her life and may make changes at any point in his/her career. The word "career" is used to refer to one's progress through his/her working life, particularly in a certain profession or line of work. When we talk about a "career in teaching" or a "career in technology" we mean that a person will study and then work in teaching or in technology, perhaps changing jobs from time to time in the interests of advancement. The goals that one has for one's working life are called "career goals," and planning how we will reach them is called setting a "career path." Carpentry, engineering, nursing, hospitality, social work, banking, and farming are just a few of the many possible careers people might choose. From the earliest years of our lives, we are asked to consider what we want to be when we grow up. Parents and guardians carefully plan and manage their children's educational experiences in the hope of preparing them for successful careers.

As a caregiver, you are faced with the challenge of helping children and youth identify and achieve their career goals. Young people tend to have limited information about the types of jobs that are available to them. Lack of information leads many to make unrealistic decisions about careers. Many youth are not sure of what they want to do. Some of them are not even aware of their own talents. You can help them get the information they need to make realistic and satisfying career choices. Another of your roles as a caregiver is to help children and youth develop the qualities they need to be successful in the job market. Certain qualities can contribute to success, such as: the willingness to work hard and do more than the bare minimum; good spoken and written communication skills; dependability; and the ability to work well with others. Career guidance becomes more and more challenging as the realities of the workplace change. At one time the types of work available and the skills required changed very little from one generation to another. Now, times are changing so quickly that it's hard to predict what the next 20, 10, or even 5 years will bring. In these rapidly changing times, qualities such as flexibility, creativity, and the desire to be a lifelong learner have become important.

This book helps to explore ways that you as a caregiver can help children and youth to decide on a career plan and gain the skills and knowledge they need to be successful in the job market, now and in the future.

I thank all members of my team who have helped in the preparation of the book. My special thanks go to "Random Publications" who have published the book.

—Etash Ranjan

Contents

1

Vocational Education

Vocational education or Vocational Education and Training (VET), also called Career and Technical Education (CTE), prepares learners for jobs that are based in manual or practical activities, traditionally non-academic and totally related to a specific trade, occupation or vocation, hence the term, in which the learner participates. It is sometimes referred to as *technical education*, as the learner directly develops expertise in a particular group of techniques or technology.

Generally, vocation and career are used interchangeably. Vocational education might be classified as teaching procedural knowledge. This may be contrasted with declarative knowledge, as used in education in a usually broader scientific field, which might concentrate on theory and abstract conceptual knowledge, characteristic of tertiary education.

Vocational education can be at the secondary or post-secondary level and can interact with the apprenticeship system. Increasingly, vocational education can be recognised in terms of recognition of prior learning and partial academic credit towards tertiary education (e.g., at a university) as credit; however, it is rarely considered in its own form to fall under the traditional definition of a higher education.

Up until the end of the twentieth century, vocational education focused on specific trades such as for example, an automobile mechanic or welder, and was therefore associated with the activities of lower social classes. As a consequence, it attracted a level of stigma. Vocational education is related to the age-old apprenticeship system of learning.

However, as the labour market becomes more specialized and economies demand higher levels of skill, governments and businesses are increasingly investing in the future of vocational education through publicly funded training organizations and subsidized apprenticeship or traineeship initiatives for businesses. At the post-secondary level vocational education is typically provided by an institute of technology, or by a local community college.

Hope

Hope is the state which promotes the desire of positive outcomes related to events and circumstances in one's life or in the world at large. Despair is often regarded as the opposite of hope. Hope is the "feeling that what is wanted can be had or that events will turn out for the best" or the act of "look[ing] forward to something with desire and reasonable confidence" or "feel[ing] that something desired may happen". Other definitions are "to cherish a desire with anticipation"; "to desire with expectation of obtainment"; or "to expect with confidence". In the English language the word can be used as either a noun or a verb, although hope as a concept has a similar meaning in either use.

In Leadership

Leadership- Napoleon Bonaparte said, "A leader is a dealer in hope." Robert Mattox, social activist and futurist, proposes a social change theory based on the hope phenomenon. There is significant research on the ability of leadership to effect change, but little research exists that examines the conditions of leadership necessary to initiate and successfully lead change.

Many leadership theories presuppose that an individual who does the right things will be an effective leader. Dr. Larry Stout postulates that certain conditions must exist before even the most talented leaders can lead change. Dr. Stout highlights four conditions necessary to lead change:

1. people (who) 2. place (where) 3. position (what) 4. period (when) If a leader has a green light in all four conditions, they will be able to lead change.

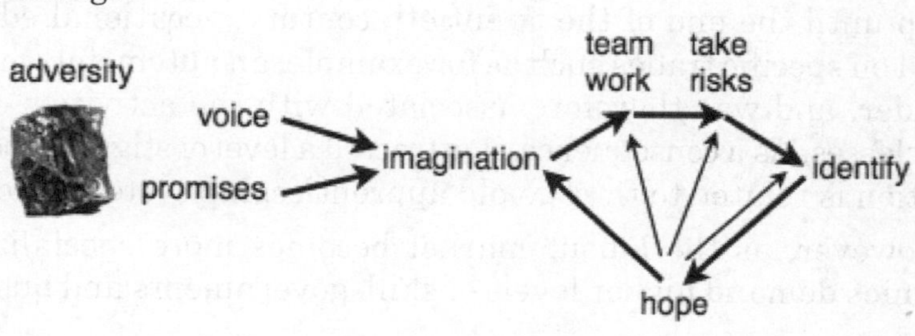

Considering these leadership conditions among other macro social change drivers, Robert Mattox proposes a change management theory. Dealers in Hope explores four leadership profiles- Steve Jobs, Barack Obama, Mike Morhaime, and the historical figure Moses who succeeded or failed to lead change based on whether or not they were a dealer in hope. Robert Mattox prescribes how a leader can lead change and shape culture within their community or organization by creating a hopescape and harnessing the hope system- illustrated using a "hope diamond" metaphor (from coal to diamond process).

In Psychology

Dr. Barbara L. Fredrickson, Principal Investigator of the Positive Emotions and Psychophysiology Lab and Professor at the University of North Carolina, Chapel Hill, argues that hope "...comes into play when our circumstances are dire", when "things are not going well or at least there's considerable uncertainty about how things will turn out". She states that "hope literally opens us up...[and] removes the blinders of fear and despair and allows us to see the big picture become creative" and have "belief in [a] better future".

"Psychologist, C.R. Snyder and his colleagues say that hope is cultivated when we have a goal in mind, determination that a goal can be reached, and a plan on how to reach those goals". Hopeful people are "like the little engine that could, [because] they keep telling themselves "I think I can, I think I can".

Hope is distinct from positive thinking, which refers to a therapeutic or systematic process used in psychology for reversing pessimism. The term "false hope" refers to a hope based entirely around a fantasy or an extremely unlikely outcome.

History of Hope

Alfred Adler said: "We cannot think, feel, will, or act without the perception of a goal"

Hope can first be seen in ancient Greek mythology with the story of Zeus and Prometheus. Prometheus stole fire from the god Zeus, which infuriated the supreme god. In turn, Zeus created a box that contained all manners of evil, unbeknownst to the receiver of the box. Pandora opened the box after being warned not to, and those evils were released into the world; hope, which lay at the bottom of the box, remained. This is the beginning of the tale of hope.

Understanding Hope

Charles Snyder, Ph.D, one of the first developers of positive psychology, embellished upon the overlaying topic of "hope" relaying its subject matter within a psychological construct. Snyder created his "hope theory" while on sabbatical from the University of Kansas. Instead of finding evidence in a book in the library, he was inspired to observe people and interact with them. Through his observations, Snyder was able to determine his own definition of "hope"; "Hope is the sum of the mental willpower and waypower that you have for your goals" Snyder continues his definition with these 3 underlying concepts:

- Goals: "Goals are objects, experiences, or outcomes that we imagine and desire in our minds." Snyder determines that "the goals involving hope fall somewhere between an impossibility and a sure thing."
- Willpower: "Willpower is the driving force in hopeful thinking" (pg.9) Willpower draws on the perception of our desired goal as well as one's mental energy. It also depends on how well we understand our goal. Within psychotherapy, techniques are used to home in on one's desires and wishes, on how to focus on our goals, on how to obtain or attain them, "...based on tacit knowledge."
- Waypower: "Waypower reflects the mental plans or road maps that guide hopeful thought" There are important versus less important goals that play a part in one's ability to plan through a goal, to map out a plan. Snyder says that hope is the "mental willpower and waypower for goals" Research has found that "persons with willpower thinking may not have waypower thoughts to their goals".

Measuring Hope

Several researchers, after defining their concept of hope, have devised ways of how to measure the actual psychological construct. Snyder's proposed "Hope Scale" measures a person's intended succession in congruence to their goals. Overall, their determination to achieve their goal is their measured hope.

Fibel and Hale measure hope by combining Snyder's Hope Scale with their own Generalized Expectancy for Success Scale (GESS) to empirically measure hope.

In Snyder's book, "Hope Theory", a differentiation between adult-measured hope and child-measured hope is given. The adult Hope Scale by Snyder contains 12 questions; 4 measuring 'pathways thinking', 4 measuring 'agency thinking', and 4 that are simply fillers. Each subject responds to each question using an 8-point scale.

Hope Versus Optimism

The difference between hope and optimism: hope entails pathways and thoughts to an intended goal. Optimism leads one to "expect the best, but it does not necessarily provide any critical thinking about how we are going to arrive at this improved future".

Snyder says that "we can best understand emotion and self-esteem as a by-product of how effective we are in the pursuit of goals".

Dr. Barbara Frederickson states that, "Because positive emotions arise in response to diffuse opportunities, rather than narrowly focused threats, positive emotions momentarily broaden people's attention and thinking, enabling them to draw on higher-level connections and a wider-than-usual range of percepts or ideas through cognitive, psychology, physical, or social resources". Frederickson is explaining hope in a moment of great need. With the sense of hope come positive emotions such as happiness and joy, courage, and empowerment. She describes these "positive emotions" as coming from four different areas of one's self: from a cognitive, psychological, social, or physical perspective.

In Philosophy

Contemporary Philosopher Richard Rorty understands hope as more than goal setting. Hope assumes a metanarrative, a story that serves as a promise or reason for expecting a better future. Rorty believes the Christian story and Marxism both proved to be false hopes because neither delivered. Jesus Christ promised to return but he hasn't. Communism promised equality for all but the economic system folded. Rorty says a new document of promise is needed for social hope to exist again.

As a Literary Concept

Hope is a common theme in cultural works across the world, and has a strong place in both classical and contemporary western literature as well as in works of world literature.

A classic reference which has generally entered modern language is the concept that "Hope springs eternal" taken from Alexander Pope's *Essay on Man*, the phrase reading "Hope springs eternal in the human breast, Man never is, but always *to be* blest:" Another popular reference, "Hope is the thing with feathers," is from a poem by Emily Dickinson.

Hope is a key concept in many classic and contemporary fictional works. It can be used as a plot device and is often a motivating force for change in dynamic characters. A commonly understood reference from western popular culture is the subtitle "A New Hope" from the original first installment (now considered Episode IV) in the Star Wars science fiction space opera. The subtitle refers to one of the lead characters, Luke Skywalker, who is expected in the future to allow good to triumph over evil within the plot of the films.

Symbolism

The anchor symbolises hope. This is because a seaman's last resort would be putting the anchor down. A dove also symbolises hope.

In Religion

Hope is a key concept in most major world religions, often signifying the "hoper" believes an individual or a collective group will reach a concept of heaven.

In Christianity

"In many traditional Christian texts, the word is an indication of certainty and a positive expectation of future reward. "Hope" in the HolyBible means "a strong and confident expectation." Though archaic today in modern terms, hope is akin to trust and a confident expectation". The author of the book of Romans, Paul the Apostle, argued that hope was a source of salvation for Christians. Romans 8:24-25 states "For in hope we have been saved, but hope that is seen is not hope; for why does one also hope for what he sees? 25 But if we hope for what we do not see, with perseverance we wait eagerly for it".

According to the *Holman Bible Dictionary*, hope is a "[t]rustful expectation, particularly with reference to the fulfillment of God's promises. Hope, is the anticipation of a favourable outcome under God's guidance[;]... the confidence that what God has done for us in the past guarantees our participation in what God will do in the future.

The concept is considered one of the three theological virtues of the Christian religion. "Hope is an essential and fundamental element of Christian life, so essential indeed, that, like faith and love, it can itself designate the essence of Christianity".

Teaching as a Vocation

One of the most important things that teachers should always keep in mind is the fact that teaching is not only a profession but also considered as a vocation. None of them could become effective and efficient teachers if they will only work for the sake of the degree that they have earned in college or just for the sake of the salary they get from their employers.

So that we can see why teaching is considered as a vocation, first, let's take a look at the difference between profession and vocation. According to the Oxford dictionary, "profession" is a paid occupation that involves prolonged training and a formal qualification while "vocation" is a strong feeling of suitability for a particular career or occupation, especially regarded as worthy and requiring dedication.

If we are going to see the difference between this two, profession is more of the work needed to be done for a salary. In contrast, vocation is more of the work that needs to be done not for salary but for service. And if we will be evaluating those two words deeper, both of them involve work but only one emphasizes dedication – which is vocation.

Yes, anyone can become a sales lady but not everyone can become a priest. Anyone can work over time but not everyone can go to mountains and serve those needy people. Therefore, a vocation is only for some who are really dedicated not just to work but also to serve other people.

Teacher Mark is treated as a teacher for teaching his students the lessons every day. He teaches everything he knows, showing off his mastery of the subject, but not even considering the feelings of his students towards difficult topics. On the other hand, a volunteer named Joy is addressed as a teacher for teaching and serving the children of a far rural community.

She travels almost 20 kilometres everyday for the sake of her students learning and development. Who do you think practices teaching as a vocation? That's right, it's Joy. Although Mark is doing everything professionally as a teacher, still he forgets something which is more important than teaching. And that is service, which Joy really shows in her deeds towards her work and towards the people whom she's working with.

Teaching is technically a profession where it normally involves occupation and the salary that is being awarded to a teacher after hard days of work. However, unlike any other profession, it requires dedication and service in order for an individual to be considered as a real teacher. That's the reason why teaching should not just be treated as a simple profession but also a serious vocation where other people and service is over self and salary.

Need and Objectives of Providing Educational Guidance to Students

The need and objective of educational guidance can be properly discussed in the light of above discussion: However, we can summarize the reasons for the justification of such guidance at the present juncture in the following way:

Need of Checking the Wastage and Stagnation in Education: We find that there is a huge wastage and stagnation in education. Many students fail repeatedly and remain in the same class for a number of years. They feel difficulty in learning or acquiring some or the other piece of knowledge and skill. It leads to the wastage of human as well as national resources. Such wastage and stagnation can only be checked through a suitable programme of educational guidance.

Need of Realizing the Aims and Objectives of Education: The function is now not limited to impart mere instruction in some school subjects. It has a quite brooder base. The all round progressive and harmonious and development of all the innate abilities and capacities of an individual is only possible through a well organized programme of educational guidance. With its help the teachers can realize the maximum educational development of their children within the specific time and limited resources.

The Need of Making Right Educational Choices: Educational guidance is necessary for making right educational choices. The students, while taking education, are, often, confronted with the problem of making selection or choice. There are diversified courses where they have to make selection of the subjects or activities.

The wrong choice of a subject or activity may doom their career and future. Therefore, they should be helped by guidance in making right choice with regard to subjects or courses of study, co-curricular activities, methods of learning, style of speaking, writing and reading and books and other literature for study etc.

The Need of Proper Educational Adjustment: Adjustment to prevailing educational environment is essential for the proper educational growth and well being of children. The child enters the school directly from his home environment. Here he finds a formal environment of education and gels experiences that are quite novel and strange to him. He needs to be adjusted to these educational situation:, and environmental conditions. He has to read, write, speak and participate in the learning process.

Drill work and home assignments have to be complete. Participation in co-curricular activities is required. Regularity and punctuality in educational process is to be observed. Some times he has to drive-benefit from the new techniques and devices of teaching. He has to prepare himself for the desired tests and evaluation. In this way the child faces so many adjustment problems with regard to his educational environment and therefore needs proper educational guidance.

Teaching Guidance and Counselling in Schools.

Guidance and counselling is a very important programme in our schools. It is the process by which students are given advice on how to deal with emotional conflicts and personal problems both in school and how to incorporate the same in their daily life. Some sessions involve career guidance where students are advised on which courses to do and which jobs to expect when one does a particular course. The following are some of the benefits of guidance and counselling:

1. Students are given solutions on how to deal with psychological problems which might affect their studies. Through this, the students are able to develop problem solving skills which to an extent helps them deal with particular issues surrounding their lives.
2. Students are advised on how to cope with different situations facing them in their school life. For instance, on how to relate with their peers.
3. It helps to shape a student's behaviour and instill discipline in students. Students who are guided and counselled in a right way tend to know what to do and how to do such things.
4. Students get to learn how to live in harmony with others in the school community. In so doing, they also learn to appreciate the people around the and come to harmony with their environment.
5. It bridges the gap between the students and the school administration, since can channel their problems through guidance and counselling office.
6. Students get comprehensive pieces of advice on careers, courses and jobs which enables them to have an informed choice on what to do after school.

It allows students to talk about various things which they feel uncomfortable talking about with their parents which include things like drug abuse. It also allows the students to become better people because they are taught by the counsellors about how to behave in a proper manner.

It enables students undergoing difficulty in their lives have a good place to ask for questions and clarity from the guiding and counselling office. There are some questions that one may find difficult to ask even his/her parents. One can ask any question without fear because the persons in charge are very willing to help.

Career Construction Theory

Career construction theory provides a way of thinking about how individuals choose and use work. The theory presents a model for comprehending vocational behaviour across the life-cycle as well as methods and materials that career counsellors use to help clients make vocational choices and maintain successful and satisfying work lives. It seeks to be comprehensive in its purview by taking three perspectives on vocational behaviour: the differential, developmental, and dynamic. From the perspective of individual differences psychology, it examines the content of vocational personality types and *what* different people prefer to do. From the perspective of developmental psychology, it examines the process of psychosocial adaptation and *how* individuals cope with vocational development tasks, occupational transitions, and work traumas. From the perspective of narrative psychology, it examines the dynamics by which life themes impose meaning on vocational behaviour and *why* individuals fit work into their lives in distinct ways. In coordination, the three perspectives enable counsellors and researchers to survey how individuals construct their careers by using life themes to integrate the self-organization of personality and the self-extension of career adaptability into a self-defining whole that animates work, directs occupational choice, and shapes vocational adjustment.

Rationale

Career construction theory is one of many career theories that seek to explain occupational choice and work adjustment, each interrogating a different aspect of vocational behaviour. Career theories that have risen to prominence have done so because they effectively address important questions. For example, the model of person-environment fit emerged early in the 20th century to address the question of how to match workers to work. The model of vocational development emerged in the middle of the 20th century to address the question of how to advance a career in one organization or profession.

These theories of vocational personality types and vocational development tasks remain useful today when considering how to match workers to work and develop a career in an organization. However, the global economy of the 21st century poses new questions about career, especially the question of how individuals can negotiate a lifetime of job changes without losing their sense of self and social identity.

Career construction theory responds to the needs of today's mobile workers who may feel fragmented and confused as they encounter a restructuring of occupations, transformation of the labour force, and multicultural imperatives. This fundamental reshaping of the work world is making it increasingly difficult to comprehend careers with just person-environment and vocational development models that emphasize commitment and stability rather than flexibility and mobility. The new job market in our unsettled economy calls for viewing career not as a lifetime commitment to one employer but as selling services and skills to a series of employers who need projects completed. In negotiating each new project, the prospective employee usually concentrates on salary yet also seeks to make the work meaningful, control the work environment, balance work-family responsibilities, and train for the next job.

While the form of career changes from stability to mobility to reflect the labour needs of post-industrial societies, career construction theory seeks to retain and renovate the best concepts and research from the 20th century career models for use in the 21st century. For example, instead of measuring personality traits as realist concepts and trying to prove construct validity, the theory concentrates on how individuals use what they have. In replacing scores with stories, career construction theory focuses on how individuals use their vocational personality to adapt to a sequence of job changes while remaining faithful to oneself and recognizable by others. The theory does this by focusing on the meaning that structures an individual's career as it plays out across the ten or more different jobs that a worker today can expect to occupy during her or his work life.

Life Themes

Career construction theory, simply stated, holds that individuals build their careers by imposing meaning on vocational behaviour. Personality types and developmental transitions deal with what a person has done and how they have done it. However, they do not address the question of why they do what they do, nor do they focus on the spirit that animates nor the values that guide the manifold choices and adjustments that build a career. Thus, career construction theory emphasizes the interpretive and interpersonal processes through which individuals impose meaning and direction on their vocational behaviour. It uses social constructionism as a meta-theory with which to reconceptualize vocational personality types and vocational development tasks as processes that have possibilities, not realities that predict the future. From a constructionist viewpoint, career, or more precisely subjective career, denotes a moving perspective that imposes personal meaning on past memories, present experiences, and future aspirations by weaving them into a pattern that portrays a life theme. Thus, the subjective career that guides, regulates, and sustains vocational behaviour emerges from an active process of making meaning, not discovering preexisting facts.

The life theme component of career construction theory addresses the subject matter of work life and focuses on the *why* of vocational behaviour. Career stories reveal the themes that individuals use to make meaningful choices and adjust to work roles. By dealing with the *why* of life themes along with the *what* of personality types and the *how* of career adaptability, career construction seeks to be comprehensive in its purview. Although the content of personality and process of adaptation are both important, studying vocational personality and career adaptability as separate variables misses the dynamics that integrate personality and adaptability into a self-defined whole. The essential meaning of a career, and the dynamics of its construction, are revealed in self-defining stories about the vocational development tasks, occupational transitions, and work traumas that an individual has faced. In chronicling the recursive interplay between self and society, career stories explain why individuals make the choices that they do and the private meaning that guides these choices. From these prototypical stories about work life, counsellors attempt to comprehend the life themes that construct careers and understand the motives and meaning that pattern work life.

The life theme component of career construction theory emerged from Donald E. Super's postulate that in expressing vocational preferences, individuals put into occupational terminology their ideas of the kind of people they are; that in entering an occupation, they seek to implement a concept of themselves; and that after stabilizing in an occupation, they seek to realize their potential and preserve self-esteem. This core postulate leads to the conceptualization of occupational choice as implementing a self-concept, work as a manifestation of selfhood, and vocational development as a continuing process of improving the match between the self and situation. From this perspective on the self, work provides a context for human development and an important location in each individual's life, a place that matters.

The life theme perspective highlights the view that careers are about *mattering*. Counselling for career construction aims to help clients understand how their life project matters to themselves and to other people. In career construction theory, the theme is what matters in the life story. It consists of what is at stake in that person's life. On the one hand, the theme matters to individuals in that it gives meaning and purpose to their work. It makes them care about what they do. On the other hand, what they do and contribute to society matters to other people. The belief that what they do matters to others sharpens identity and promotes a sense of social meaning and relatedness. What individuals choose to do is the subject matter of vocational personality.

Vocational Personality

Vocational personality refers to an individual's career-related abilities, needs, values, and interests. Individuals form personalities in their families of origin and develop these personalities in the neighbourhood and school as they prepare to eventually enter the work world. Before these characteristics are expressed in occupations, they are rehearsed in activities such as household chores, games, hobbies, reading, and studying.

Career construction theory prefers to view interests and other career-related "traits" as strategies for adapting rather than as realist categories. Concepts such as interests should not be reified as factors or traits. They do not reside within an individual and they cannot be excavated from within by interest inventories. They should not be treated as objects by counsellors; they are verbs not nouns. Career-related abilities, interests, and values are relational phenomena that reflect socially-constituted meanings. They are dynamic processes that present possibilities, not stable traits that predict the future. From this perspective, individuals can adopt or drop selected strategies as situations call for them. Of course, long-practised strategies do coalesce into a tested style. This style can be compared to that of other people to form types or groups, but these socially-constructed categories should not be privileged as anything more than similarities.

Career construction theory asserts that vocational personality types and occupational interests are simply *resemblances* to socially-constructed clusters of attitudes and skills. They have no reality or truth value outside themselves because they depend on the social constructions of time, place and culture that support them. Regulated similarities in work environments produce vocational personality types and occupational groups from among individuals with heterogeneous potentials. Thus, career construction theory regards vocational personality types and occupational interests as relational phenomena that reflect emergent and socially-constituted meanings. For this reason, career construction theory views vocational personality as an individual's *reputation* among a group of people. Accordingly, the theory concentrates on what individuals can become in doing work, not what they are before they go to work. Work, as a context for human development, provides the outer form of something intensely private; it is the bridge between public and private. Crossing the bridge between self and society is called adaptation.

Career Adaptability

In concert with life themes and vocational personality, the third central component in career construction theory is career adaptability. Life themes guide the expression of personality in work, while the expression itself is managed by the process of career adaptation. Viewing career construction as a series of attempts to implement a self--concept in social roles focuses attention on adaptation- to a series of transitions from school to work, from job to job, and from occupation to occupation. Career construction theory views adaptation to these transitions as fostered by five principal types of behaviours: orientation, exploration, establishment, management, and disengagement. These constructive activities form a cycle of adaptation that is periodically repeated as new transitions appear on the horizon. As each transition approaches, individuals can adapt more effectively if they meet the change with growing awareness, information-seeking followed by informed decision making, trial behaviours leading to a stable commitment projected forward for a certain time period, active role management, and eventually forward-looking deceleration and disengagement. For example, an employee begins a new job with a period of growth in the new role, including ex-ploration of the requirements, routines, and rewards of that role. Then she becomes established in the role, manages- the role for a certain time period, and eventually dis-engages from it either voluntarily when further growth readies her to change jobs or involuntarily when organizational changes make her position redundant. In post-industrial economies people do not work at one job for thirty years. New technology, globalization, and job redesign require workers to more actively construct their careers. They change jobs often and make frequent transitions, each time repeating the cycle of orientation, exploration, stabilization, management, and disengagement. The ability to adapt to new circumstances is enhanced by certain coping resources for solving the unfamiliar, complex, and ill-defined problems presented by developmental tasks, occupational transitions, and work traumas.

In considering adaptability, career construction theory highlights a set of specific attitudes, beliefs, and competencies – the ABCs of career construction— which shape the actual problem-solving strategies and coping behaviours that individuals use to synthesize their vocational self-concepts with work roles. The ABCs are grouped into four dimensions of adaptability: concern, control, curiosity, and confidence. Thus, the adaptive individual is conceptualized as (a) becoming *concerned* about the vocational future, (b) increasing personal *control* over one's vocational future, (c) displaying *curiosity* by exploring possible selves and future scenarios, and (d) strengthening the *confidence* to pursue one's aspirations. Increasing a client's career adaptablity is a central goal in the goal of career construction counselling.

Counselling For Career Construction

Counselling for career construction begins with an interview that poses a uniform set of questions to a client. The *Career Style Interview* elicits self-defining stories that enable counsellors to identify and appreciate the thematic unity in a client's life. In addition to revealing the life theme, data from a *Career Style Interview* also manifest the client's vocational personality and career adaptability.

It is critical that neither the counsellor nor the client view the career stories as determining the future; instead, they should view storying as an active attempt at making meaning and shaping the future. The stories guide adaptation by evaluating opportunities and constraints as well as by using vocational personality traits to address tasks, transitions, and traumas. In telling their stories, clients are re-membering the past in a way that constructs a possible future. Clients seem to tell counsellors the stories that they themselves need to hear; from all their available stories, they narrate those stories that support current goals and inspire action. Rather than reporting historical facts, individuals reconstruct the past so that prior events support current choices and lay the groundwork for future moves. This narrative truth often differs from historical truth because it fictionalizes the past in order to preserve dispositional continuity and coherence in the face of psychosocial change.

In attempting to discern the life theme while listening to an individual's career stories, counsellors and researchers can become disoriented by the numerous particulars of a life. To prevent becoming confused by a client's complexities and contradictions, they can listen not for the facts but for the glue that holds the facts together as they try to hear the theme or secret that makes a whole of the life. Arranging the seemingly random actions and incidents reported in career stories into a plot can be done in many ways. Career construction theory proposes for this purpose that the listener try to hear the quintessence of the stories a client tells. Counsellors and researchers approach this task by assuming that the archetypal theme of career construction involves turning a personal preoccupation into a public occupation. As they listen to a client narrate his or her stories, they concentrate on identifying and understanding his or her personal paradigm for turning essence into interest, tension into intention, and obsession into profession. The progress narrative in the 20th century career model that told about climbing the occupational ladder is thus transformed into a progress narrative that tells how individuals can use work to actively master what they have passively suffered and thus move from a felt minus to a perceived plus. Thus, in its counselling application, career construction theory assists clients to fully inhabit their lives and become more complete as they sustain themselves and contribute to their communities.

2

Aspiration Management

Psychologist David McClelland studied workplace motivation extensively and theorized that workers as well as their superiors have needs that influence their performance at work. One of these needs is Achievement Motivation - which can be defined as an individual's need to meet realistic goals, receive feedback and experience a sense of accomplishment. To create a work environment that helps employees experience a sense of accomplishment, we need to understand employee aspirations and provide the means to accomplishment, through aspiration management. According to McClelland, understanding human motivation ought to be a good thing as it opens up opportunities of self-development if we apply motivational principles to pursuing our goals in life.

Aspirations and Goals

Many people view Goals and Aspirations to be similar, but they are quite different. The origin of the word "goal" comes from the Old English word "gol" which means obstacle or boundary, and is related to the world gælan which is "to hinder." We typically use goals as a way of overcoming these barriers. Think about sports, such as American football. You push hard and struggle to move the ball past 400 pound linebackers with the ultimate objective to move past the goal line; your destination.

Conversely, look up "aspiration" and you will find that its origins are similar to the words "spirit" and "inspire". They are all derived at some level from the Latin word aspirare which means "to breathe upon." It is believed that the connotation is "to breath life into" or "panting with desire." Quite simply put, goals are logical and calculated. Aspirations are emotional and inspirational.

Goals are typically about convergence, narrowing, and focusing in on an outcome. On the other hand, aspirations are expansive. They create new possibilities. There are many paths and options for you. And you have a wide peripheral vision, sensing new opportunities as they arise. In other words, Aspirations are emotional and inspirational, panting with desire. It is the inspirationally felt need that the individual aspires to achieve. It talks about "What" to achieve. Goals provide the specific direction to achieve an aspiration. This talks about "How" to achieve. The vision of a CEO is aspiraitonal and hence it inspires the team which works towards actualizing it. It tells you "What" to achieve. It is inspirational and hence motivates the team to breath life into and make the vision a reality. Aligning people to the business vision or goal alignment in aspiration management context is about creating the right balance between organizational and individual aspirations and goals which in turn creates the synergy that helps the team panting with desire to work towards aspiration actualization of both the organization and self.

Vision outlines what the organization wants to be, or how it wants the world in which it operates to be (an "idealized" view of the world). It is a long-term view and concentrates on the future. It can be emotive and is a source of inspiration. For example, a charity working with the poor might have a vision statement which reads "A World without Poverty." In a business context, the business strategy and business plan defines the goals which talks about how to get there. Once goals are defined, it has its own boundaries with the many obstacle that needs to be overcome as we move towards actualization.

Employee Aspirations and Self-Actualization

The term Self-actualization was originally introduced by the organismic theorist Kurt Goldstein for the motive to realize one's full potential. In his view, "the tendency to actualize itself as fully as possible is the basic drive...the drive of self-actualization." However, the concept was brought most fully to prominence in Abraham Maslow's hierarchy of needs theory as the final level of psychological development that can be achieved when all basic and mental needs are fulfilled and the "actualization" of the full personal potential takes place. As each individual progressed towards self-actualization, all of Maslow's subjects reported the frequent occurrence of peak experiences (temporary moments of self-actualization). These occasions were marked by feelings of ecstasy, harmony, and deep meaning.

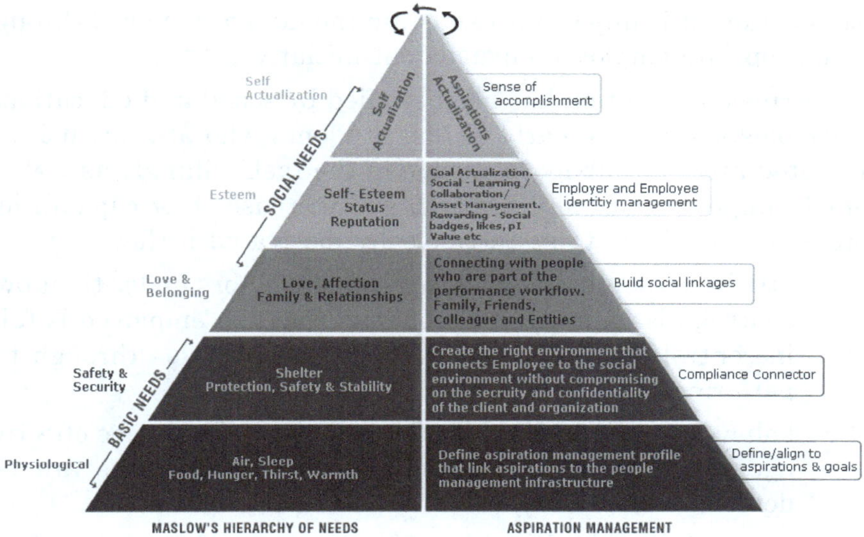

Figure: *Hierarchy of Needs and Aspiration Management.*

These temporal moments of peak experience happens as frequently as the aspirations and goals related to Physiological, Safety, Belongingness and Love, Esteem, and Self-Actualization needs are actualized or accomplished.

Motivation Theories and Employee Aspiration Management

Motivation plays a critical role in influencing workplace behaviour and performance. At one time, employees were considered just another input into the production of goods and services. It is key for organizations to understand and to structure the work environment to encourage productive behaviours and discourage unproductive behaviour. Carl Rogers wrote of "the curative force in psychotherapy - *man's tendency to actualize himself, to become his potentialities...*to express and activate all the capacities of the organism." There are many motivation theories that contribute towards structuring the work environment that fosters individual and team Aspirations Management so that they can actualize their fullest potentialities.

Motivation Concepts

Intrinsic and Extrinsic Motivation: Intrinsic motivation refers to motivation that is driven by an interest or enjoyment in the task itself, and exists within the individual rather than relying on any external pressure or stimulus. For example, an employee who actualizes his or her career aspiration is intrinsically motivated to put in their best efforts as it provides the peak experience of aspirations actualization. It is important to sustain the motivation level through the appropriate employee engagement initiatives.

Intrinsic motivation has been studied by social and educational psychologists since the early 1970s. Students who are intrinsically motivated are more likely to engage in the task willingly as well as work to improve their skills, which will increase their capabilities. Employees are likely to be intrinsically motivated if they:

- attribute their employment results to factors under their own control, also known as autonomy, that the employee is fully in control of all dependencies with other roles through the performance workflow environment.
- believe they have the skill that will allow them to be effective agents in reaching desired goals (i.e. the results are not determined by luck),
- are ambitious, self-motivated, exercise self-control and are interested in mastering their role and performing, rather than performing just for the incentives. (Douglas McGregor theory Y)

Extrinsic motivation refers to the performance of an activity in order to attain an outcome. Motives can be divided into two types: external and internal. Internal motives are considered as the needs that every human being experience, while external indicate the presence of specific situations where these needs arise. Extrinsic motivation comes from outside of the individual. Common extrinsic motivations are rewards like money and grades, coercion and threat of punishment. Competition is in general extrinsic because it encourages the performer to win and beat others, not to enjoy the intrinsic rewards of the activity. A crowd cheering on the individual and trophies are also extrinsic incentives.

Social psychological research has indicated that extrinsic rewards can lead to overjustification and a subsequent reduction in intrinsic motivation. In one study demonstrating this effect, children who expected to be (and were) rewarded with a ribbon and a gold star for drawing pictures spent less time playing with the drawing materials in subsequent observations than children who were assigned to an unexpected reward condition. For those children who received no extrinsic reward, self-determination theory proposes that extrinsic motivation can be internalized by the individual if the task fits with their values and beliefs and therefore helps to fulfill their basic psychological needs.

Theories of Motivation and Aspiration Actualization

There are many theories of motivation which include, Abraham Maslow's hierarchy of needs, Herzberg's two-factor theory. Alderfer's ERG theory, Goal-setting theory, Models of behaviour change, Organismic theory, theory X and theory Y. These are some of the motivation theories that has an influence on employee aspirations actualization and work motivation.

Kurt Goldstein's Theory

Kurt Goldstein's book *The Organism: A Holistic Approach to Biology Derived from Pathological Data in Man* (1939), presented self-actualization as "the tendency to actualize, as much as possible, [the organism's] individual capacities" in the world. The tendency towards self-actualization is "the only drive by which the life of an organism is determined". However, for Goldstein self-actualization cannot be understood as a kind of goal to be reached sometime in the future. At any moment the organism has the fundamental tendency to actualize all its capacities, its whole potential, as it is present in exactly that moment in exactly that situation in contact with the world under the given circumstances. From Goldstein's theory, if an individual has an aspiration, he or she has "the tendency to actualize, as much as possible, to the individual capacities."

Behavioural Approach to Motivation

The behavioural approach to workplace motivation is known as Organizational Behavioural Modification. This approach applies the tenets of behaviourism developed by B.F. Skinner to promote employee behaviours that an employer deems beneficial and discourage those that are not. Any stimulus that increases the likelihood of a behaviour increasing is a reinforcer. An effective use of positive reinforcement would be frequent praise while an employee is learning a new task. An employee's behaviour can also be shaped during the learning process if approximations of the ideal behaviour are praised or rewarded. The frequency of reinforcement is an important consideration. While frequent praise during the learning process can be beneficial, it can be hard to sustain indefinitely.

A variable-ratio schedule of reinforcement, where the frequency of reinforcement varies unpredictably, can be also be highly effective if used in instances where it is ethical to do so. Providing praise on a variable-ratio schedule would be appropriate, whereas paying an employee on an unpredictable variable-ratio schedule would not be. Compensation and other reward programmes provide behavioural reinforcement, and if carefully crafted, can provide powerful incentives to employees. Behavioural principles can also be used to address undesirable behaviours in the workplace, but punishment should be used judiciously. If overused, punishment can negatively impact employee's perception of fairness in the workplace. In general, the less time that elapses between a behaviour and its consequence, the more impactful a consequence is likely to be. This theory highlights the importance of various reinforcers that can help improve performance and optimize productivity.

Maslow's Hierarchy of Needs

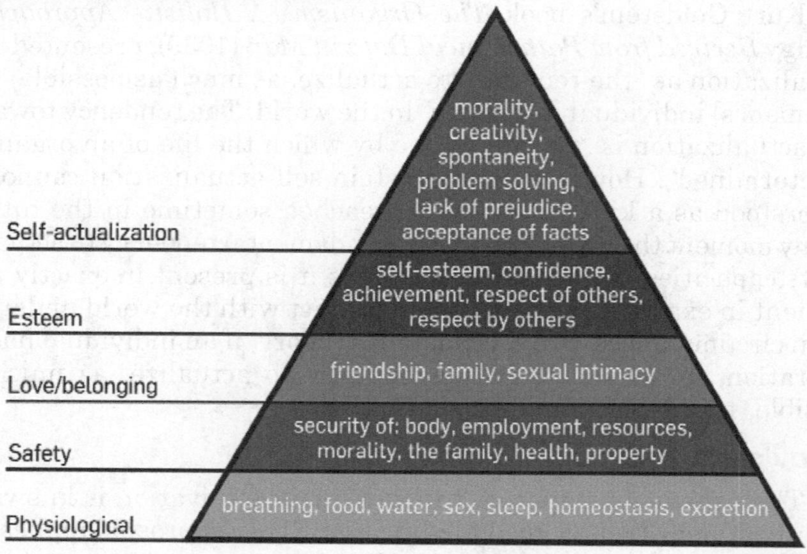

***Figure:** An interpretation of Maslow's hierarchy of needs, represented as a pyramid with the more basic needs at the bottom.*

Maslow's hierarchy of needs is a theory in psychology, proposed by Abraham Maslow in his 1943 paper "A Theory of Human Motivation." Maslow subsequently extended the idea to include his observations of humans' innate curiosity. His theories parallel many other theories of human developmental psychology, all of which focus on describing the stages of growth in humans. Maslow use the terms Physiological, Safety, Belongingness and Love, Esteem, and Self-Actualization needs to describe the pattern that human motivations generally move through.

The term Self-actualization was originally introduced by the organismic theorist Kurt Goldstein for the motive to realize one's full potential. In his view, "the tendency to actualize itself as fully as possible is the basic drive...the drive of self-actualization." Carl Rogers similarly wrote of "the curative force in psychotherapy - *man's tendency to actualize himself, to become his potentialities*...to express and activate all the capacities of the organism." However, the concept was brought most fully to prominence in Abraham Maslow's hierarchy of needs theory as the final level of psychological development that can be achieved when all basic and mental needs are fulfilled and the "actualization" of the full personal potential takes place.

The term was later used by Abraham Maslow in his article, *A Theory of Human Motivation*, Maslow explicitly defines self-actualization to be "the desire for self-fulfillment, to become actualized in what he is potentially. Maslow used the term self-actualization to describe a desire, not a driving force, that could lead to realizing one's capabilities. Maslow did not feel that self-actualization determined one's life; rather, he felt that it gave the individual a desire, or motivation to achieve budding ambitions. Each individual is motivated to work towards actualizing their aspiration or ambitions. All of Maslow's subjects reported the frequent occurrence of peak experiences (temporary moments of self-actualization). These occasions were marked by feelings of ecstasy, harmony, and deep meaning.

Goal-setting Theory

Employers and Managers need to designing task-related goals for their employees that are:

- attainable
- specific
- appropriately difficult,
- feedback providing

in hopes of rousing tunnel vision focus in the employees. Following S.M.A.R.T criteria is also suggested.

Letter	*Major Term*	*Minor Terms*
S	Specific	Significant, Stretching, Simple
M	Measurable	Meaningful, Motivational, Manageable
A	Attainable	Appropriate, Achievable, Agreed, Assignable, Actionable, Ambitious, Aligned, Aspirational, Acceptable, Action-focused
R	Relevant	Results-oriented, Realistic, Resourced, Resonant
T	Timely	Time-oriented, Time framed, Timed, Time-based, Timeboxed, Time-bound, Time-Specific, Timetabled, Time limited, Trackable, Tangible

Studies have shown both feedback from the employer and self-efficacy (belief in one's capabilities to achieve a goal) within the employee must be present for goal-setting to be effective. However, because of the tunnel vision focus created by goal-setting theory, several studies have shown this motivational theory may not be applicable in all situations. In fact, in tasks that require creative on-the-spot improvising, goal-setting can even be counterproductive. Furthermore, because clear goal specificity is essential to a properly designed goal-setting task, multiple goals can create confusion for the employee and the end result is a muted overall drive. Despite its flaws, Goal-setting Theory is arguably the most dominant theory in the field of I–O psychology; over one thousand articles and reviews published in just over thirty years.

Locke suggested several reasons why goals are motivating: they direct attention, lead to task persistence and the development of task strategies for accomplishing the goal. In order for a goal to be motivating, the employee or work group must first accept the goal. While difficult goals can be more motivating, a goal still needs to appear achievable, which in turn will lead to greater goal acceptance. The person or group should have the necessary skills and resources to achieve the goal, or goal acceptance could be negatively impacted. Specific goals that set a performance expectation are more motivating than those that are vague. Similarly, more proximal goals have greater motivation impact than those that are very long range or distal goals. Hence if an employee has a personal or organizational goal which is proximal and that leads to actualizing an aspiration, they will be motivated to work towards actualizing those goals. It can be a personal goal based task of getting a credit card, to an organization goal of based task of filling a timesheet. Since the organization attaches a performance indicator value for encouraging employees towards accomplishing organizational goals through the performance management and rewards system, the employee is motivated to take up those rewarding proximal goals on priority. Feedback while the employee or group is striving for the goal is seen as crucial. Feedback keeps employees on track and reinforces the importance of the goal as well as supporting the employees in adjusting their task strategies.

Goal-setting Theory has strong empirical support dating back thirty years. However, there are some boundary conditions that indicate in some situations, goal-setting can be detrimental to performance on certain types of tasks. Goals require a narrowing of one's focus, so for more complex or creative tasks, goals can actually inhibit performance because they demand cognitive resources. Finally, too many goals can become distracting and counterproductive, especially if they conflict with one another and hence a day to day performance management strategy is needed to ensure that too many long terms goals don't distract and become counterproductive.

Holistic Work Motivation and Aspiration Management

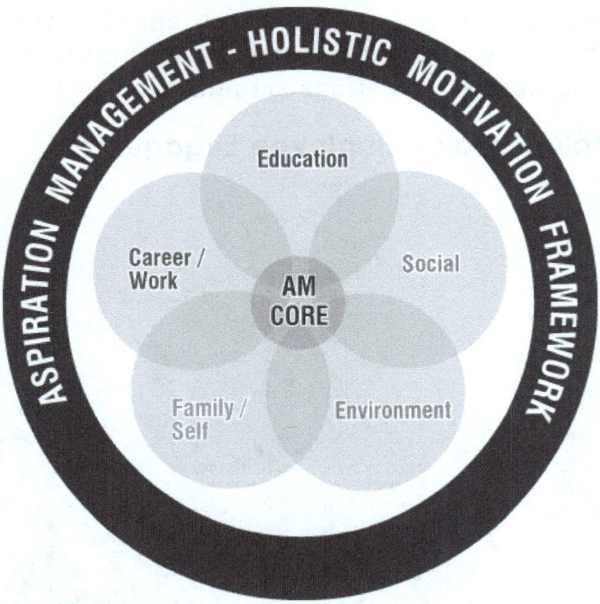

Figure: *Holistic Motivation Framework.*

Work motivation "is a set of energetic forces that originate both within as well as beyond an individual's being, to initiate work-related behaviour, and to determine its form, direction, intensity, and duration". A holistic work motivation environment fosters both intrinsic motivation and extrinsic motivation. The external stimulus comes from peers, organization and managers. The internal stimulus is driven by the inner drive to work towards each individuals aspiration. Employee aspiration management driven work environment provides a holistic motivation work environment by providing both Intrinsic and extrinsic motivation stimulus for motivating employees so that excess extrinsic rewards does not lead to overjustification and subsequent reduction in intrinsic motivation.

Aspiration's management is based on the assumption that each individual is motivated to work towards actualizing their aspiration and that productivity can be optimized by providing an organizational infrastructure or work culture that fosters employee aspirations actualization. Aspiration's management is a people management methodology and is built on a framework that focuses on the need and urge of individual's to actualize their aspirations and considers an employee as a whole (part of society with multiple roles) and not just as a resource or capital which is part of an organization or corporate who will perform, if remunerated. It tries to built in the theories of motivation and provides a system which enriches the core people management systems of an organization by linking to many peripheral interfaces that fosters aspirations actualization.

Work Life Balance and Employee Engagement

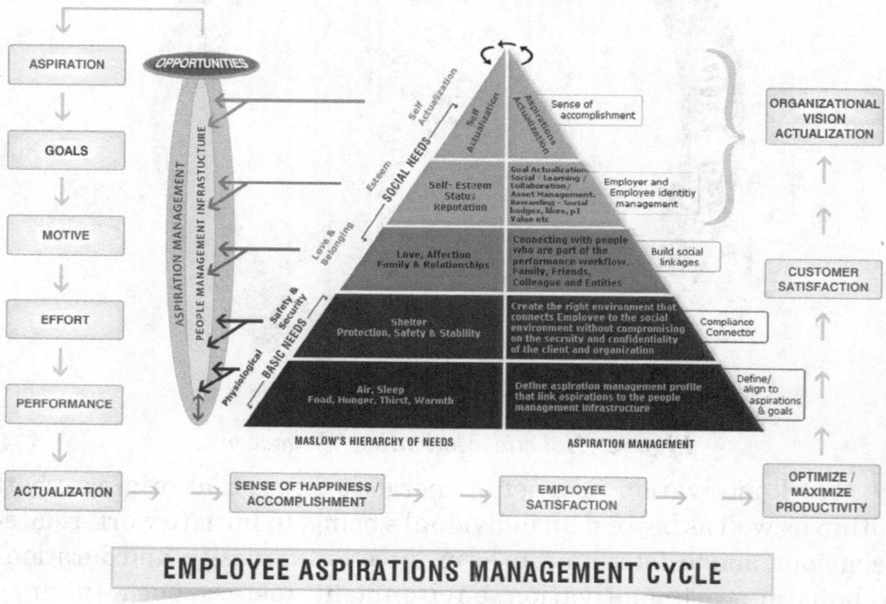

Figure: *Employee Aspiration Management Cycle.*

Based on the multiple roles that an individual has in life, an Employee has multiple role based aspirations. The organization through its recruitment, career planning or the succession planning process identifies the right fit (career aspiration fitment) from within the organization or from the potential talent pool to help actualize the organizations aspirations (vision). Managing these helps aligns organizational vision to individual needs by providing an organizational environment or infrastructure that helps employees actualize their goals as they contributing to the success of the organization. This alignment is deployed through the aspirations management system, which supports implementation of Aspirations management. The integration of the core people management infrastructure and the multiple peripheral interfaces collectively form the Aspirations Management System that generates opportunities within the system for employees to actualize their goals.

Every level in the hierarchy of employee needs has an aspiration and goal actualization cycle, which leads to employee satisfaction, productivity maximization, and ultimately creating a work culture that improves the emotional connect between organization (role, peers, managers, work environment) and employees, and hence creating engaged employees who contribute towards the business vision. This integration needs to provide maximum opportunities for the employees to actualize their needs, which can be provided for any of the level in the hierarchy of employee needs. The objective is to strike the right balance between the organizational growth opportunities (career aspirations) and social opportunities (personal aspirations) that the organization intents to provides through the system.

Personnel Management – Human Resource Management – Human Capital Management – Aspiration Management

The transition from personnel management, Human Resources Management, Human Capital Management to Aspiration Management needs to be viewed through the prism of people management in changing times and in context of the industry that is being studied. Personnel Management was seen as being administrative in nature and the Personnel Administration team was expected to ensure that the needs of the workforce as they pertain to their immediate concerns are taken care of. Personnel Management was also seen as a predominantly mediatory function and it typically played the role of mediators between the management and the employees and hence there was always the feeling that personnel management was not in tune to meet the objectives set by the management. Some of the personnel management functions included, employee record keeping, adherence to the policies related to recruitment, training and wage administration, administering welfare measures like medical care, housing etc., attempting to increase productivity through salary increases and training, enforcement of standards derived from work studies, dealing with trade unions, trying to solve industrial disputes through collective bargaining and other industrial relations approaches, conducting performance appraisals or report card of past performance to determine salary fitment and promotions.

With the advent of resource centric organizations, it became imperative to put "people first" at the same time secure the management's objectives of maximizing the ROI (Return on Investment) on resources. This has led to the development of the modern HRM function which aimed at the fulfillment of management objectives. In the process of transition from Human Resources Management to Human Capital Management, the work force considered as "resources" now became "assets" or "capital" and a valuable source of competitive advantage. The thrust of people management shifted focus to aligning employees to the business vision and ensuring goal alignment to maximize productivity. People Management processes at this stage is optimized through the use of technology providing detailed analytics and metrics required for decision making. With social networking becoming popular, many people management functions like Recruitment, Learning and Development and performance management has taken the social route. The transition to aspiration management is marked by the need to actualize human potential, since process optimization using technology, managing people as Resources or as a capital that has an economic value did not have the requisite motivational framework to optimize productivity. Aspiration's management is based on the assumption that each individual is motivated to work towards actualizing their aspirations and that productivity can be optimized and human potential can be actualized through the deployment of the holistic motivational framework that creates the balance between intrinsic and extrinsic motivation based employee engagement initiatives by extending maximum opportunities for employee aspiration actualization.

Integrating the Motivational Framework to HRM and HCM

Succession Planning in Aspiration Management: Organizations have highly qualified people who may be performing well in the current role. Expecting them to do well in which ever role the organization wants the Employee to work in is what works against the theory of self-determination. Career aspiration fitment built in through the appropriate Motivational framework is the key. The self-determination theory is based on the work of Edward Deci and Richard Ryan. They believed that self-determination is achieved by intrinsic motivation which can provide the person satisfaction without any reward. The challenge for Aspiration Management practitioners is to built in the right balance between intrinsic and extrinsic motivation, so as to provide a work environment that helps actualize human potential. This intrinsic motivation is achieved by a feeling of autonomy, by not feeling controlled, feelings of competence through training and positive performance feedback. Expectancy theory, hierarchy of needs, and goal setting also have relevance in the succession planning process. There are many factors to be considered in order to built in the right motivational framework to help optimize productivity and actualize human potential

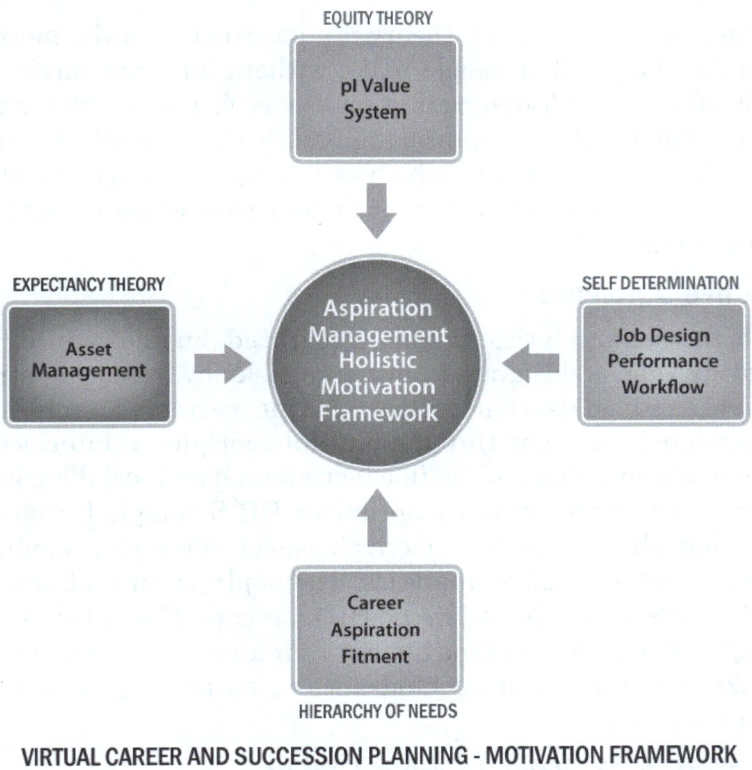

Figure: *Aspiration Management Holistic Motivation Framework for Succession Planning.*

- Interest: Ensure that career aspiration fitment is integral to your succession planning process.
- Autonomy: Has the organization created a work environment that ensures performance work flow. Are they provided with the right tools and support to accomplish their tasks and goals without being dependent?
- Enjoyment: Do you love what you are currently doing? What is challenging about the next role that the individual is going to take-up?

- Competence: Is the person ready or is there a competency development plan to ensure smooth transition to the higher role.
- Job Satisfaction: Design jobs that are meaningful and foster a sense of contribution to the organization. Can the employee expect balance between work and lifestyle.

The self determination theory is concerned with the motivation behind the choices that people make without any external influence and interference. Self-determination theory focuses on the degree to which an individual's behaviour is self-motivated and self-determined. Passion follows ownership, which is important to achieve the end objective "To Create a work environment that helps in Actualizing Human Potential."

Corrective Analytics

Corrective analytics is the integrated business intelligence technology that is designed to mitigate risks by executing strategic objectives and goals that reflects in the corrected scorecard for organizational functions through multiple peripheral interfaces that enables execution of risk mitigation using inbuilt and scalable corrective modules. Corrective analytics optimizes HR Strategic Initiatives by integrating the strategic objectives based corrective modules to predictive and actionable analytics. The deployment and analysis of corrective modules reflected in the HR scorecard. Corrective analytics is integral to aspiration management as it aims to mitigate or reduce the risks that are potential hindrance to optimizing or actualizing human potential.

Integrating Work Ethics to Work Culture

An Organizational culture determines ethical behaviour of the workforce and it determines how they go about doing their work with honesty and integrity. Employers are expected to implement appropriate work ethics management processes, policies and systems that help reflect an authentic track record of managing internal and external customers. The policies of a company should have good ethical foundation to promote morality in the employer, employee and customer relationship. This behaviour becomes part of the work culture. Authentic Track Record (ATR), a peripheral aspiration management system, provides the power of the source of truth or source data that can contribute towards building a value driven organization and contribute towards productivity optimization. It delivers productivity optimization through its integration with the multiple source data which are updated at the various points of authorized origin. As part of the integration process, the organization defines its benchmark work ethics policy that will determine the level of compliance delivered through the compliance connector with the various external and internal entities and includes, equal opportunities for career growth, ethical employee joining process, ethical exist process, workplace infrastructure safety compliance, customer support compliance, statutory compliance connectors, authentication connectors, and other such benchmarks required to ensure that a process driven system is deployed to ensure organizational value compliance.

Any Time Manpower - HR ATM

An aspiration management peripheral system that integrates the recruitment process, fast tracks talent acquisition, provides equal opportunity, broadens the talent pool and reaches out to right candidate, from the remotest corners. Career placement from any place in the world is the vision behind the world's first HR ATM integrated with the ATM compliance technology that enables a candidate to walk into an HR ATM, complete the process, and walk out with the hard copy of the offer letter, from any company, anywhere in the world.

Effects of Achievement Motivation on Behaviour

Motivation can be defined as the driving force behind all the actions of an individual. The influence of an individual's needs and desires both have a strong impact on the direction of their behaviour. Motivation is based on your emotions and achievement-related goals. There are different forms of motivation including extrinsic, intrinsic, physiological, and achievement motivation. There are also more negative forms of motivation. Achievement motivation can be defined as the need for success or the attainment of excellence. Individuals will satisfy their needs through different means, and are driven to succeed for varying reasons both internal and external.

Motivation is the basic drive for all of our actions. Motivation refers to the dynamics of our behaviour, which involves our needs, desires, and ambitions in life. Achievement motivation is based on reaching success and achieving all of our aspirations in life. Achievement goals can affect the way a person performs a task and represent a desire to show competence (Harackiewicz, Barron, Carter, Lehto, & Elliot, 1997). These basic physiological motivational drives affect our natural behaviour in different environments. Most of our goals are incentive-based and can vary from basic hunger to the need for love and the establishment of mature sexual relationships. Our motives for achievement can range from biological needs to satisfying creative desires or realizing success in competitive ventures. Motivation is important because it affects our lives everyday. All of our behaviours, actions, thoughts, and beliefs are influenced by our inner drive to succeed.

Implicit and Self-Attributed Motives

Motivational researchers share the view that achievement behaviour is an interaction between situational variables and the individual subject's motivation to achieve. Two motives are directly involved in the prediction of behaviour, implicit and explicit. Implicit motives are spontaneous impulses to act, also known as task performances, and are aroused through incentives inherent to the task. Explicit motives are expressed through deliberate choices and more often stimulated for extrinsic reasons. Also, individuals with strong implicit needs to achieve goals set higher internal standards, whereas others tend to adhere to the societal norms. These two motives often work together to determine the behaviour of the individual in direction and passion (Brunstein & Maier, 2005).

Explicit and implicit motivations have a compelling impact on behaviour. Task behaviours are accelerated in the face of a challenge through implicit motivation, making performing a task in the most effective manner the primary goal. A person with a strong implicit drive will feel pleasure from achieving a goal in the most efficient way. The increase in effort and overcoming the challenge by mastering the task satisfies the individual. However, the explicit motives are built around a person's self-image. This type of motivation shapes a person's behaviour based on their own self-view and can influence their choices and responses from outside cues. The primary agent for this type of motivation is perception or perceived ability. Many theorists still can not agree whether achievement is based on mastering one's skills or striving to promote a better self-image (Brunstein & Maier, 2005). Most research is still unable to determine whether these different types of motivation would result in different behaviours in the same environment.

The Hierarchal Model of Achievement Motivation

Achievement motivation has been conceptualized in many different ways. Our understanding of achievement-relevant effects, cognition, and behaviour has improved. Despite being similar in nature, many achievement motivation approaches have been developed separately, suggesting that most achievement motivation theories are in concordance with one another instead of competing. Motivational researchers have sought to promote a hierarchal model of approach and avoidance achievement motivation by incorporating the two prominent theories: the achievement motive approach and the achievement goal approach. Achievement motives include the need for achievement and the fear of failure. These are the more predominant motives that direct our behaviour towards positive and negative outcomes. Achievement goals are viewed as more solid cognitive representations pointing individuals towards a specific end. There are three types of these achievement goals: a performance-approach goal, a performance-avoidance goal, and a mastery goal. A performance-approach goal is focused on attaining competence relative to others, a performance-avoidance goal is focused on avoiding incompetence relative to others, and a mastery goal is focused on the development of competence itself and of task mastery. Achievement motives can be seen as direct predictors of achievement-relevant circumstances. Thus, achievement motives are said to have an indirect or distal influence, and achievement goals are said to have a direct or proximal influence on achievement-relevant outcomes (Elliot & McGregor, 1999).

These motives and goals are viewed as working together to regulate achievement behaviour. The hierarchal model presents achievement goals as predictors for performance outcomes. The model is being further conceptualized to include more approaches to achievement motivation. One weakness of the model is that it does not provide an account of the processes responsible for the link between achievement goals and performance. As this model is enhanced, it becomes more useful in predicting the outcomes of achievement-based behaviours (Elliot & McGregor, 1999).

Achievement Goals and Information Seeking

Theorists have proposed that people's achievement goals affect their achievement-related attitudes and behaviours. Two different types of achievement-related attitudes include task-involvement and ego-involvement. Task-involvement is a motivational state in which a person's main goal is to acquire skills and understanding whereas the main goal in ego-involvement is to demonstrate superior abilities (Butler, 1999). One example of an activity where someone strives to attain mastery and demonstrate superior ability is schoolwork. However situational cues, such as the person's environment or surroundings, can affect the success of achieving a goal at any time.

Studies confirm that a task-involvement activity more often results in challenging attributions and increasing effort (typically in activities providing an opportunity to learn and develop competence) than in an ego-involvement activity. Intrinsic motivation, which is defined as striving to engage in activity because of self-satisfaction, is more prevalent when a person is engaged in task-involved activities. When people are more ego-involved, they tend to take on a different conception of their ability, where differences in ability limit the effectiveness of effort. Ego-involved individuals are driven to succeed by outperforming others, and their feelings of success depend on maintaining self-worth and avoiding failure. On the other hand, task-involved individuals tend to adopt their conception of ability as learning through applied effort (Butler, 1999). Therefore less able individuals will feel more successful as long as they can satisfy an effort to learn and improve. Ego-invoking conditions tend to produce less favourable responses to failure and difficulty.

Competence moderated attitudes and behaviours are more prevalent in ego-involved activities than task-involved. Achievement does not moderate intrinsic motivation in task-involving conditions, in which people of all levels of ability could learn to improve. In ego-involving conditions, intrinsic motivation was higher among higher achievers who demonstrated superior ability than in low achievers who could not demonstrate such ability (Butler, 1999). These different attitudes towards achievement can also be compared in information seeking.

Task- and ego-involving settings bring about different goals, conceptions of ability, and responses to difficulty. They also promote different patterns of information seeking. People of all levels of ability will seek information relevant to attaining their goal of improving mastery in task-involving conditions. However they need to seek information regarding self-appraisal to gain a better understanding of their self-capacity (Butler, 1999). On the other hand people in ego-involving settings are more interested in information about social comparisons, assessing their ability relative to others.

Self-Worth Theory in Achievement Motivation

Self-worth theory states that in certain situations students stand to gain by not trying and deliberately withholding effort. If poor performance is a threat to a person's sense of self-esteem, this lack of effort is likely to occur. This most often occurs after an experience of failure. Failure threatens self-estimates of ability and creates uncertainty about an individual's capability to perform well on a subsequent basis. If the following performance turns out to be poor, then doubts concerning ability are confirmed. Self-worth theory states that one way to avoid threat to self-esteem is by withdrawing effort. Withdrawing effort allows failure to be attributed to lack of effort rather than low ability which reduces overall risk to the value of one's self-esteem. When poor performance is likely to reflect poor ability, a situation of high threat is created to the individual's intellect. On the other hand, if an excuse allows poor performance to be attributed to a factor unrelated to ability, the threat to self-esteem and one's intellect is much lower (Thompson, Davidson, & Barber, 1995).

A study was conducted on students involving unsolvable problems to test some assumptions of the self-worth theory regarding motivation and effort. The results showed that there was no evidence of reported reduction of effort despite poorer performance when the tasks were described as moderately difficult as compared with tasks much higher in difficulty. The possibility was raised that low effort may not be responsible for the poor performance of students in situations which create threats to self-esteem. Two suggestions were made, one being that students might unconsciously withdraw effort, and the other stating that students may reduce effort as a result of withdrawing commitment from the problem. Regardless of which suggestion is true, self-worth theory assumes that individuals have a reduced tendency to take personal responsibility for failure (Thompson, Davidson, & Barber, 1995).

Avoidance Achievement Motivation

In everyday life, individuals strive to be competent in their activities. In the past decade, many theorists have utilized a social-cognitive achievement goal approach in accounting for individuals striving for competence. An achievement goal is commonly defined as the purpose for engaging in a task, and the specific type of goal taken on creates a framework for how individuals experience their achievement pursuits. Achievement goal theorists commonly identify two distinct ideas towards competence: a performance goal focused on demonstrating ability when compared to others, and a mastery goal focused on the development of competence and task mastery. Performance goals are hypothesized to produce vulnerability to certain response patterns in achievement settings such as preferences for easy tasks, withdrawal of effort in the face of failure, and decreased task enjoyment. Mastery goals can lead to a motivational pattern that creates a preference for moderately challenging tasks, persistence in the face of failure, and increased enjoyment of tasks (Elliot & Church, 1997).

Most achievement goal theorists conceptualize both performance and mastery goals as the "approach" forms of motivation. Existing classical achievement motivation theorists claimed that activities are emphasized and oriented towards attaining success or avoiding failure, while the achievement goal theorists focused on their approach aspect. More recently, an integrated achievement goal conceptualization was proposed that includes both modern performance and mastery theories with the standard approach and avoidance features. In this basis for motivation, the performance goal is separated into an independent approach component and avoidance component, and three achievement orientations are conceived: a mastery goal focused on the development of competence and task mastery, a performance-approach goal directed towards the attainment of favourable judgements of competence, and a performance-avoidance goal centred on avoiding unfavourable judgements of competence. The mastery and performance-approach goals are characterized as self-regulating to promote potential positive outcomes and processes to absorb an individual in their task or to create excitement leading to a mastery pattern of achievement results. Performance-avoidance goals, however, are characterized as promoting negative circumstances. This avoidance orientation creates anxiety, task distraction, and a pattern of helpless achievement outcomes. Intrinsic motivation, which is the enjoyment of and interest in an activity for its own sake, plays a role in achievement outcomes as well. Performance-avoidance goals undermined intrinsic motivation while both mastery and performance-approach goals helped to increase it (Elliot & Church, 1997).

Most achievement theorists and philosophers also identify task-specific competence expectancies as an important variable in achievement settings. Achievement goals are created in order to obtain competence and avoid failure. These goals are viewed as implicit (non-conscious) or self-attributed (conscious) and direct achievement behaviour. Competence expectancies were considered an important variable in classical achievement motivation theories, but now appear to only be moderately emphasized in contemporary perspectives (Elliot & Church, 1997).

Approach and Avoidance Goals

Achievement motivation theorists focus their research attention on behaviours involving competence. Individuals aspire to attain competence or may strive to avoid incompetence, based on the earlier approach-avoidance research and theories. The desire for success and the desire to avoid failure were identified as critical determinants of aspiration and behaviour by a theorist named Lewin. In his achievement motivation theory, McClelland proposed that there are two kinds of achievement motivation, one oriented around avoiding failure and the other around the more positive goal of attaining success. Atkinson, another motivational theorist, drew from the work of Lewin and McClelland in forming his need-achievement theory, a mathematical framework that assigned the desire to succeed and the desire to avoid failure as important determinants in achievement behaviour (Elliot & Harackiewicz, 1996).

Theorists introduced an achievement goal approach to achievement motivation more recently. These theorists defined achievement goals as the reason for activities related to competence. Initially, these theorists followed in the footsteps of Lewin, McClelland, and Atkinson by including the distinction between approach and avoidance motivation into the structure of their assumptions. Three types of achievement goals were created, two of which being approach orientations and the third an avoidance type. One approach type was a task involvement goal focused on the development of competence and task mastery, and the other being a performance or ego involvement goal directed towards attaining favourable judgements of competence. The avoidance orientation involved an ego or performance goal aimed at avoiding unfavourable judgements of competence. These new theories received little attention at first and some theorists bypassed them with little regard. Motivational theorists shifted away and devised other conceptualizations such as Dweck's performance-learning goal dichotomy with approach and avoidance components or Nicholls' ego and task orientations, which he characterized as two forms of approach motivation (Elliot & Harackiewicz, 1996).

Presently, achievement goal theory is the predominant approach to the analysis of achievement motivation. Most contemporary theorists use the frameworks of Dweck's and Nicholls' revised models in two important ways. First, most theorists institute primary orientations towards competence, by either differentiating between mastery and ability goals or contrasting task and ego involvement. A contention was raised towards the achievement goal frameworks on whether or not they are conceptually similar enough to justify a convergence of the mastery goal form (learning, task involvement and mastery) with the performance goal form (ability and performance, ego involvement, competition). Secondly, most modern theorists characterized both mastery and performance goals as approach forms of motivation, or they failed to consider approach and avoidance as independent motivational tendencies within the performance goal orientation (Elliot & Harackiewicz, 1996).

The type of orientation adopted at the outset of an activity creates a context for how individuals interpret, evaluate, and act on information and experiences in an achievement setting. Adoption of a mastery goal is hypothesized to produce a mastery motivational pattern characterized by a preference for moderately challenging tasks, persistence in the face of failure, a positive stance towards learning, and enhanced task enjoyment. A helpless motivational response, however, is the result of the adoption of a performance goal orientation. This includes a preference for easy or difficult tasks, effort withdrawal in the face of failure, shifting the blame of failure to lack of ability, and decreased enjoyment of tasks. Some theorists include the concept of perceived competence as an important agent in their assumptions. Mastery goals are expected to have a uniform effect across all levels of perceived competence, leading to a mastery pattern. Performance goals can lead to mastery in individuals with a high perceived competence and a helpless motivational pattern in those with low competence (Elliot & Harackiewicz, 1996).

Three motivational goal theories have recently been proposed based on the tri-variant framework by achievement goal theorists: mastery, performance-approach, and performance-avoidance. Performance-approach and mastery goals both represent approach orientations according to potential positive outcomes, such as the attainment of competence and task mastery. These forms of behaviour and self-regulation commonly produce a variety of affective and perceptual-cognitive processes that facilitate optimal task engagement. They challenge sensitivity to information relevant to success and effective concentration in the activity, leading to the mastery set of motivational responses described by achievement goal theorists. The performance-avoidance goal is conceptualized as an avoidance orientation according to potential negative outcomes. This form of regulation evokes self-protective mental processes that interfere with optimal task engagement. It creates sensitivity to failure-relevant information and invokes an anxiety-based preoccupation with the appearance of oneself rather than the concerns of the task, which can lead to the helpless set of motivational responses. The three goal theories presented are very process oriented in nature. Approach and avoidance goals are viewed as exerting their different effects on achievement behaviour by activating opposing sets of motivational processes (Elliot & Harackiewicz, 1996).

Intrinsic Motivation and Achievement Goals

Intrinsic motivation is defined as the enjoyment of and interest in an activity for its own sake. Fundamentally viewed as an approach form of motivation, intrinsic motivation is identified as an important component of achievement goal theory. Most achievement goal and intrinsic motivational theorists argue that mastery goals are facilitative of intrinsic motivation and related mental processes and performance goals create negative effects. Mastery goals are said to promote intrinsic motivation by fostering perceptions of challenge, encouraging task involvement, generating excitement, and supporting self-determination while performance goals are the opposite. Performance goals are portrayed as undermining intrinsic motivation by instilling perceptions of threat, disrupting task involvement, and creating anxiety and pressure (Elliot & Harackiewicz, 1996).

An alternative set of predictions may be derived from the approach-avoidance framework. Both performance-approach and mastery goals are focused on attaining competence and foster intrinsic motivation. More specifically, in performance-approach or mastery orientations, individuals perceive the achievement setting as a challenge, and this likely will create excitement, encourage cognitive functioning, increase concentration and task absorption, and direct the person towards success and mastery of information which facilitates intrinsic motivation. The performance-avoidance goal is focused on avoiding incompetence, where individuals see the achievement setting as a threat and seek to escape it (Elliot & Harackiewicz, 1996). This orientation is likely to elicit anxiety and withdrawal of effort and cognitive resources while disrupting concentration and motivation.

Personal Goals Analysis

In recent years, theorists have increasingly relied on various goal constructs to account for action in achievement settings. Four levels of goal representation have been introduced: task-specific guidelines for performance, such as performing a certain action, situation-specific orientations that represent the purpose of achievement activity, such as demonstrating competence relative to others in a situation, personal goals that symbolize achievement pursuits, such as getting good grades, and self-standards and future self-images, including planning for future goals and successes. These goal-based achievement motivation theories have focused almost exclusively on approach forms behaviour but in recent years have shifted more towards avoidance (Elliot & Sheldon, 1997).

Motivation is an important factor in everyday life. Our basic behaviours and feelings are affected by our inner drive to succeed over life's challenges while we set goals for ourselves. Our motivation also promotes our feelings of competence and self-worth as we achieve our goals. It provides us with means to compete with others in order to better ourselves and to seek out new information to learn and absorb. Individuals experience motivation in different ways, whether it is task- or ego-based in nature. Some people strive to achieve their goals for personal satisfaction and self-improvement while others compete with their surroundings in achievement settings to simply be classified as the best. Motivation and the resulting behaviour are both affected by the many different models of achievement motivation. These models, although separate, are very similar in nature and theory. The mastery and performance achievement settings each have a considerable effect on how an individual is motivated. Each theorist has made a contribution to the existing theories in today's achievement studies. More often than not, theorists build off of each other's work to expand old ideas and create new ones. Achievement motivation is an intriguing field, and I find myself more interested after reviewing similar theories from different perspectives.

Expanding Achievement Motivation Theory: How Motivational Psychology Relates to Other Fields

Scott T. Rabideau's paper, "Effects of Achievement Motivation on Behaviour," effectively summarized current research and theories in the field of motivational psychology. Rabideau's paper detailed the basic aspects of motivational theory in educational psychology, such as intrinsic and extrinsic motivation, and described its finer aspects, such as how seeking information about a task can depend on whether the task is motivated by approach goals or avoidance goals.

Although the paper was competent in this regard, I find it surprising that it focused so little on how research into motivation theory relates and can be applied to more well-known, traditional psychological schools of thought, such as behaviourism and cognitive psychology. Indeed, many of the ideas presented in this paper are strongly tied to traditional psychological fields. In this paper I will attempt to link some of these fields with the theories and concepts presented in Rabideau's paper.

Cognitive psychology is one such field that has strong ties to motivation theory. According to motivation theory, the perception one has of ones self and ones perceived abilities have an effect on task motivation. Furthermore, self-worth theory as described by Rabideau tells us that people take personal responsibility for a failure, and in this case will likely avoid that task in the future. It seems reasonable therefore that challenging negative perceptions would have a strong positive effect on motivation. This echoes the principles dealt with in some aspects of cognitive psychology. For instance, Aaron T. Beck's cognitive theory of depression works in much the same manner, by challenging automatic negative thoughts, which are a causal factor in depression (Martin & Pear, 2003). Likewise, Albert Ellis has gained a significant following based on his development of rational-emotive behaviour therapy, which deals with identifying irrational thoughts that cause negative emotions (Martin & Pear, 2003). These cognitive theories have had tremendous effect on developing effective therapies for individuals suffering from depression, and I believe that their core principles could be used in achievement motivation theory.

Motivation theory also has very strong ties to behavioural psychology. In fact, I believe much of the goals behind motivation as described by Rabideau can be described in terms of positive reinforcement. Both intrinsic and extrinsic motivation can usually be attributed to a desired positive outcome, whether it is pleasure gained by accomplishing the task, or rewards such as money or social status that is expected in the future. The behavioural field of psychology has much to say about education and teaching, and a lot of it echoes what is presented in motivation theory. Although behavioural psychology is more often used in an educational environment to treat problematic and disruptive behaviours, much success has been made applying behavioural methods to strengthen positive academic behaviours, both with normal and mentally disabled students. Furthermore, behavioural psychology has been gaining support in physical training and education (Martin & Pear, 2003). Rabideau's paper identifies many potential causes for poor motivation, which stem from a variety of internal and external (such as social) reasons. I believe that despite the varied nature of causes for poor motivation, behaviour therapy techniques can be used to have a positive effect on problem areas. There are many behaviour modification techniques and methodologies available to therapists and educators who are working in the field of achievement motivation. Some strategies include token economies, shaping, extinction, and intermittent reinforcement, all of which have proven to provide measurable levels of improvement in target behaviours (Martin & Pear, 2003). I believe that through these and other techniques, it is possible to increase achievement motivation, even in cases where it may lacking due to one or more problems, or in cases of avoidant motivation (which will not drive an individual towards mastery of a task), such as the fear of failing to look competent by peers. By helping to create motivation based on implicit enjoyment of completing a task, behaviour therapy can not only drive motivation towards mastery of a task, but also help in cases where treating a cause of poor motivation is not always possible. This certainly may be the case in some of the causes Rabideau mentioned, such as low motivation that stems from past failure or a fear of peer criticism.

Finally, Rabideau's paper also tied in strongly with the field of social psychology. Competence relevant to peers plays a big role in motivation theory, both in approach and avoidance goals. Often times motivation for a task comes from seeking a level of proficiency, or avoiding a failure. It would have been interesting to see how the outcome of peer criticism or support in the face of a failure effects future task motivation, as in some areas of psychology peer support can have a large effect on the progression of emotional problems.

Benefits of Avoiding

All of the achievement motivation theories presented by Rabideau seem to agree that mastery and approach-type goals or motives lead to constructive behaviour in addition to personal advancement and success. Meanwhile, avoidance-type goals or motives lead to negative personal outcomes, inefficiency, and inner-turmoil.

Although it seems idealistic to have one's motivation completely based on receiving positive reinforcement and self-improvement in order to achieve personal success, perhaps it is not realistic. Motivation based on avoidance characteristics may be detrimental to one's self in excess, but it may be a necessary tool in some regards towards the development of long-term approach and mastery goals. A delicate balance of both approach and avoidance motivation may lead to a more well-rounded and successful individual.

Imagine a workplace scenario in the modern fast-paced American business world in which there are no deadlines, no bosses, and no competition. Sure this would be the ideal place for mastery and approach type goals in which an individual could spend all of his or her time developing their skills and knowledge, but this is not the case. No matter how much enjoyment people receive from their work, people in the business world must unavoidably perform tasks in the midst of deadline threats and competition in order to persevere. They most definitely face some anxiety and fear about not meeting their employers' standards and perform tasks based on avoidance motivation in order to prevent from losing their jobs. They may also aim to perform tasks better in comparison with co-workers both for an ego-boost and for avoiding social incompetence.

These anxiety and stress-inducing situations may not be what we desire as individuals or what is desired for optimal human success, but they are undoubtedly present and encountered in our lifestyles. Without them would anything ever get done? If mastery goals are an individual's only source of motivation and they receive purely pleasure out of performing a task I doubt they would ever make the statement, "well this is good enough." How could they feel they have accomplished their goal if something can always be improved upon? They would always continue to strive for the mastery of the particular task or skill.

Another similar example would be students attending colleges and universities in western society. Unless they are there for the sole purpose of expanding their knowledge, the majority of the students enrolled in any particular university are probably there to receive a higher-level education in the pursuit of employment for sustenance. This long-term goal is not achieved through solely positive reinforcement; there is plenty of stress, anxiety, and sometimes failure as well. In fact the goal itself could be considered an avoidance goal and motivate a student based on the fear of becoming a social pariah or the inability to provide for oneself.

In regards to class work and assignments, a student might be motivated to excel in his or her particular area of study. Although If student is forced to attend a required class not related to their area of interest and study he/she might be motivated by the avoidance of receiving poor marks or negative feedback by the professor, which would be detrimental to their college career from an overall perspective. The avoidance would lead to completion of course work and material and actually benefit the student in the long run.

In contrast too much motivation through means of avoidance would follow the motivational theories as described by Rabideau and completely "undermine intrinsic motivation." With a deprivation of approach and mastery type goals an individual may lack the inner-drive needed to succeed in life. Instances as described in the "self-worth" theory may occur in which an individual chooses the easiest route and removes most or all task-related effort in order to avoid failure and low self-esteem.

It would be interesting to explore further into this realm and see how motivations through avoidance type goals are related to depression, particularly unipolar disorders. Perhaps the continuation of motivation through stress, anxiety and fear leads an individual through a downward spiral into a depressive state. Cognitive therapy may assist these individuals in developing more approach-type goals and counter the effects described in the "self-worth" theory.

What's My Motivation? It May Not Be Yours

The most interesting concepts explored in this paper concerned the identification of various types of motivation. Obviously motivation drives human behaviour and there are many different forms motivation can take, but how do these different types of motivation interact to describe behaviour? Whether motivational cues are taken directly from the environment or imposed by individuals, there is always a choice to be made, be it conscious or unconscious. Nobody can make an individual do anything, a person's perception of reality shapes that person's motivation.

To better illustrate this phenomenon, an actual [observed] scenario describing two students will be described. One student, receives a poor grade on an exam while the other receives an "A." Why did the first student do so poorly? Obviously he was motivated to take the test and he was also motivated to receive a passing grade so he could advance. But what was the goal? Let us explore the many different forms that motivation can take. This author discusses numerous types of motives starting with achievement goals including: performance-approach, in which a student would focus on attaining mere competence relative to his classmates, a performance-avoidance goal mindset would mean the student was trying to avoid incompetence, and finally if the student was facing a mastery goal he would try to become an expert in the material regardless of what was required for the test. Student one is very bright, highly task-involved and seeks to acquire knowledge as well as skills and understanding, in direct contrast to ego-involvement were the goal here is to prove superiority over the rest of the class.

Now let us contrast the first student with one of his classmates who is not that gifted and is demonstrating performance-avoidance. He is terrified he will fail the class and is extrinsically motivated- he is not studying for his own betterment; he is motivated to both please others and avoid punishment. The future is looking fairly grim for student number two so he begins to withdraw effort. According to self-worth theory, the reason for this is to lessen his inevitable cognitive dissonance from failing the class, that way if he fails it would be due to a lack of preparation rather than his own lack of academic ability.

Student number one studied for the pure joy of learning to master the material while the second students performance-avoidance goals put him between a rock and a hard place; paralyzed with fear of failure he faced task anxiety and helpless achievement outcomes. But student number one gets a "C" on the test and student number two gets an "A." What happened? What happened was a cultural component exerting more power than any other types of motivation. Student number one faced persecution from his peers by "breaking the curve" and student number two cheated to please his parents with his grade. In this case simply understanding motivation did not predict *behaviour*, only motive. Seldom is a person driven by a solitary, isolated motive that is easily defined. The author touches on this point and discusses a variety of motives that are possible, but sometimes predicting behaviour by understanding motivation requires a model containing numerous and sometimes contradicting motivations.

Interestingly, both students altered their behaviours in ways some would consider unexpected. However, the second student broke societies rules by cheating while the first override his desire to receive a high grade with one lower than what he truly deserved. Similarities also come from the fact that both students felt cognitive dissonance, obviously for two different reasons, but the first student was implicitly motivated the second was explicitly motivated. The first student damaged himself for the benefit of the group [to ultimately protect himself from persecution] while the second student took advantage of the group to better himself. One intriguing possibility is that simple implicit or explicit motivations can predict the possible inclusion of other types of behaviours.

External/ internal perceived locus of causality (Gollowitzer, 1996) describes persons with an internal perceived locus as more in control of their density. As a result these persons, like student number one are flexible with regards to the environment and are better equipped to handle situations that require in-depth understanding of how their moral code interacts with the outside world. This may account for this student deciding on task-mastery while at the same time allowing himself to give in to peer pressure to achieve the second goal of group acceptance. It is also possible that student number one receives far less dissonance that student number two who has an external perceived locus of causality. This student feels that his actions could only have been justified by the limited options he perceives are as a result of his own shortcoming. In short, persons who exhibit avoidance achievement motivations are more likely to be susceptible to external influence the opposite is true for those seeking task-mastery.

Motivational Theory From a Different Perspective

Charbonneau introduced the relation between motivational theory with both the cognitive area of psychology and the school of behaviourism. His points were very interesting and I agree they could have enhanced my original argument and allowed me to further articulate and describe different aspects of motivational theory. He mainly focused on ideas for enhancing motivation and suggested how these areas of psychology could be related to a motivational therapy. As for the cognitive field, I agree that the perceptions people have of themselves indeed play a strong role in affecting their motivation. It would be interesting to conduct a future study of how depression therapy techniques could possibly be used to aid in motivation. Charbonneau's other argument focused on behavioural therapy and how it could be used in motivation treatments. I found these arguments to be quite interesting and would also be interested in seeing the results of a study based on Charbonneau's ideas. However, I still feel that motivation is most strongly tied to the social aspect of psychology.

Segovia provided an interesting counter-argument concerning avoidance and motivation. His idea that a balance of approach and avoidance motivation would create a more well-rounded person seems quite intriguing. I believe Segovia makes a strong case in his argument that avoidance achievement goals are completely necessary for daily functioning, not only for working adults but for college students as well. His points about students taking classes unrelated to their primary studies and adults performing tasks at work just to avoid failure or avoid being fired is something I should have considered including in my original presentation. Like Segovia, I would be interested in seeing a study performed that might assess how avoidance goals can help people succeed in life, and also how avoidance goals may be related to mental disorders such as depression.

Swerdlow presented an interesting example of how task mastery and avoidance goals can sometimes result in unexpected outcomes and how motivational drives are different for individual people. His example using the two students was quite provocative and fascinating.

He emphasized how observed behaviour of an individual can differ from the motivational drives of that individual by introducing environmental and cultural factors. I agree that these factors can strongly influence an individual's behaviour despite their own intrinsic motives for success.

Fostering the Talents of Vocational-Technical Students

A developmental approach to examining career aspiration is holistic, intertwining the person and the environment. This approach focuses on the interplay between individuals and the environments and then looks at that relationship over time. Such an approach is necessary to understand career pathways of the gifted. Prior to 1980, career development theorists examined the individual in isolation from the environment. Gottfredson and others reformulated career development theory and drew attention to the interrelatedness and interdependence of the environment on career decisions. Gottfredson (1981) hypothesized, after reviewing the cognitive development literature that there are four basic stages of development: orientation to size and power (ages 3-5), orientation to sex roles (ages 6-8), orientation to social evaluation (about ages 9-13), and orientation to the internal, unique self (beginning at about age 14). She states that the major vocationally relevant elements of gender, social class background, intelligence, vocational interests, competencies, and values are incorporated into a vocational self-concept at different stages of development.

The literature on counselling the gifted and talented provides strategies for meeting the needs of the gifted, but does not include comprehensive programming models. Taylor (1993) integrated components from the Enrichment Triad Model (Renzulli, 1977; Renzulli & Reis, 1985) with a developmental approach to heightening career aspirations of gifted and talented students. The Enrichment Triad Model allows both the nurturing of creative productivity during school years as well as fostering the lifelong process of career development. The model also provides a broadened conception of giftedness for identifying students.

The Enrichment Triad Model was adapted to include an integrated career development model, Focus On (Taylor, 1993). This monograph proposes an implementation process that takes into account the needs of students as they travel through the stages of career development. Students are provided with enrichment opportunities which expands their exposure to various fields (modified Type I); process skills, including critical and creative thinking, specific methodological skills, and career development skills (modified Type II), and creative productive investigations (modified Type III) which can be used to explore potential career interests and allow students to see themselves in the role of practicing professionals and begin to visualize a different sense of self. In this study using the Focus On Model, significantly heightened career aspirations were found for students who had participated in creative productivity.

In order to reach and nurture a broader spectrum of gifted and talented students, changes must be made in some of the practices currently being used. New approaches are needed for providing conceptual frameworks, identification processes, and implementation strategies for gifted and talented programmes. Conceptions of giftedness must go beyond schoolhouse giftedness and include potentially creative productive behaviours. Broadened screening practices should be utilized which look for this potential creative productivity in a range of fields. Finally, creative productive behaviour should be nurtured through activities which may influence a lifelong process of career development.

Career Aspirations: A Developmental Approach

Prior to 1980, career development theorists examined the individual in isolation from the environment. Gottfredson and others reformulated career development theory and drew attention to the interrelatedness and interdependence of the environment on career decision making and development (Fleming & Hollinger, 1994).

A developmental approach to examining career aspiration is holistic, intertwining the person and the environment. This approach focuses on the interplay between individuals and their environments and then looks at that relationship over time. From a developmental perspective, career aspiration is not a stable trait, it is a process that "unfolds" throughout the life span (Csikszentmihalyi & Robinson, 1986). As a person's concept of himself and herself and a future career image evolve internally, external environmental forces are thought to have differing effects at different times in the life span (Gottfredson, 1981).

A recent longitudinal study of technical creative ability revealed the identification of factors that are necessary for adult creative technical performance and should be nurtured during childhood. Among these factors was the opportunity to try out and experiment with technological items in the environment; prior experience and technical expertise moderated the ability to creatively problem solve in the technical arena (Hany, 1994).

Other important career development variables that have been revealed through factor analysis of the most widely used career assessment instruments include career interest, the amount of knowledge one has about the world of work and important aspects of career decision making, extensiveness of involvement in career-planning activities, certainty of career interests, and decision-making style (Jepsen & Prediger, 1981). Gifted students have been found to have general knowledge relevant to career decision making, they know how many years of study a particular career may take, but needed to understand exactly what is done within these career environments and how to gain entry to specialized career paths (Kelly & Cobb, 1991).

Holland's Theory of Career Development

Holland's (1966, 1973, 1979, 1987) theory of personality style and career development describes different ways in which an individual can interact with his/her environment. He developed a type of measure of an individual's cognitive interaction with his/her environment and distinguishes those with styles that are adept at finding/solving problems.

Holland (1973) has suggested that vocational satisfaction, stability, and achievement depend on the match between one's personality style and the opportunities and rewards offered in the environment in which one interacts. He believes that people search for environments that will let them exercise their skills and abilities, express their attitudes and values, and take on agreeable problems and roles.

A key assumption of this theory is that behaviour is determined by an interaction between one's personality style and the prevailing environmental characteristics. Holland proposes that an individual's personality style can be described by a profile of six interest areas: realistic, investigative, artistic, social, enterprising, and conventional. Occupational environments can also be grouped in terms of the same six areas as functions of the types of experiences, challenges, and opportunities they provide. Congruence refers to the match between an individual's preferences and personality style, and the opportunities and rewards offered by the environment. An individual with an investigative personality style would be best suited for a career in an investigative field, such as scientific research.

Holland's model is an important aspect of the *Strong-Campbell Vocational Inventory* which is often given to college students when they are making career decisions. This inventory has been used with gifted high school students and has potential as a powerful career counselling tool (Perrone, 1991). Kerr found that even a one day career guidance workshop could affect how female students reported personality styles as measured by Holland's test (Kerr, 1983). Positive changes in congruence, or the match between personality style and occupational choice, are known to occur when adolescents explore a variety of career alternatives and choose a career that matches their style (Grotevant, Cooper, & Kramer, 1986).

Gottfredson's Developmental Theory of Career Aspirations

Gottfredson (1981, 1986, Gottfredson & Becker 1981) has proposed a developmental theory of career aspiration. She hypothesized after reviewing the cognitive development literature that there are four basic stages of development: orientation to size and power (ages 3-5), orientation to sex roles (ages 6-8), orientation to social evaluation (about ages 9-13), and orientation to the internal, unique self (beginning at about age 14). She states that the major vocationally relevant elements of gender, social class background, intelligence, vocational interests, competencies, and values are incorporated into a vocational self-concept at different stages of development. Perrone (1991) argues for a fifth stage that would incorporate an integrated worldview and would occur in late adolescence or young adulthood.

The first stage of development summarized by Gottfredson, from her synthesis of the literature, is that of orientation to size and power (ages 3-5), begins when children grasp the concept of being an adult. They are considered to have intuitive thought processes at this stage, have not yet achieved object constancy, and are beginning to perceive the difference between themselves and others with respect to little versus big. Their occupational perceptions include occupations as adult roles. The orientation to sex roles occurs during the ages of 6 to 8. Thought processes during this period are concrete, objects are classified by simple groupings, and gender becomes a new element to perception of self and others. Gender becomes the new element in occupational perception and preferences.

Orientation to social valuation (ages 9-13) is accompanied by less concrete thought processes and two-factor groupings in classification. The new elements in perceptions of self and others include social class and intelligence. Prestige level appears in the occupational perception.

In this stage the individual becomes sensitized to peer group evaluations and then to more general social expectations, values, and evaluations. The differences between children in their perceptions is believed to come from the emergence of class differences with respect to aspirations. Youngsters are found to identify with the socioeconomic group from which they come and to adopt those standards. Parents' aspirations for their children are reflected in what they consider acceptable career choices. The lower the social class of the mother, the lower the level of the position that would be acceptable to her (Dillard & Campbell, 1981; Rosen, 1959).

Parental influence has been found to be a factor affecting occupational aspirations along with socioeconomic status. Frasier (1987) states that the key ingredient in a family's orientation towards achievement is a supportive home environment, regardless of socioeconomic status. Parental encouragement of higher education was found to be the primary predictor of career aspirations for African American and White, male and female tenth graders (McNair & Brown, 1983). In this study socioeconomic status was found to have a greater negative impact on males than females. Ginzberg, Gusburg, Axeland, and Herma (1951) found that from a group of high ability, 11-year-old boys, only the boys from disadvantaged backgrounds did not plan on going on to college.

Differences in career aspirations between students of varying abilities occur at the same stage as socioeconomic factors. More able students were found to aspire to higher-level jobs, though the higher social class children had the higher aspirations within all ability groups (Sewell & Hauser, 1975; Sewell & Shah, 1968). Students of higher abilities and social class levels were more likely to actually plan to go to college whether encouraged or not. They are much more likely to aspire to college if they are encouraged. These complex links between education, social class, and work develop by grades 6 through 8.

Finally, in the last stage, an orientation to an internal, unique self occurs along with the shift to more abstract thought processes. The ability to process multi-factor groupings has developed. Personal interests, values, and competencies have evolved as elements in the perception of self and of others, and occupational perceptions now include field of work. In this fourth stage of development, youngsters seem to shift from accommodating directly from external socially defined goals to pursuing self-defined goals. The concern with external similarities of self with others has been replaced by a concern with one's unique capabilities. The shift towards a more unique and internally based definition of self is said to be accompanied by a shift towards inner direction and internal sources of self-knowledge. Adolescents are thought to be still dependent on adults for knowledge and direction, but they are beginning to seek independence.

This time of transition is often accompanied by varying levels of high self-consciousness, unstable self-concepts, low self-esteem, and even depression. Rosenberg (1979) found that self-concept is often unsettled during junior high school and then stabilizes to some degree during high school. One study found that only 25% of high school students in grades 10 or 12 had reached the stage of development where the orientation to the internal, unique self occurs (Van den Daele, 1968). As Gottfredson states, this implies that students may have problems in coping with the developmental tasks that they face in high school and early in their careers.

Gottfredson's (1981) circumscription theory states that young children define themselves, sex roles, and occupations according to concrete, external, observable appearances, and behaviours. Vocationally relevant self-concepts are developed and incorporated in an order corresponding to their concrete and external visibility: first, gender identity, then social class, and finally feelings and values. "With age, youngsters develop more sophisticated and complex views of the world, relating many disparate pieces of information into more unified and coherent understandings of themselves and others" (p. 556). As children develop and incorporate new pieces of information into their view of self, they continue to redefine their occupational image. In each stage, new criteria are added to help them with their image: sex type of occupation, prestige level, and field of work.

The youngsters are actually aware of the new dimensions in the stage preceding its incorporation. Children are aware of gender differences in stage one, but only in stage two are these differences associated with perceptions of both self and others. Henderson, Hesketh, and Tufflin (1988) directly tested this part of the theory and found that gender did influence occupational preferences at a younger age than social class. As the process evolves, preferences become more complex but more narrow. It is believed that movement between each stage includes the elimination of alternatives that are incompatible with adult occupations (rather than magical or nonhuman states of being), followed by sex type, prestige or difficulty, and finally particular interests and abilities.

Gottfredson's circumscription theory, just described, is based on the development of cognitive processes. Visible and concrete attributes, such as gender, are built into the self-concept and influence career preferences at an earlier stage than social class, interests, and values. Gottfredson's (1981) compromise theory predicts that elements internalized at an earlier age will be more resistant to change than those factors that are internalized later and emphasizes accordingly, the importance of gender and social status. A later study (Hesketh, Elmslie, & Kaldor, 1990) suggests that interest, the process of finding the unique self, is an important and complex factor. These researchers suggest the process is cumulative and that the final stage incorporates the input from all other stages, making interest, or orientation to the unique self of utmost importance. In this modification of Gottfredson's model, the importance of developing interests that may override decisions based singly on gender or social status is a key concept.

Research has shown by grade 8, students have an adult-like awareness of sex-roles, social class, and occupational prestige differences, and an understanding of the link between education, social class, and work (Goldstein & Oldham, 1979). Youngsters from a higher social class have the higher aspirations (Sewell & Shah, 1968). Students were found, without intervention, not to vary significantly in their level of aspiration between grades 9 and 12 (Gottfredson & Becker, 1981). The early development of a vocational identity based on sex-roles, underestimation of ability, and social class roles can limit the range of later development of one's unique personal identity based on specific interests and abilities.

Career Development of Gifted and Talented Students

Sanborn (1979) believes that gifted and talented students often travel a developmental pathway of self-discovery. His years of work with gifted and talented students at the University of Wisconsin Research and Guidance Laboratory suggest that appropriate educational activities should be generated for the particular style and needs of the student. Programmes should be designed to help these children learn about their own styles and abilities and to attempt to relate these qualities to opportunities open to them both in the present and in the future.

The literature on counselling the gifted and talented provides strategies for meeting the needs of the gifted, but does not include comprehensive programming models (Colson, Borman, & Nash 1978; Fredrickson, 1979; Hoyt & Hebeler, 1974; Kerr, 1983, 1986; Kerr &

Colangelo, 1988; Kerr & Ghrist-Priebe, 1988; Perrone, 1991; Sanborn, 1979; VanTassel-Baska, 1989). One of the recurring themes in this literature is multipotentiality. The gifted possess many potentialities and varied interests that may complicate their selection of a career. The investment of time is another important issue since the gifted often look towards careers that will take a large investment of time and energy. The need for self-discovery and independence, along with the need for direct exploratory career experiences are also common issues.

In some of the literature on the social-emotional needs of the gifted, the need for life/career counselling is discussed. The approach that is usually recommended is a separate career counselling component that may consist of group seminars on selective topics, career nights, college visitations, internships in selected career areas, planning of annual courses of study, and clinical counselling on problem areas (VanTassel-Baska, 1989). VanTassel-Baska stresses the need for a partnership model, involving teachers, counsellors, and parents. An example she uses involves a teacher in designing courses that utilize academic and career constructs. As part of the curriculum the course would involve speakers who represent key career areas to address certain topics. VanTassel-Baska suggests certain strategies for intervention of counselling needs such as the teaching of creative problem solving, encouraging positive and expressive outlets, and creating a "safe" environment to experiment with failure. Unfortunately, these constructs are not intertwined in her summary charts with the goals of career development. Existing programmes for the gifted and talented do not actually intertwine academic enrichment activities with career exploration. Recognition of the importance of career development can be seen in aspects of the Purdue Secondary Model (Feldhusen & Reilly, 1983) and the Autonomous Learner Model (Betts & Knapp, 1980).

The Enrichment Triad Model

The Enrichment Triad Model allows us a pathway to nurture creative productivity during school years and to foster the process of lifelong career development. One major goal of the Triad Model is to have students discover through general exploration (Type I enrichment), an area of interest where they can learn skills (Type II enrichment), and apply their talents to create a unique product (Type III enrichment). Research on students who have pursued creative productivity within a Triad Programme has revealed significant increases in perceived characteristics such as study skills, work habits, positive feelings towards school, and awareness of thought processes, personal strengths, and weaknesses (Starko, 1988). Studies had reported that involvement in general enrichment activities and Type III projects allowed for career exploration (Delcourt, 1988), and affected students' career choice (Starko, 1988).

Components from the Secondary Enrichment Triad Model (Reis & Renzulli, 1985) and the elementary model, the Schoolwide Enrichment Model (Renzulli, 1977; Renzulli & Reis, 1985) have been integrated with a developmental approach to heightening career aspirations of gifted and talented students. In the Focus On Model (Taylor, 1993), students are provided with enrichment opportunities which broaden their exposure to various fields (modified Type I); process skills, including critical and creative thinking, specific methodological skills, and career development skills (modified Type II); and modified Type III investigations. These opportunities can be used to explore potential career interests, experience the role of practicing professionals, and visualize a different sense of self.

The Focus on Model: Broadening Conceptions, Screening Processes, and Implementation

Broadening Conceptions of Giftedness: Creative Productivity: A broadened conception of giftedness is based on the premise that many who have achieved recognition because of their contributions to society have displayed an interplay of attributes (Cox, 1926; Renzulli, 1978, 1986, 1988; Roe, 1952; Torrance, 1969; Wallach, 1976). Hoyt (1965) reviewed 46 studies dealing with the relationship between traditional indicators of academic success and post-college performance in the fields of business, teaching, engineering, medicine, scientific research, and other areas such as the ministry, journalism, and government. This extensive review revealed that traditional indications of academic success have no more than a very modest correlation with various indicators of success in the adult world. These studies reinforce broadening the conception of giftedness from a sole reliance on test-scores as an indicator of future potential.

Studies on the Secondary Enrichment Triad Model (Reis & Renzulli, 1985) and the Schoolwide Enrichment Model (Renzulli, 1977; Renzulli & Reis, 1985) have demonstrated that multiple cognitive and affective factors underlie the concept of creative productive giftedness (Delisle & Renzulli, 1982; Gubbins, 1982; Reis & Renzulli, 1985). In the model, giftedness is viewed as an interaction of above average ability, task commitment, and creativity brought to bear upon a specific performance area. These clusters of traits are known to interact with personality and environmental factors that can determine whether gifted behaviour emerges (Delcourt, 1988; Schack, 1989; Starko, 1988). Burns (1990) found that although barriers to creative production do exist, proactive measures can be designed to counteract the personal or environmental factors. These barriers to success can also be identified as they affect the individual over time (Gottfredson, 1981). As described in the Focus On Model, the factors of parental influence, gender issues, social orientation, and self-concept all sequentially affect development and will determine if creative productive potential will be expressed (Taylor, 1993).

Barron (1963) and MacKinnon (1965, 1978) completed the most extensive studies of highly creative individuals and found that they are characterized by such personality traits as inventiveness, independence, individuality, enthusiasm, determination, and industry. Barron states that a special fascination for and involvement with the subject matter of one's field are the invariable precursors of original and distinctive work. These are the types of characteristics that must be nurtured in those individuals who show creative productive promise.

Broadening the Screening Process

The Enrichment Triad Model (Reis & Renzulli, 1985; Renzulli, 1977; Renzulli & Reis, 1985; Renzulli, Reis, & Smith, 1981) has at its core a screening process that recognizes a broadened definition of giftedness. The model nurtures the development of talents or gifts by utilizing a multifaceted screening process, providing opportunities designed to encourage exploration and skill building, and to ultimately stimulate creative production in a field of endeavour.

The Revolving Door Identification Model (Renzulli, Reis, & Smith, 1981), stresses the importance of using multiple criteria to find students who have the potential for creative productive behaviour; those capable of an interplay above average ability, creativity, and task commitment. The process consists of obtaining four types of information about the student: psychometric, developmental, sociometric, and performance.

Psychometric data generally refer to tests of cognitive processes such as intelligence, aptitude, creativity, and school achievement. The type of tests that are used should take into account the characteristics of the population being tested. For example, a programme that was targeting gifted students at a vocational-technical school utilized the spatial and mechanical intelligence scales on the *Differentiatal Aptitude Tests* (Taylor, 1993). Students from low-income environments do not fair well on standardized tests. Therefore, these students should be examined as a group and not compared against national norms.

Developmental information, knowledge about how the students interact with their environment, is suggested to be obtained from teacher rating scales, such as the *Scales for Rating the Behavioural Characteristics of Superior Students (SCRBSS,* Renzulli, Smith, White, Callahan, & Hartman, 1976). The *SCRBSS* consists of ten dimensions, each of which is named for the specific ability area it is designed to evaluate: Learning, Motivation, Creativity, Leadership, Art, Music, Dramatics, Communication (Precision), Communication (Expressiveness), and Planning. The first four scales are recommended for use in the nomination process. These scales have also been modified for use with students of low socioeconomic status (Baldwin, 1985). Other suggested sources of developmental information include ratings and biographical information from parents and student self-ratings or nominations. Developmental barriers to success should also be examined for possible impact on the screening process. For example, gender issues may begin to impact development in primary age students, and gender issues may begin to mask future potential. This underlies importance of using a variety of sources for screening data.

Sociometric information is defined as information about an individual that is provided by members of the peer group. Peer rating scales are available and can be used for this purpose. Performance information includes actual examples of creative production by the students. Anecdotal records, observational reports, performance evaluations, or rating scales can all be used to gather evidence of this component of the screening process. The growing use of portfolios in education provides an excellent resource for information. Actual student products from a variety of sources can be utilized in the screening process.

In establishing a talent pool of students who will be eligible to receive services, two basic criteria plus an alternative pathway approach is recommended (Renzulli, Reis, & Smith, 1981). A student who qualifies on either psychometric or developmental information would gain immediate access to services by automatically being placed in a talent pool. A student who is nominated by sociometric or performance criteria would have been considered for placement in the talent pool, pending a review by a selection committee.

Implementation: Broadening Services

Enrichment Triad Model

The Schoolwide Enrichment Model (Renzulli & Reis, 1985) provides a structural framework for meeting the needs of gifted and talented students at the elementary or middle school level. The resource teacher makes sure the needs of the students are met in the regular classroom, in classroom extension activities, and in activities that may originate in a resource room. Some enrichment activities may target a schoolwide population, some classrooms, and yet others may specifically target members of an identified talent pool.

The Secondary Enrichment Triad Model (Reis & Renzulli, 1985) was designed to meet the demands of providing services for gifted and talented students at the high school level. The model provides a framework for dealing with problems including scheduling, finding time for creative productive work in content oriented classes, and developing administrative and staff support. The services suggested in the model are blended into already existing options such as advanced placement, honours classes, and extracurricular activities. The formation of an Interdisciplinary Planning Team provides a mechanism for classroom and resource teachers to plan and organize programme goals and activities. The team, including faculty members who volunteer to participate from each of the major academic areas, meets on a regular basis to discuss curriculum compacting options for students and to plan schoolwide enrichment opportunities.

The Secondary Triad Model involves the formation of talent pool classes which differ considerably from the traditional honours or accelerated classes. These classes are established as Triad Programmes within any given subject. Classes include more intensive and individualized studies of the course content. The course content itself should be modified to reflect types of topics or areas of study not covered in the regular curriculum. All talent pool students receive an orientation to the programme and are interviewed about interest in the talent pool classes. Even if eligible students do not enroll in talent pool classes, they can participate in enrichment activities and meet on a regular basis with the resource teacher for discussion, counselling, and any other intervention activity. Curriculum compacting allows for classroom time to be utilized for enrichment activities when the student has demonstrated mastery of required concepts.

Several kinds of services and three types of enrichment activities are included as the basis of the Secondary Enrichment Triad Model. One component of the model includes a talent pool class which provides three types of enrichment activities: Type I or general exploratory activities, Type II or group training activities, including investigative methodologies and process skills, and Type III or individual or small group investigations of real problems. The goal of the enrichment activities is to activate three interlocking clusters or attributes of giftedness that are necessary for creative productivity: above average ability, creativity, and task commitment.

An Integrative Model of Career Development

Gifted and talented programmes could be modified to incorporate the processes of career development. Activities that are very similar to Renzulli's Type I (general exploratory), Type II (skill training), and Type III (opportunities for creative production) could be utilized with an orientation towards career exploration. These activities should also be recognized to affect students differently, taking into account their developmental levels.

Gifted programmes provide services to children in all four stages of career development summarized by Gottfredson (1981). During stage one (ages 3-5), as children orient to size and power, they begin to grasp the concept of being an adult. Programmes that service preschool students could focus on orienting youngsters about opportunities available to them as adults. Elementary and middle school programmes should reflect the importance of gender issues, the major focus of the second stage Gottfredson discusses, along with social orientation, prominent in stage three, as individuals begin to develop and narrow their career aspirations. High school programmes must incorporate the struggle to define the unique self, her fourth stage, into the programming of services required at this stage of development. Finally, the importance of parental influence on career development has been documented (Dillard & Campbell 1981; Frasier, 1987; McNair & Brown, 1983; Rosen, 1959) and must become an integrated part of any programme designed to nurture the untapped potential in underserved populations. The Focus On Model incorporates strategies of gifted and talented programming with the issues students face during career development.

Focus on Parental Influence

Since parental influence has been found to be a major factor influencing occupational aspirations, parents need to be included in programming designed to meet the needs of gifted and talented students. Meetings should be held to include parents in the planning and implementation of a gifted programme. They need to understand and recognize the need for them to encourage their child in the development of his/her giftedness and career aspirations. Delcourt

(1988) has reported that parental behaviours important in nurturing creative productivity include encouragement of independence, risk taking behaviours, and experiencing the value and love of learning. Current research by Robinson (personal communication, 1991) describes a programme that provides career guidance for parents of low socioeconomic students right in their homes. Parents need to be brought into the picture as schools strive to help a broader spectrum of students reach their full potential.

Focus on Gender Issues

The primary years, kindergarten through grade 3 or ages 6-8, encompass the stage where, according to career development theory, an orientation to sex roles occurs. Gender becomes a new element to perception of self and others in this stage. Type I exploratory activities should reflect the breadth of involvement of males and females in all fields of endeavour. The Type II skills would utilize critical and creative thinking skills and specific methodological skills associated with various career fields. Classroom integration of skills used in different fields could include units on the methodologies of architecture, engineering, and paleontology.

The Type III creative productive investigations would provide opportunities for students to realize that occupations exist to solve problems. These activities could build a base for an understanding that choosing an occupation means selecting problems that one is interested in working on. Type III training activities, modelling and training of the creative production process, would be important at these early stages of development.

Focus on Social Orientation

Career development stage of orientation to social evaluation manifest itself during grades 4 and 5 (ages 9-13). The new elements in perceptions of self and others include social class and intelligence (Gottfredson, 1981). In this stage, the individual becomes very sensitized to peer group evaluations and then to more general social expectations, values, and evaluations. The origin of differences between children in their perceptions is believed to come from the emergence of class differences in aspirations (Ginzberg, Gubsburg, Axelrad, & Herma, 1951; McNair & Brown, 1983; Rosen, 1959; Sewell & Shah, 1968). Youngsters are found to identify with the socioeconomic group from which they come and to adopt those standards. Exploration of activities outside of those found in the immediate socioeconomic environment will be very important for some populations; therefore Type I activities should stress a breadth of activities.

Additional Type II skills should be recognized and considered in a developmental perspective. VanTassel-Baska (1989) lists strategies to address the needs that should be dealt with directly with students in this stage. An understanding of differences, between self and others can be handled through bibliotherapy, group discussions, and individual dialogues. The existence of learning styles and Holland's (1985) personality types could be springboards for discussions of the range of differences that exist in populations. An appreciation for their own individuality and the differences of others can be promoted through biographical study, recognizing and honouring diverse talents, and special seminars. Gowan (1979) strongly suggested a seminar type homeroom where high creative potential students could share unique interests in a safe environment to avoid the "herd instinct" that can prevent creative development at this stage. The Autonomous Learner Model has an individual development dimension which includes activities to develop learning skills, personal understanding, interpersonal skills, and career involvement (Betts & Knapp, 1980). However these skills are not integrated with the enrichment activities and the in-depth study dimensions of the model. Within the process of creative production, Type III level enrichment activities, powerful opportunities for career exploration and the raising of ceilings that may have been placed on students aspirations.

Focus on the Unique Self

During development, youngsters are found to shift from accommodating directly from external socially defined goals to pursuing self-defined internal goals (Gottfredson, 1981). The concern with external similarities of self with others has been replaced by a concern with one's unique capabilities. The shift towards a more unique and internally based definition of self is said to be accompanied by a shift towards inner direction and internal sources of self knowledge. This time of transition is often accompanied by varying levels of high self-consciousness, unstable self-concepts, low self-esteem, and even depression. Self-concept is often unsettled during junior high school and then stabilizes to some degree during high school. One study found that only 25% of high school students in grades 10 or 12 had reached the stage of development where the orientation to the internal, unique self occurs (Van den Daele, 1968). As Gottfredson states, this implies that students may have problems in coping with the developmental tasks that they face in high school and early in their careers. Self-concept development has been found to be positively affected by enrichment activities. Self-concept constructs such as the courage to be different were mentioned as being perceived as the most important benefit of gifted programmes by students and parents (Moon & Feldhusen, 1994).

Type I activities at this stage should continue to broaden the fields of study that students encounter. Type II training skills, including critical and creative thinking, and specific methodological skills may take on new importance as students enter into more sophisticated stages of thinking. Type II skills, as they relate to career development or career development skills, deserve much attention at this stage. As students orient towards a unique self they will need to gain a realistic assessment of their abilities, learn to harness critical and creative thinking abilities to make life decisions, and plan for their future. Self assessment procedures should be provided for the students by school personnel. Interest inventories such as the *Strong-Campbell,* and personality surveys such as *Myers-Briggs* can be used to help students focus on their own individual interests. Decision making and problem solving strategies can be applied to these real-life concerns.

Type III creative productive investigations are important to youngsters at this stage. It is important to provide opportunities that will leave students feeling competent in their explorations of particular fields of endeavour. Examples of modified Type I, Type II, and Type III enrichment activities from a high school programme utilizing Focus On can be found in Appendix A. Bloom (1985), in his discussions of the development of talent, stresses the importance of the small successes that result in a child's increasing interest and greater commitment to a career field. The falling in love with a topic that often occurs during creative productivity can become intertwined with a future career image and predict future creative achievement (Torrance, 1981).

Type III investigations can be used to explore potential career interests, allow students to see themselves in the role of practicing professionals, and begin to visualize a different sense of self. This process is especially important for those who had limited their aspirations during development due to limits placed on sex-roles, underestimation of ability or confinements of social class. Involvement in the creative productive process would allow an individual to reassess his or her vocational identity. The process involves a bringing together of abilities, creative potential, and commitment to a problem that is of interest to an internal self. The nature of this "real" problem would then bring students in contact with the materials and methods used by professionals in many diverse fields. Students may develop a mentor relationship with a professional, making personal connections while exploring the field of interest.

The importance of gifted and talented programming on career aspirations can be seen in a college application of a high school student who had been involved in a programme that utilized Focus On. This student, who had completed a Type III investigation, wrote, "Being a part of the Gifted and Talented Programme has expanded my knowledge of many different fields. It has given me many insights on different occupations, and has gotten me interested in becoming a lawyer."

Research on the Focus on Model

The effectiveness of using the Focus On Model in heightening career aspirations was assessed. The following research question was posed:

What are the effects of levels of enrichment in the Secondary Enrichment Triad Model and participation in a self-awareness and career focusing component on career aspiration?

Methods and Procedures

A mid-sized vocational-technical high school was selected as the site for this study because it met several criteria. The first of those criteria was that a gifted and talented programme, based on the Secondary Enrichment Triad Model, had been in place for six years, four years with the same coordinator. A talent pool of 60 students was identified as having the potential to exhibit gifted and talented behaviour. The students were identified using procedures based on the Revolving Door Identification Model. The students received three types of enrichment, Type I (general exploratory), Type II (group training), and Type III (individual or small group investigation of real problems), as described in the Secondary Enrichment Triad Model (Reis & Renzulli, 1985) and Schoolwide Enrichment Model (Renzulli & Reis, 1985).

Another criteria met by this study site was that variability existed in the career aspirations of this gifted and talented population although the sample was both socioeconomically and ethnically homogeneous and was representative of the population in the school. The sample consisted of 7 females and 53 males. There were 59 students from

White lower to middle class families, 1 from a African American middle class family.

Research Design

This research study used a posttest only control-group experimental type group design (Borg & Gall, 1989). Pretest information was gathered in order to assess group equivalence. Sixty subjects were randomly assigned to experimental (n=30) and control groups (n=30) that were involved in the career counselling component of the study. Random assignment was not used according to level of enrichment. The students chose the level of enrichment. The assignment of treatment and control groups was stratified randomly by level of enrichment to ensure equivalence. There were 14 subjects in the no enrichment group, 26 in the Type I group, and 20 in the Type III group. The cells of the experimental design were proportional.

Student records were used to determine the level of enrichment. Students were grouped for the 3 x 2 analysis of variance (ANOVA) by their level of enrichment: no enrichment (only identified), general exploratory enrichment (Type I), or creative production (Type III). They were grouped for analysis according to their participation (treatment) or non-participation (control) in the self-awareness and career focusing (SACF) counselling component. Students were placed in the Type III group if they had completed products during the last two years.

A pretest was administered to both groups, a questionnaire including one question from the *Student Descriptive Questionnaire* (College Entrance Examination Board, 1989). Both groups were administered the *Strong-Campbell Interest Inventory,* for assessment purposes and the *Myers-Briggs Type Indicator* for assessment purposes only. The treatment, explained below, was administered to the experimental group but not the control group. The same instrument was used as a pretest and posttest and was administered to both groups.

Treatment

Students in the treatment group participated in a self-awareness and career focusing (SACF) counselling component modelled after interventions planned at career laboratories for the gifted and talented at Texas A & M University (Colson, Borman, & Nash, 1978) and at the University of Iowa (Kerr, 1986; Kerr & Colangelo, 1988). The programme involved assessment of the *Strong-Campbell Interest Inventory (SCII)* and the *Myers-Briggs Type Indicator (MBTI)* and an individual (50 minutes) counselling session. A school psychologist assessed the results of the instruments and provided the individual counselling sessions. The psychologist followed a structured interview schedule designed to clarify interests, needs, and values and to encourage goal setting behaviour. The interview began with a career information sheet that was filled in by the student and provided information to the counsellor on interests and aspirations. The Strong-Campbell Interpretive report results were discussed: general occupation themes and basic interest scales along with a description of Holland's hexagon of themes. The occupations of people with similar interests to the students were reviewed. For example, a student with high Realistic, Conventional, and Investigative type scores would have similar interests to people in computer programming, engineering, and systems analysis. The *Myers-Briggs* results would then be discussed and relationship between Holland themes and *Myers-Briggs* types examined using explanation of types from manual (Myers & McCaully, 1985).

Students' original aspirations from the information sheet were discussed along with these results and cognitive ability results information from the *Differential Aptitude Tests.* On the basis of the test results, it was demonstrated to students how they were unique or special, and how these qualities could be related to career choices. Students were guided in setting appropriate career goals that reflected their abilities and their interests and encouraged to utilize school and community resources to reach their goals.

The *Strong-Campbell Interest Inventory (SCII;* Campbell & Hansen, 1985) is a commonly used career counselling tool for college students that has high validity and reliability measures (Pinkney, 1983). The instrument incorporates Holland's personality types with a wide range of occupational scales and determines congruent career options. The *Myers-Briggs Type Indicator (MBTI)* is often used along with *SCII* to provide an "excellent start for relating self-understanding to career planning" (Pinkney, 1983). The *MBTI* generates preference scores that describe a person's interactions on four dimensions. The integration of these two instruments is regarded as useful in encouraging active participation in the counselling process (Miller, 1988) and will potentially increase the individual's self-awareness, underlying decision making process, and the understanding of preferences scales (Pinkney, 1983).

A questionnaire included a question from the *College Board's Student Descriptive Questionnaire* (College Entrance Examination Board, 1989). The question on career aspiration determined how many years of further education or training the students were planning.

The College Board studies on this questionnaire, and other studies using similar self-reported descriptive information have been shown to have high reliability scores ranging from 0.76 to 0.95 (Freeberg, 1988). Information from this instrument should be applicable to a number of educational purposes for which student biographical information has been used in the past (Freeberg, 1988). Other studies that have measured career aspiration have shown that expressed career plans have as high predictive validity as do measured interest (Bartling & Hood, 1981).

Results

Preliminary Analysis: The data were initially examined to determine if the underlying assumptions of analysis of variance (ANOVA) were met. These included the examination of the distribution of the sample variances to determine if they were significantly different. The means and the variance between the control and treatment groups of the pretest on the number of years of college planned did not significantly differ. The pretest mean for the control group was 3.5, the standard deviation 2.2. The pretest mean for the treatment group was 2.9, and the standard deviation 1.9. To examine another underlying assumption of ANOVA, the distribution of the sample was checked for normality. A univariate analysis was conducted on the dependent variable, career aspiration. The curve was found to be positively skewed and the data were transformed logarithmically.

Anova Analysis

The results of the Analysis of Variance (ANOVA) determining the effects of the levels of enrichment experienced in the talent pool classes and participation in a self-awareness and career focusing component are found in table below.

The first main effect concerns the participation in a career counselling component (SACF) in addition to Triad enrichment and its effects on career aspiration. The analysis of variance on these data revealed no significant difference between participation in a career counselling component (SACF) with respect to career aspiration.

There is a significant difference, a main effect, $F(2,54) = 7.784$, $p<.001$, $MS=0.457$ between the levels of enrichment in the Secondary Enrichment Triad Model with respect to career aspiration. The students who did not decide to pursue enrichment opportunities had a mean of 1.5 years of college planned. Those who participated in Type I, general exploratory activities had a mean of 2.6 years of college to which they were aspiring. The students who had completed investigations of real problems, Type III activities, had a mean of 4.0 years of college planned. Therefore, students who had participated in the enrichment activities had more years of college planned.

The question of a significant interaction of the levels of enrichment in the Secondary Enrichment Triad Model and participation in a self-awareness and career focusing component (SACF) on career aspiration was analyzed. No significant interaction was found between the levels of enrichment in the Secondary Enrichment Triad Model and participation in a self-awareness and career focusing component (SACF) on career aspiration.

Table: *Results of 3 x 2 Analysis of Variance*

Source	*Sum-of-Squares*	*DF*	*Mean-Square*	*F-Ratio*	*P*
SACF	0.011	1	0.011	0.190	0.665
LEVELS	0.915	2	0.457	7.784	0.001*
SACF X LEVELS	0.123	2	0.061	1.044	0.359
Error	54 3.173				

*p< .001

Post Hoc Analysis

A Tukey Post hoc analysis was conducted in order to determine where the significant differences existed between levels. Significant differences were found between no enrichment and Type III, and Type I and Type III. The Q value reported for the levels, no enrichment and Type III was 5.78 and was significant at the p<.01 level. The Q value determined between the levels Type I and Type III was 6.08 and was significant at the p<.01 level. There were no significant differences, a Q value of 2.48, found between providing no enrichment and providing Type I enrichment experiences. Therefore, the Type III enrichment activities that are significantly related to the career aspirations of the students in this study.

Discussion

The Focus On Model significantly heightened career aspirations of high school students who had participated in exploratory activities and creative productivity. The students participated in enrichment activities in such fields as cultural arts, computer arts, engineering, environmental science, and architectural design. Standard career development types of activities such as familiarization, exploration, and preparation were intertwined with the enrichment activities of the gifted and talented programme. Although the exploratory activities did heighten career aspirations as measured in the number of years of college planned, it was the involvement as a creative productive "practicing professional" that had the greatest impact on the students.

Table: *Results of Post Hoc Analysis Using Tukey Method*

Levels	Means	Q values#
0	1.5	
1	2.6	2.48 (0 & 1)
3	4.0	5.78* (0 & 3) 6.08* (1 & 3)

*p< .01. # Q values obtained using logarithmically transformed data

Table: *Description of Type I and Type III Activities*

Student	Type I Area	Topic	Type III - Enrichment Activity Product	Audience
1	c, a, en	writing	poetry	publication
2	c, en, eg	environment	Earth Day	school/community
3	c, en, eg	environment	Earth Day	school/community
4	c, a, en, eg	environment	Earth Day	school/community
5	c, eg	engineering	invention	competitions
6	c, eg	engineering	invention	patent attorney
7	c, eg	engineering	invention	competitions
8	c, g	politics	speech	U.S. Congress
9	c, ar	architecture	model	school, museum
10	c, a, g	advertising	commercial	radio producer
11	c, a, ar	architecture	home design	architects
12	c, a, ar	architecture	home design	architects
13	c, a, ar	design	commercial	business
14	c, a, eg	computer/art	design	school
15	c, eg	advertising	commercial	radio producer
16	c, a, eg	advertising	commercial	radio producer
17	c, a, eg	drawing	design	art college
18	c, a, eg	advertising	commercial	radio producer
19	c, eg	engineering	invention	competitions
20	c, a, eg	computer	music	community

c=cultural, a=arts, eg=engineering, en=environmental, g=general, ar=architectural

This study examined the effects of the Schoolwide Enrichment Model (Renzulli, 1977; Renzulli & Reis, 1985) integrated with a career development component, Focus On (Taylor, 1993). The Enrichment Triad Model allows a pathway to not only nurture creative productivity during school years, but to foster the process of lifelong career development by engaging students as active participants in a real-world oriented learning process. Explorations were offered in many fields of endeavour and there were opportunities to interact with and simulate professional levels of study.

The results support the developmental theory of career aspiration proposed by Gottfredson (1981). She hypothesized after reviewing the cognitive development literature that there are four basic stages of development: orientation to size and power (ages 3-5), orientation to sex roles (ages 6-8), orientation to social evaluation (about ages 9-13), and orientation to the internal, unique self (beginning at about age 14). The vocationally relevant elements of gender, social class background, intelligence, vocational interests, competencies, and values were thought to be incorporated into a vocational self-concept at different stages of development. We would expect a successful intervention to be able to remove barriers due to gender in the primary grades.

The subjects from the vocational-technical high school and identified as members of a talent pool who did not opt for enrichment opportunities had a mean of 1.5 years of college planned. Students who participated in Type I, general exploratory experiences, had a mean of 2.6 years of college aspirations. The students who had completed investigations of real problems, Type III experiences, had significantly heightened career aspirations, they had a mean of 4.0 years of college planned. The career development of students involved in this study was intertwined with the development of their creative productivity. Possible explanations of this relationship may be found in Gottfredson's theory of career development. According to Gottfredson (1981), all students pass through a developmental career pathway. The important objectives of the later stages of career development, such as those involving high school students, are to orient towards the internal, unique self. One of the major goals of the Triad Model is for students to discover through general exploration (Type I enrichment) an area of intense self interest. It is not surprising then that a connection was found between involvement in creative productivity and heightened career aspirations. Involvement in the creative productive process would allow an individual to reassess his or her vocational identity. The process brings together abilities, creative potential, and commitment to a problem that is of interest to an internal self. The nature of this "real" problem would then put students in contact with the materials and methods used by professionals in many diverse fields. Students may develop a mentor relationship with a professional, making personal connections while exploring the field of interest. Most importantly, students are allowed to view themselves in the role of practicing professionals and begin to visualize a different sense of self. This process would be especially important for those who had limited their aspirations during development due to constraints placed on sex-roles, underestimation of ability, or confinements of social class.

Although this study has been conducted on a small scale, the results are encouraging when considering the career development of special populations. Aspirations can be heightened of students who have experienced early constraints on gender roles and social class. Dreams that have been narrowed in scope, can again be broadened through programming that is responsive to the developmental processes occurring when those dreams are being spun.

Potential exists in youth from every socioeconomic group for participating in a range of career fields, and for solving the societal problems that will arise. Studies have shown that students from lower socioeconomic families often underestimate their potential in a chosen career field (Ginzberg et al., 1951; McNair & Brown, 1983; Rosen, 1959; Sewell & Shah, 1968). There is a ceiling created by societal expectations, placed upon the educational potential of these students.

Research has shown by grade eight, students have an adult-like awareness of sex-roles, social class and occupational prestige differences, and an understanding of the link between education, social class, and work (Gottfredson, 1981, 1986). The early development of a vocational identity based on sex-roles, underestimation of ability, and social class roles can limit the range of later development of one's unique personal identity based on specific interests and abilities.

With intervention, vocational identities can be influenced by involvement in gifted and talented programming. Focus On, an integrative model of career development, allows students to explore a full range of opportunities, developing interests and aspirations that can prevent environmental factors from narrowing their options. Thomas Edison in discussing the intervention of home schooling that his mother provided for him after only three months of formal schooling related:

The good effects of her early training I can never lose. If it had not been for her appreciation and her faith in me at a critical time in my experience, I should very likely never have become an inventor. You see, she believed that many of the boys who turned out badly by the time they grew to manhood would have become valuable citizens if they had been handled in the right way when they were young. Her years of experience as a school teacher taught her many things about human nature and especially about boys. I was always a careless boy, and with a mother of a different character I should have probable turned out badly. (Gudeman, 1984, p. 53).

What Influences a Young Person's Career Decisions?

Many things influence the career decisions of young people. However, you might be surprised to hear that you, as their parent, are likely to have the strongest influence. This influence comes through your interactions with them and through your values and beliefs; your comments and your encouragement of their use of their strengths and interests. However daunting that may sound, rest assured. We are here to partner you.

Their career development will be a process and few students are in the same place in this process at the same time. It's a process that shouldn't be rushed; a process that can be tackled systematically and a process that can empower them. You can engage with them at any stage but their influences could be a good place to start. Let's take a look at some of them:

You

- To what extent is your child interested in what you do for a living?
- Are they keen to follow the same career path and, if so, have they considered any alternatives?
- Could you discuss with them what you do, and how you made career decisions?
- What effects do you think your occupation; background; career history; finances; education; skills and values might have on your child's career thinking and approach to job seeking?
- How might your relationships with them, and with other people, play a part in this?

Their Friends

- How well would you say that you knew their friends?
- Do they look up to some of them more than others and if so, why?
- Which of their friends have made career plans and what are they?
- How did they reach those decisions?
- What interests their friends and what do they value in life?
- Do their friends still live near them or have they moved away?

- To what extent do you think they are opting for safe and known career ideas?

Their Culture

- In what ways would you say that their culture; their background and where they live might influence your child's career aspirations?
- For example, what importance might they place on the status of the job? On the potential to earn a good salary? On opportunities for personal and professional development? On their ability to save for their future?
- Equally, is their culture one in which they may be expected to show respect for the wishes of their elders; to care for family members; to support their family financially; to work outside of New Zealand or to seek work in a particular range of roles?

Their Family

- You, and your child's siblings (particularly older brothers and sisters), can instil aspirations in them – also expectations.
- Does your child have brothers or sisters who have been to university? Are they in work? Do they share their experiences of both with your child – the good and the bad? How did they tackle decisions that they took on work and study?
- Is there a type of work that is prevalent in your family? If so, to what extent might your child be considering that option?

The Media

- Film; television and related media can offer great insights into possible careers. Equally however, these may not be in any depth and may create unrealistic portrayals of occupations.
- As a result, consider how you might encourage your child to use such media critically. Is there a particular genre of film and television that they enjoy? What roles do the actors play? Which of these might interest your child – and why? Media can be a good, relatively un-threatening way of engaging your child in a discussion about their career thoughts.
- When your child is ready, encourage them to use the media as part of their research into possible careers; employment sectors; employers and the labour market.

Their Tutors

- Students often have very strong views on 'good' and 'bad' tutors. Chances are the good are ones who show a passion for the subject they are teaching and have great skills in engaging their students.
- Tutors may well have links with employers, knowledge of the careers that their students pursue on graduation and knowledge of your child that they can use if being asked to be a referee.

Government Policy

- Perhaps subtly, government policy may have a part to play. This can be through efforts to encourage young people to enter career areas where the country is experiencing significant skill shortage, or to open access to certain roles to greater numbers from a particular gender; certain backgrounds and so on.
- Additionally, state financial support for tertiary education can make it easier, or harder, to pursue university study; to do so as a distance student rather than on-campus; to study particular disciplines and to study at a particular institution.

It is crucial to note that no study or career decision that your child makes need be for life. Indeed, they may find themselves doing a job that has yet to be invented! Also, most graduates will have a number of jobs over their working life and some will change career direction as well as role and employer.

3

Institutional Pedagogy

Institutional pedagogy is a practice of education that is centred on two factors: 1. the complexity of the learner, and the "unconscious" that he or she brings to the classroom. This unconscious is another name for the diversity of social, economic, cultural and other unspoken elements that an educator interacts with in an institutional setting; and 2. the role of the institution in the process of intervening in both those psycho-social factors and in what is known by a student.

But even more than this, as conceived by its founder, Fernand Oury, Institutional Pedagogy is a constant calling into question of the institutional context itself. Thus the classroom is never a presupposed and static setting. The movement of Institutional Pedagody is thus in direct opposition to the prevailing trends of education prior to the late 1960s, almost all of which tended to homogenize socio-cultural differences amongst learners, psycho-social factors in learning and most important the presence of the "unconscious" in the classroom itself.

Thus the use of 'institution' in Institutional Pedagogy is broader than in its more colloquial sense. To Oury the institution could be defined as:

> *"the places, moments, status of each according to his/ her level of performance, that is to say according to his/ her potentialities, the functions (services, posts, responsibilities), roles (president, secretary), diverse meetings (team captains, different levels of classes, etc.), and the rituals that maintain their efficacy."*

Industry-oriented Education

Industry Oriented Education has been applied to vocational education. It was only offered to sub-degree education and industry training until 2004. Since 2004 Industry Oriented Education has been introduced to undergraduate degree and Master's degree.

Industry oriented education is an approach to learning from an industry perspective. With traditional technical teaching methodologies in educational environments, the conventional pathway is to build the foundation learning through subject based teaching of maths, physics and science independently. Subjects based on the knowledge required for the discipline usually follow on from this. The problem with this traditional methodology of learning is that there is no close relationship with industry requirements.

Students may well graduate with no industrial oriented learning experience prior to their first job. Industrial oriented methodology is an approach to learning from an industry perspective. As an example, the course of Electronics Technology in the Bachelor of Applied Technology is directly linked to industry and the focus is on an industrial product such as a Switch-mode power supply. Initially students will receive a demonstration and the product enclosure will be opened to investigate inside. The internal components form the topics for study: this includes the mechanical design for the enclosure, electronic design including the PCB (Printed Circuit Board) and embedded software design. The focus for learning is product design, application and operation of electronic components and circuitry. The industrial product will be activated under simulated industry conditions where students will gain invaluable insight of design technology, operational procedure and programming techniques. All foundation skills can be achieved within these studies and the students are well prepared to develop further knowledge and skills required for their industry project required in their final year through cooperative education with industry. Mathematics is not taught here as an independent course of study, but totally integrated into the compulsory technical courses. As an example, the course of Electronics Technology taught in the Bachelor of Applied Technology uses Fast Fourier Transform series to explore the method of Electromagnetic Interference (EMI) in Switch-mode power supplies. Initially students will receive a demonstration and the product which is a commercial product, will be opened for internal investigation of the enclosure. The internal components form the topics for study: this includes the mechanical design for the enclosure, electronic design including the PCB (Printed Circuit Board) and embedded software design. The focus for learning is product design, application and operation of electronic components and circuitry.

An example in post-graduate programme is a "bridge" technology course designed for the first year students in Master of Design programme before they start their projects. It is to enable a Bachelor of Design graduate to entry this technology oriented programme.

Professional Development

In workplaces, *professional development* refers to the acquisition of skills and knowledge both for personal development and for career advancement. Professional development encompasses all types of facilitated learning opportunities, ranging from college degrees to formal coursework, conferences and informal learning opportunities situated in practice. It has been described as intensive and collaborative, ideally incorporating an evaluative stage. There are a variety of approaches to professional development, including consultation, coaching, communities of practice, lesson study, mentoring, reflective supervision and technical assistance.

History

The Oxford English Dictionary notes the use of the phrase "professional development" from 1857 onwards.

In the training of school staff in the United States, "[t]he need for professional development [...] came to the forefront in the 1960's".

Who Participates and Why

A wide variety of people, such as teachers, military officers and non-commissioned officers, health care professionals, lawyers, accountants and engineers engage in professional development. Individuals may participate in professional development because of an interest in lifelong learning, a sense of moral obligation, to maintain and improve professional competence, to enhance career progression, to keep abreast of new technology and practices, or to comply with professional regulatory organizations. Many American states have professional development requirements for school teachers. For example, Arkansas teachers must complete 60 hours of documented professional development activities annually. Professional development credits are named differently from state to state. For example, teachers: in Indiana are required to earn 90 Continuing Renewal Units (CRUs) per year; in Massachusetts, teachers need 150 Professional Development Points (PDPs); and in Georgia, must earn 10 Professional Learning Units (PLUs). American and Canadian nurses, as well as those in the United Kingdom, have to participate in formal and informal professional development (earning Continuing education units, or CEUs) in order to maintain professional registration. Other groups such as engineering and geoscience regulatory bodies also have mandatory professional development requirements.

Approaches

In a broad sense, professional development may include *formal* types of vocational education, typically post-secondary or poly-technical training leading to qualification or credential required to obtain or retain employment. Professional development may also come in the form of pre-service or in-service professional development programmes. These programmes may be formal, or informal, group or individualized. Individuals may pursue professional development independently, or programmes may be offered by human resource departments. Professional development on the job may develop or enhance process skills, sometimes referred to as leadership skills, as well as task skills. Some examples for process skills are 'effectiveness skills', 'team functioning skills', and 'systems thinking skills'.

Professional development opportunities can range from a single workshop to a semester-long academic course, to services offered by a medley of different professional development providers and varying widely with respect to the philosophy, content, and format of the learning experiences. Some examples of approaches to professional development include:

- Case Study Method - The case method is a teaching approach that consists in presenting the students with a case, putting them in the role of a decision maker facing a problem (Hammond 1976).
- Consultation - to assist an individual or group of individuals to clarify and address immediate concerns by following a systematic problem-solving process.
- Coaching - to enhance a person's competencies in a specific skill area by providing a process of observation, reflection, and action.
- Communities of Practice - to improve professional practice by engaging in shared enquiry and learning with people who have a common goal

- Lesson Study - to solve practical dilemmas related to intervention or instruction through participation with other professionals in systematically examining practice
- Mentoring - to promote an individual's awareness and refinement of his or her own professional development by providing and recommending structured opportunities for reflection and observation
- Reflective Supervision - to support, develop, and ultimately evaluate the performance of employees through a process of enquiry that encourages their understanding and articulation of the rationale for their own practices
- Technical Assistance - to assist individuals and their organization to improve by offering resources and information, supporting networking and change efforts

Professional development is a broad term, encompassing a range of people, interests and approaches. Those who engage in professional development share a common purpose of enhancing their ability to do their work. At the heart of professional development is the individual's interest in lifelong learning and increasing their own skills and knowledge.

Online Professional Development

The 21st century has seen a significant growth in online professional development. Content providers incorporate collaborative platforms such as discussion boards and wikis, thereby encouraging and facilitating interaction, and optimizing training effectiveness.

In the education industry, the use of online sources of professional development represents a significant shift. Whereas many other industries have used online sources of continuing education and professional practices for many years, traditionally educators have turned solely to internal professional development departments, local education agencies (LEAs), and local colleges and universities to acquire the necessary education to meet the required hours/units for renewal of their state teaching-licenses.

However, the economic pressures facing school districts combined with a greater conviction that online professional development can be effective has led to increased interest in this option. Rather than replacing traditional sources of professional development, online sources and providers have served to augment existing options and can bring a widening access to topics and a broader scope to "learning communities". As teacher performance comes under increased scrutiny, a study conducted by Boston College found that English and math teachers who took professional development courses online improved their instructional practices and boosted their subject knowledge scores, producing modest performance gains for their students.

> *"A series of online professional development courses that focus on specific content and target student learning needs can have positive effects on teacher knowledge and instructional practices," said Boston College Associate Professor of Education Laura O'Dwyer. "The studies also show that teacher participation in online professional development can translate into improvements in targeted student outcomes."*

This type of research-based and outcomes-focused study has lent credibility to the idea that online professional development can and will serve an important role in supporting the educational goals of the United States Department of Education.

Initial Professional Development

Professional development may be separated into two distinct phases, Continuing Professional Development and Initial Professional Development. Initial Professional Development (IPD) is defined by the UK Initial Professional Development Forum as "a period of development during which an individual acquires a level of competence necessary in order to operate as an autonomous professional". Professional bodies may recognise the successful completion of IPD by the award of chartered or similar status.

The Institute of Mathematics and its Applications defines IPD as "a pattern of learning undertaken by a graduate mathematician to develop the range of skills and competencies needed to achieve professional status".

The Institution of Structural Engineers states that "Initial Professional Development (IPD) comprises the acquisition and development of the specialist knowledge and skills, and their practical application, that are needed to practise as a structural engineer. It bridges the gap between your educational base and attaining professional qualifications. The Institution defines IPD in terms of Core Objectives, which are defined to minimum standards".

The Institution of Mechanical Engineers states that Initial Professional Development builds upon academic skills and leads to registration as a Chartered Engineer or Incorporated Engineer. IPD must be challenging and based upon the level of educational achievement reached. It can be undertaken prior to, during or after the completion of a course of study.

Training and Development

Human Resource Management, training and development is the field which is concerned with organizational activity aimed at bettering the performance of individuals and groups in organizational settings. It has been known by several names, including human resource development, and learning and development.

Harrison observes that the name was endlessly debated by the Chartered Institute of Personnel and Development during its review of professional standards in 1999/2000. "Employee Development" was seen as too evocative of the master-slave relationship between employer and employee for those who refer to their employees as "partners" or "associates" to feel comfortable with. "Human Resource Development" was rejected by academics, who objected to the idea that people were "resources" &m dash; an idea that they felt to be demeaning to the individual. Eventually, the CIPD settled upon "Learning and Development", although that was itself not free from problems, "learning" being an overgeneral and ambiguous name. Moreover, the field is still widely known by the other names. Training and development (T&D) encompasses three main activities: training, education, and development. Garavan, Costine, and Heraty, of the Irish Institute of Training and Development, note that these ideas are often considered to be synonymous. However, to practitioners, they encompass three separate, although interrelated, activities:

- Training: This activity is both focused upon, and evaluated against, the job that an individual currently holds.
- Education: This activity focuses upon the jobs that an individual may potentially hold in the future, and is evaluated against those jobs.
- Development: This activity focuses upon the activities that the organization employing the individual, or that the individual is part of, may partake in the future, and is almost impossible to evaluate.

The "stakeholders" in training and development are categorized into several classes. The *sponsors* of training and development are senior managers. The *clients* of training and development are business planners. Line managers are responsible for coaching, resources, and performance. The *participants* are those who actually undergo the processes. The *facilitators* are Human Resource Management staff. And the *providers* are specialists in the field. Each of these groups has its own agenda and motivations, which sometimes conflict with the agendas and motivations of the others.

The conflicts that are the best part of career consequences are those that take place between employees and their bosses. The number one reason people leave their jobs is conflict with their bosses. And yet, as author, workplace relationship authority, and executive coach, Dr. John Hoover points out, "Tempting as it is, nobody ever enhanced his or her career by making the boss look stupid." Training an employee to get along well with authority and with people who entertain diverse points of view is one of the best guarantees of long-term success. Talent, knowledge, and skill alone won't compensate for a sour relationship with a superior, peer, or customer.

Talent Development

Talent development, part of human resource development, is the process of changing an organization, its employees, its stakeholders, and groups of people within it, using planned and unplanned learning, in order to achieve and maintain a competitive advantage for the organization. Rothwell notes that the name may well be a term in search of a meaning, like so much in management, and suggests that it be thought of as selective attention paid to the top 10% of employees, either by potential or performance.

While talent development is reserved for the top management it is becoming increasingly clear that *career development* is necessary for the retention of any employee, no matter what their level in the company. Research has shown that some type of career path is necessary for job satisfaction and hence job retention. Perhaps organizations need to include this area in their overview of employee satisfaction.

The term *talent development* is becoming increasingly popular in several organizations, as companies are now moving from the traditional term *training and development*. Talent development encompasses a variety of components such as training, career development, career management, and organizational development, and training and development. It is expected that during the 21st century more companies will begin to use more integrated terms such as *talent development*.

Washington Group International, in their paper "The Nuclear Renaissance, A Life Cycle Perspective" defined two logical laws of talent development:

- First law of talent development: "The beginnings of any technology-rich business are all characterized by a shortage of large numbers of technically trained people needed to support ultimate growth"
- Second law of talent development: "The resources will come when the business becomes attractive to the best-and brightest who adapt skills to become part of an exciting opportunity"

Talent development refers to an organization's ability to align strategic training and career opportunities for employees.

Reflective Practice

Reflective practice is "the capacity to reflect on action so as to engage in a process of continuous learning", which, according to the originator of the term, is "one of the defining characteristics of professional practice". According to one definition it involves "paying critical attention to the practical values and theories which inform everyday actions, by examining practice reflectively and reflexively. This leads to developmental insight".

Reflective practice can be an important tool in practice-based professional learning settings where individuals learning from their own professional experiences, rather than from formal teaching or knowledge transfer, may be the most important source of personal professional development and improvement. As such the notion has achieved wide take-up, particularly in professional development for practitioners in the areas of education and healthcare. The question of how best to learn from experience has wider relevance however, to any organizational learning environment. In particular, people in leadership positions have a tremendous development opportunity if they engage in reflective practice.

History and Background

Reflective Practice was introduced by Donald Schön in his book *The Reflective Practitioner* in 1983, however, the concepts underlying reflective practice are much older. John Dewey was among the first to write about Reflective Practice with his exploration of experience, interaction and reflection. Other researchers such as Kurt Lewin, Jean Piaget, William James and Carl Jung were developing theories of human learning and development. Marcus Aurelius' Meditations has also been described as an example of reflective practice.

Dewey's works inspired writers such as Donald Schön and David Boud to explore the boundaries of reflective practice. Central to the development of reflective theory was interest in the integration of theory and practice, the cyclic pattern of experience and the conscious application of that learning experience. For the last 30 years, there has been a growing literature and focus around experiential learning and the development and application of Reflective Practice. Reflective practice also contributes to learning and expressing our own and others' stories (Ivan, 2012).

Donald Schön's 1983 book introduces concepts such as 'reflection on action' and 'reflection in-action' where professionals meet the challenges of their work with a kind of improvisation learned in practice. Reflective Practice has now been widely accepted and used as developmental practices for organisations, networks, and individuals. As Boud *et al* state: "Reflection is an important human activity in which people recapture their experience, think about it, mull it over and evaluate it. It is this working with experience that is important in learning." Reflective Practice can be seen and has been recognised in many teaching and learning scenarios, and the emergence in more recent years of blogging has been seen as another form of reflection on experience in a technological age.

Models of Reflective Practice

The concept of Reflective Practice centres around the idea of lifelong learning in which a practitioner analyses experiences in order to learn from them. Reflective Practice is used to promote independent professionals who are continuously engaged in the reflection of situations they encounter in their professional worlds. Several models of reflection exist and are used to draw lessons out of experiences.

Argyris and Schön 1978

Argyris and Schön pioneered the idea of single loop and double loop learning in 1978. The theory was built around the recognition and amendment of a perceived fault or error. Single loop learning is when a practitioner or organisation, even after an error has occurred and a correction is made, continues to rely on current strategies, techniques or policies when a situation again comes to light. Double loop learning involves the modification of personal objectives, strategies or policies so that when a similar situation arises a new framing system is employed.

Schön himself introduced some years later the concept of Reflection-in-action and Reflection-on-action. Reflection-in-action can be described as the ability of a practitioner to 'think on their feet', otherwise known as 'felt-knowing'. It revolves around the idea that within any given moment, when faced with a professional issue, a practitioner usually connects with their feelings, emotions and prior experiences to attend to the situation directly. Reflection-on-action on the other hand is the idea that after the experience a practitioner analyses their reaction to the situation and explores the reasons around, and the consequences of, their actions. This is usually conducted through a documented reflection of the situation.

Kolb 1975

Kolb was highly influenced by the research conducted by Dewey and Piaget in the 1970s. Kolb's reflective model highlights the concept of experiential learning and is centred around the transformation of information into knowledge. This takes place after the situation has occurred and entails a practitioner reflecting on the experience, gaining a general understanding of the concepts encountered during the experience and then testing these general understandings on a new situation. In this way the knowledge that is gained from a situation is continuously applied and reapplied building on a practitioners prior experiences and knowledge.

Gibbs 1988

Graham Gibbs discussed the use of structured debriefing to facilitate the reflection involved in Kolb's "experiential learning cycle". He presents the stages of a full structured debriefing as follows:

- (Initial experience)
- Description: "What happened? Don't make judgements yet or try to draw conclusions; simply describe."
- Feelings: "What were your reactions and feelings? Again don't move on to analysing these yet."
- Evaluation: "What was good or bad about the experience? Make value judgements."
- Analysis: "What sense can you make of the situation? Bring in ideas from outside the experience to help you."

  "What was really going on?"

  "Were different people's experiences similar or different in important ways?"

- Conclusions (general): "What can be concluded, in a general sense, from these experiences and the analyses you have undertaken?"
- Conclusions (specific): "What can be concluded about your own specific, unique, personal situation or way of working?"
- Personal action plans: "What are you going to do differently in this type of situation next time?"

  "What steps are you going to take on the basis of what you have learnt?"

Gibbs' suggestions are often cited as Gibbs' reflective cycle or Gibbs' model of reflection (1988), and simplified into the following six distinct stages:

- Description
- Feelings
- Evaluation
- Analysis
- Conclusions
- Action plan.

Johns 1995

Johns' model is a structured mode of reflection that provides a practitioner with a guide to gain greater understanding. It is designed to be carried out through the act of sharing with a colleague or mentor, which enables the experience to become learnt knowledge at a faster rate than reflection alone. Johns highlights the importance of experienced knowledge and the ability of a practitioner to access, understand and put into practice information that has been acquired through empirical means. In order for this to be achieved reflection occurs though 'looking in' on ones thoughts and emotions and 'looking out' at the situation experienced. Johns draws on the work of Carper (1978) to expand on the notion of 'looking out' at an experience. Five patterns of knowing are incorporated into the guided reflection, having a practitioner analyse the aesthetic, personal, ethical, empirical and the reflexive elements experienced through the situation. Johns' model is comprehensive and allows for reflection that touches on many important elements.

Brookfield 1998

Critically reflective practitioners constantly research their assumptions by seeing practice through four complementary lenses:

the lens of their autobiography of learners of reflective practice, the lens of learners eyes, the lens of colleagues' perception and the lens of theoretical, philosophical and research literature. Reviewing practice through these lens makes us more aware of the power dynamics that infuse all practice settings It also helps us detect hegemonic assumptions-assumptions that we think are in our own best interests but actually work against us in the long run (BROOKFIELD 1998) To become critically reflective Brookfield thinks that the four lenses stated above will reflect back to us stark and differently highlighted picture of who we are and what we do. Lens 1 Our autobiography as a learner is an important source of insight into practice. As we talk to each other about critical events in our practice, we start to realize that individual crises are usually collectively experienced dilemmas. Analysing our autobiographies allows us to draw insight and meanings for practice on a deep visceral emotional level Lens 2 Our learners Eyes. Seeing ourselves through learners eyes we discover that learners are interpreting our actions in the way that we mean them.

But often we are surprised by the diversity of meanings people read into our words and actions. A cardinal principle of seeing ourselves through learners eyes is that ensuring the anonymity of their critical opinions. You have to make students feel safe. Seeing our practice through learners eyes help us teach more responsively Lens 3 Our colleagues' Experiences. Our colleagues serve as critical mirrors reflecting back to us images of our actions. Talking to colleagues about problems and gaining their perspective increases our chance finding some information that can help our situation. theory can help us "name"our practice by illuminating the general elements of what we think are idiosyncratic experiences

Rolfe 2001

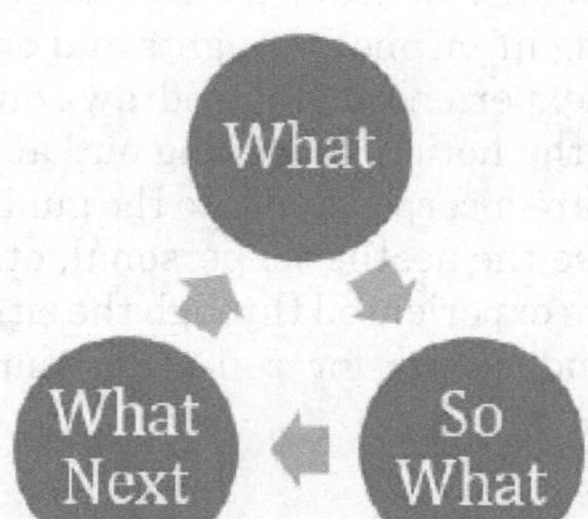

***Figure:** Adaptation of the Rolfe Reflective Model*

Rolfe's reflective model is based around Borton's 1970 developmental model. A simplistic cycle composed of 3 questions which asks the practitioner, What, So What and Now What. Through this analysis a description of the situation is given which then leads into the scrutiny of the situation and the construction of knowledge that has been learnt through the experience. Subsequent to this, ways in which to personally improve and the consequence of ones response to the experience are reflected on.

Application

Reflective Practice has been described as an unstructured approach directing understanding and learning, a self regulated process, commonly used in health and teaching professions, though applicable to all professions. Reflective practice is a learning process taught to professionals from a variety of disciplines by practitioners, with the aim of enhancing abilities to communicate and making informed/ balanced decisions. The practice has historically been applied most in the educational and medical field. When reflection in action and reflection on action described by Donald Schon are utilized in practice and when practitioners are able to identify these actions they become better at reflective practice. Professional Colleges such as the College of Nurses and College of Dental Hygienists are recognizing the importance of reflective practice and require practitioners to prepare reflective portfolios as a requirement to be licensed, and for yearly quality assurance purposes.

Education

In education, reflective practice refers to the process of the educator studying his or her own teaching methods and determining what works best for the students. It involves the consideration of the ethical consequences of classroom procedures on students.

The appeal of the use of reflective practice for teachers is that as teaching and learning are complex, and there is not one right approach, reflecting on different versions of teaching, and reshaping past and current experiences will lead to improvement in teaching practices. Schön's reflection-in-action assists teachers in making the professional knowledge that they will gain from their experience in the classroom an explicit part of their decision-making.

As Larrivee argues, Reflective Practice moves teachers from their knowledge base of distinct skills to a stage in their careers where they are able to modify their skills to suit specific contexts and situations, and eventually to invent new strategies. In implementing a process of Reflective Practice teachers will be able to move themselves, and their schools, beyond existing theories in practice. Larrivee concludes that teachers should "resist establishing a classroom culture of control and become a reflective practitioner, continuously engaging in a critical reflection, consequently remaining fluid in the dynamic environment of the classroom".

Health Professionals

Reflective Practice is associated with learning from experience, and is viewed as an important strategy for health professionals who embrace lifelong learning. Due to the ever changing context of healthcare and the continual growth of medical knowledge, there is a high level of demand on healthcare professionals' expertise. Due to this complex and continually changing environment, healthcare professionals could benefit from a programme of reflective practice.

Price (2004) recognizes that there are several reasons why a healthcare practitioner would engage in reflective practice: To further understand yourself, motives, perceptions, attitudes, values and feelings associated with client care; To provide a fresh outlook to practice situations and challenge existing thoughts, feelings as well as actions; To explore how the practice situation may be approached differently.

In the field of nursing there is concern that actions may run the risk of habitualisation, thus dehumanising patients and their needs. In utilising Reflective Practice, nurses are able to plan their actions and consciously monitor the action to ensure it is beneficial to their patient.

The act of reflection is seen as a way of promoting the development of autonomous, qualified and self-directed professionals. Engaging in Reflective Practice is associated with the improvement of the quality of care, stimulating personal and professional growth and closing the gap between theory and practice. Activities to promote reflection are now being incorporated into undergraduate, postgrduate and continuing medical education across a variety of health professions Mann (2009) found through her research that in practising professionals the process of reflection appears to be multifactorial and to include different aspects. In addition to reflection both on and during experiences that the anticipation of a challenging situation also stimulated reflection. Practicing professionals vary in their tendency and ability to reflect.

Davies (2012) identifies that there are both benefits as well as limitations to reflective practice:

Benefits to Reflective Practice

- Increased learning from an experience for situation
- Promotion of deep learning
- Identification of personal and professional strengths and areas for improvement
- Identification of educational needs
- Acquisition of new knowledge and skills
- Further understanding of own beliefs, attitudes and values
- Encouragement of self-motivation and self-directed learning
- Could act as a source of feedback
- Possible improvements of personal and clinical confidence

Limitations of Reflective Practice

- Not all practitioners may understand the reflective process
- May feel uncomfortable challenging and evaluating own practice
- Could be time consuming
- May have confusion as to which situations/experiences to reflect upon
- May not be adequate to resolve clinical problems

Environmental Management and Sustainability

There is some criticism that traditional environmental management which simply focuses on the problem at hand, fails to integrate the wider context in which the environment sits into the decision making. While research and science must inform the process of environmental management, it is up to the practitioner to integrate those results within this wider context. In order to deal with this and to reaffirm the utility of environmental management Bryant and Wilson propose that a "more reflective approach is required that seeks to rethink the basic premises of environmental management as a process". This style of approach has been found to be successful in sustainable development projects where participants appreciated and enjoyed the educational aspect of utilising reflective practice throughout, however the authors noted the challenges with melding the "circularity" of reflective practice theory with the "doing" of sustainability.

Leadership Positions

Reflective Practice provides a tremendous development opportunity for those in leadership positions. Managing a team of people requires a delicate balance between people skills and technical expertise, and success in this type of role does not come easily. Reflective Practice provides leaders with an opportunity to critically review what has been successful in the past and where improvement can be made. To support reflective learning organizations have invested in coaching programmes for their emerging and established leaders. Coaching is defined by the International Coaching Federation as partnering with clients in a thought provoking and creative process that inspires them to maximize their personal and professional potential. Leaders frequently engage in self-limiting behaviours because of their over reliance on their preferred ways of reacting and responding. To help support the establishment of new behaviours, coaching is extremely useful as it encourages reflection, critical thinking and transformative learning. Adults have acquired a body of experience throughout their life or frames of reference that define their world. Coaching programmes support the process of questioning and potentially rebuilding these pre-determined frames of reference. The goal is for a leader to maximize their professional potential and in order to do this, there must be a process of critical reflection on current assumptions.

Other Professions

Reflective Practice can help an individual to develop personally, and is useful for professions other than those discussed above. It allows professionals to continually update their skills and knowledge and consider ways to interact with their colleagues.

Suggested ways for professionals to practice reflective management include:

- Coaching;
- Keeping a journal;
- Seeking feedback;
- View experiences objectively; and
- Taking time at the end of each day, meeting, experience etc. to reflect-on-actions.
- Anecdotal Notes
- Group discussion

4

Induction Training

Induction training is a type of training given as an initial preparation upon taking up a post. To help new people get to work initially after joining a firm, a brief programme of this training can be delivered to the new worker as a way to help integrate the new employee, both as a productive part of the business, and socially among other employees. It often contains information dealing with the layout of the firm's operating facility, health and safety measures and security systems. An attempt may also be made to introduce the individual to key employees and give an impression of the culture of the organisation, it is a critical time for the employer to gain commitment from the employee, and the latter to understand the expectations, targets and so on. The induction provides a really good opportunity to socialise and brief the newcomer on the company's overall strategy, performance standards, etc. Induction training should, according to TPI-theory, include development of theoretical and practical skills, but also meet interaction needs that exist among the new employees.

This training is done systematically and is often the responsibility of the immediate supervisor to make sure that its done smoothly. If carefully done, it will save time and cost(in terms of faulty products or poor services, etc.). It is imperative that managers place their authority and power to make sure that the new employee is carefully helped to adjust to the new work surroundings and culture

Just as in schools, sometimes the work place may have bullies, who may give the new employee the wrong impression of the company or organization at first. These programmes can play a critical role under the socialization to the organization in terms of performance, attitudes and organizational commitment.

Core Competency

A core competency is a concept in management theory originally advocated by two business authors, C. K. Prahalad and Gary Hamel. In their view a core competency is a specific factor that a business sees as central to the way the company or its employees work. It fulfills three key criteria:

1. It is not easy for competitors to imitate.
2. It can be reused widely for many products and markets.
3. It must contribute to the end consumer's experienced benefits and the value of the product or service to its customers.

A core competency can take various forms, including technical/subject matter know-how, a reliable process and/or close relationships with customers and suppliers. It may also include product development or culture, such as employee dedication, best Human Resource Management (HRM), good market coverage, etc.

Core competencies are particular strengths relative to other organizations in the industry, which provide the fundamental basis for the provision of added value. Core competencies reflect the collective learning of an organization and involve coordinating diverse production skills and integrating multiple streams of technologies. It includes communication, involvement and a deep commitment to working across organizational boundaries. Few companies are likely to build world leadership in more than five or six fundamental competencies.

As an example of core competencies, Walt Disney World Parks and Resorts has three main core competencies:

- Animatronics and Show Design
- Storytelling, Story Creation and Themed Atmospheric Attractions
- Efficient operation of theme parks

A core competency results from a specific set of skills or production techniques that deliver additional value to the customer. These enable an organization to access a wide variety of markets. Executives should estimate the future challenges and opportunities of the business in order to stay on top of the game in varying situations.

In an article from 1990 titled "The Core Competence of the Corporation", Prahalad and Hamel illustrate that core competencies lead to the development of core products which further can be used to build many products for end users. Core competencies are developed through the process of continuous improvements over the period of time rather than a single large change. To succeed in an emerging global market, it is more important and required to build core competencies rather than vertical integration. NEC utilized its portfolio of core competencies to dominate the semiconductor, telecommunications and consumer electronics market. It is important to identify core competencies because it is difficult to retain those competencies in a price war and cost-cutting environment. The author used the example of how to integrate core competences using strategic architecture in view of changing market requirements and evolving technologies. Management must realize that stakeholders to core competences are an asset which can be utilized to integrate and build the competencies Competence building is an outcome of strategic architecture which must be enforced by top management in order to exploit its full capacity.

In *Competing for the Future*, the authors Prahalad and Hamel show how executives can develop the industry foresight necessary to adapt to industry changes and discover ways of controlling resources that will enable the company to attain goals despite any constraints. Executives should develop a point of view on which core competencies can be built for the future to revitalize the process of new business creation. Developing an independent point of view of tomorrow's opportunities and building capabilities that exploit them is the key to future industry leadership.

For an organization to be competitive, it needs not only tangible resources but intangible resources like core competences that are difficult and challenging to achieve. It is critical to manage and enhance the competences in response to industry changes in the future. For example, Microsoft has expertise in many IT based innovations where, for a variety of reasons, it is difficult for competitors to replicate or compete with Microsoft's core competences.

In a race to achieve cost cutting, quality and productivity, most executives do not spend their time developing a corporate view of the future because this exercise demands high intellectual energy and commitment. The difficult questions may challenge their own ability to view the future opportunities but an attempt to find their answers will lead towards organizational benefits.

Opportunity School

An opportunity school is an alternative to regular schools. Students who may be applicable to attend opportunity schools are students who have unique situations that may hinder their abilities in an average schooling environment. This may include: students who cannot work well in large groups, such as in an average classroom; students who have difficulty paying attention to their teachers or their school work; students who have been suspended or expelled from their home school and need to make up their students; students with physical or mental health problems; students who don't feel comfortable among certain teachers or classmates; students who cannot afford the cost of attending a regular school; and other unique situations.

Misconception

A common misconception is that opportunity schools are only available for "troubled youths". While this may be true in some cases, an opportunity school is not made for the sole purpose of being a holding place for "troubled youths". An opportunity school is an available option for students with various unique situations who may otherwise fail to succeed in a regular school environment. On the other hand, opportunity schools are, quite contrary to their name, often a place of little or no opportunity, with classes, prohibitions on extracurricular activities, prohibitions on socializing, and often a schedule with no time between classes and a rule forbidding being on campus before or after classes. They are often used as a punishment or a dumping ground for students the system does not want to deal with in any sort of reasonable or constructive way, such as zero-tolerance policy violators.

In the early 1950s, the Allentown School District, Allentown, Pennsylvania, began one of the earliest gifted programmes in the area. It was also called opportunity school. Students in the programme were selected through teacher recommendations and a required minimum score on a standardized IQ test. In the 1950s and 60s, the programme was for students in grades 3 through 9. In grades 3 through 6, students were given typing instruction and Spanish instruction in addition to the normal curriculum. In addition, 7th through 9th grade students were given Spanish instruction and advanced English, mathematics and science classes. Classroom activities were creative and did not follow the same curriculum as non-opportunity school students. Students were selected from each elementary school in the school district in second grade and attended classes in a central location. Students arrived at the schools where the classes were held by school buses, public transportation, or were driven by parents. In 1954, the Opportunity School classes were held at Jackson Elementary school. In the following two years, the fifth and sixth grade classes were sent to Jefferson Elementary school; they were then sent to South Mountain Junior High school for 7 through 9 grades. At the end of ninth grade, those students were then integrated back into the high school which served the geographic area where the student lived. Students who began third grade in 1961 and completed sixth grade in 1965 went to Jefferson Elementary School. They were then sent to one of four junior high schools and then to one of the two senior high schools (William Allen or Dieruff), again depending on the geographic area where the student lived.

Self-realization

Self-realization is an expression used in psychology, spirituality, and Eastern religions. In one overview, Mortimer Adler defines self-realization as freedom from external coercion, including cultural expectations, political and economic freedom, etc. The Indian mystic Paramahansa Yogananda describes Self-realization as "the knowing—in body, mind and soul—that we are one with the omnipresence of God; that we do not have to pray that it come to us, that we are not merely near it at all times, but that God's omnipresence is our omnipresence; that we are just as much a part of Him now as we ever will be. All we have to do is improve our knowing". The basic premise of self-realization is that there exists an authentic Self (or 'soul') which has to be discovered by psychological or spiritual self-striving. Self-realization can be a gradual or instantaneous phenomena depending on the school of thought but in all cases it involves extensive preparation of mind and emotions to recognize self-realization when it occurs.

Self-realization is a maturing of the ego or personality to accept its own evanescence and thus allow space for the true Self to reveal itself. The sun veiled by clouds is an apt metaphor for the Self's apparent absence in our everyday lives. The dissolution of the ego's obsessive, internal pre-occupations with its psycho-somatic complexes frees the psyche's energy to directly experience reality of the world as it is, free of any assumptions.

Eastern Understanding

Hinduism: For the Hindu religion, self-realization (*atma-jnana*) is knowledge of the true self beyond both delusion and identification with material phenomena. Self identification and not ego identification.

Advaita Vedanta

The branch of Advaita Vedanta is the one that has particularly developed this concept. According to Vedanta, God as Sat-Chit-Ananda is perfect existence, consciousness, bliss. Whereas the manifest universe which is a play of shakti or energy is temporal, the immutable principle or reality is beyond time. God is not exactly a being - in order for there to be being, there has to be non-being - and, it is said, that such dualism within the differentiated reality does not exist in that state. It cannot be described, quantified, reasoned, or explained all of which exist on a differentiated basis only directly experienced as itself. Shakti or energy, as an abstraction, is eternal but its manifestations are continually changing. Therefore, in Hinduism, God is represented in both male and female form. The male as sat-chit-anand is immutable; the female shakti is temporal. While being omnipresent and immanent in reality, sat-chit-anand is formless. Shakti is manifested but, also, exists in an unexpressed form inside of sat-chit-anand. Therefore, even if the Universe ceases to exist at one point, it will eventually be reborn because Shakti in an immaterial form is also eternal. What motivates the action is described more poetically as a dance or a play.

Life begins with consciousness. What makes an ant different from a rock is some sense of itself. Rather than existing purely causally, it has some degree of freedom, but the grosser awareness is more causally bound. In its pure form as sat-chit-anada, consciousness is said to be completely independent of causality. And therefore true freedom can only be realized in that state. Until then, the mind is bound to causal existence to greater and lesser extents. An awareness of self is present in grosser and subtler forms. Animals or even a microbe will have some form of awareness. However, in mankind, the ability to reason allows this base awareness to be refined into higher existential contemplation.

Vedanta describes the mind as being composed of sheaths or veils going from a gross awareness of self to a subtler awareness. Love - what we call love - is a very complex emotion described by as a feeling of empathy or compassion. The identification of one's self with others.

According to Vedanta, selfless love is actually an attribute of the self-realized. The mind shorn of its grossness is perfectly pure and, just like water poured from a jug into a pond mingles in an undifferentiated manner, so ultimately in nirvikalpa samadhi or enlightenment, there is a type of universal identification. This identification is not merely a delusion but actually a state of simultaneous experience. Yogis have described having a spherically expanding universal vision and a state of indescribable rapture. Scripture gives the metaphor of a voluminous lake overflowing with pure water. Paramahansa Yogananda, in his book Autobiography of a Yogi, *describes this experience as realization of ever new joy. Self-realization is not easy to achieve and requires spiritual practice, sometimes over multiple life times.*

One of the biggest reasons for this difficulty is that the thirst of the soul for material existence is not sated. Though realization is by far the greatest prize and the culmination of achievement, it is elusive. Prarabdha karma, the force of accumulated metaphysical causality, the impulses whose imprints or samskaras are in the mind where the subtle most human desires are the yearnings of the soul. Ramakrishna said that God himself has become all these forms. It is not his will that the play should come to an end. That's why self-realization is not easily achieved. Saint Jnaneshwar said that the play existed for the sport of God. It was all his forms and manifestations.

The yearnings or desires cause the soul to seek out new manifestations. At death, though the gross body and senses die, the causality of those desires does not die. It seeks out a new corporeal existence. If the motive force is good, then the bound soul will go to any number of heavens; if the motive force is bad, it will go into any number of hells. The place where it goes is precisely motivated by its own nature. Hell is a place where there is suffering and ignorance. Heaven is where there is pleasure or sensory enjoyment.

Neither residence in that heaven or hell, for the bound soul, is permanent. The soul (atman), while working off its previous karma, continually acquires new karma. Like a metal hammered with new impressions, in the course of a life, the actions we reinforce shape the quality of the mind and the subtlest part of the mind is the soul. Therefore, it is conceivable that if someone continually acquired bad karma by reinforcing bad actions they would remain in hell for a very long time. However, the soul can always be redeemed because there is the power of free will or independence from causality that originates from God himself.

Good and evil is equivalent to knowledge and ignorance. Knowledge is good. Ignorance is evil. Ignorance leads to suffering and bondage. Knowledge to happiness and liberation. The highest heaven is said to be self-realization because that state is eternal, evernew, pure, perfect, and rapturous. Therefore, it is considered to be better than any sensual heaven, such as those in the realms of the gods.

Self-realization is achieved through 4 types of spiritual practices.

- Karma yoga - without attachment to the fruit of action, acting by offering the fruit of the action to God. In other words, the practice of wholesome actions, actions that are complete, that fulfill all aspects of the present moment, leaving one in a state of fulfillment, i.e. free from desire, until the next impulse arises. All actions have a personal component which is unavoidable, be it pleasant, neutral or unpleasant. Wholesome, harmonious or in the flow actions are by definition fulfilling and therefor lead to Self Realization.

- Raja yoga - psychic control or one pointed meditation that first focuses thought onto one point and then stops thought leaving only the underlying awareness.
- Bhakti yoga - the development of love for God and other beings.
- Jnana yoga - reasoning the mind from gross most to subtle most state culminating in samadhi. This type of Jnana or knowledge is not exactly like book learning. Rather Jnana is discovering one's self and uncovering its mysteries through direct inner contemplation. Ultimately knowledge of relative phenomena dissolves and only the original Life-Force or God remains.

Ramana Maharshi

As taught by Ramana Maharshi, awareness or consciousness of "I am," plays a key role in achieving self-realization; tracing back to the source of awareness by asking oneself the question "Who am I?", the true self becomes obvious. Focussing attention on the qualified "I am" is a powerful means to achieving the end which is being one with the completely unqualified "I," the True Self which is experienced as Silence. Replacing the confused duality of Self and ego with the pristine non-dual experience of Self is the essence of Ramana's teaching.

True happiness is the manifested Self. It only seems like a result because it is not felt or known permanently before the ego is removed. As explained by Ramana Maharshi,

Happiness is inherent in man and is not due to external causes. One must realize himself in order to experience his unalloyed happiness. All spiritual scriptures are meant to make man retrace his steps to his original source.

Sahaja Yoga

The method of meditation Sahaja Yoga, created in 1970 by Shri Mataji Nirmala Devi, defines self-realization as a connection with your self or the first encounter with reality.

Buddhism

Since Buddhism denies the existence of a separate self, as explicated in the teachings of anatman and sunyata, self-realization is a *contradictio in terminis* for Buddhism. Though the tathagatagarbha-teachings seem to teach the existence of a separate self, they point to the inherent possibility of attaining awakening, not to the existence of a separate self. The dharmadhatu-teachings make this even more clear: reality is an undivided whole; awakening is the realization of this whole.

Sikhism

Sikhism propounds the philosophy of Self-realization. This is possible by "aatam-cheennea" or "Aap Pashaanae", purifying the self from the false ego:

'Atam-cheene' is self analysis, which is gained by peeping into one's self in the light of the teachings of *Sri Guru Granth Sahib*. It is the process of evaluating and analyzing oneself on the touchstone of 'naam simran' which if practised, pierces into the self and washes it from within. The filth of too much of materialism goes, the self gets purified and the mind comes in 'charhdi kala/higher state of mind". This means that the self should be assessed, examined and purified, leading to self-realization and the purification of our mind. Once purified the mind helps in ushering in oneness with the Super Power as the Guru says, "Atam-cheen bhae nirankari" (SGGS:P. 415) which means that one gets attuned to the Formless Lord through self-realization. Indirectly it means that self-realization leads to God-realization.

Guru Nanak says,

Those who realize their self get immersed into the Lord Himself.

Guru Nanak also says,

He who realizes his self, comes to know the essence.

Western Understanding

Merriam Webster's Dictionary Defines Self-realization as: Fulfillment by oneself of the possibilities of one's character or personality.

In the western world "self-realization" has gained great popularity. Influential in this popularity were psycho-analysis, humanistic psychology, the growing acquaintance with eastern religions, and the growing popularity of western esotericism.

Psycho-analysis

Though Sigmund Freud was skeptical of religion and esotericism, his theories have had a lasting influence on western thought and self-understanding. His notion of repressed memories, though based on false assumptions, has become part of western mainstream thinking.

Freud's ideas were further developed by his students and neo-psycho-analysts. Especially Carl Jung, Erik Erikson and Winnicott have been important in the western understanding of the self. But also other alternatives have been developed. Jung developed the notion of individuation, the lifelong process in which the centre of psychological life shifts from the ego to the self. Erikson described human development throughout the life-span in his theory of psychosocial development. Winnicott developed the notion of the true self. Roberto Assagioli developed his approach of Psychosynthesis, an original approach to psychology.

Humanistic Psychology

Abraham Maslow and Carl Rogers, leaders in the Humanistic Psychology movement, developed the concept of self-actualization.

Based on Maslow, the most common meaning given to self-realization is that of psychological growth. It represents the awakening and manifestation of latent potentialities of the human being -for example, ethical, esthetic, and religious experiences and activities.

Maslow

Maslow Defined Self-actualization as: The impulse to convert oneself into what one is capable of being.

Eastern Religions

While the western knowledge of eastern spirituality is still growing, the understanding of these traditions is biased by western concepts.

Aajit K. Das, in the International Journal for the Advancement of Counselling, compared and contrasted Maslow and Rogers' concept of self-actualization with the concept of self-realization in Vedandic Hinduism and the two major schools of Buddhism, Theravada and Mahayana. The author concluded in this paper that the two concepts complement each other.

Western Esotericism

Western esotericism integrates a broad variety of traditions. It views self-realization as the ultimate goal of a human being, attaining permanent happiness and complete independence and freedom from all worldly bondage. In this view, true happiness is the result of self-realization.

Self-realization and Career Development

Choosing an appropriate career path is perhaps one of the most important decisions of life. A wrong decision may lead to dissatisfaction, frustration, and a lack of interest and enthusiasm towards work. A right decision, on the other hand, can lead to happiness, satisfaction, and a sense of joy and excitement towards work.

Despite the importance of the decision, many a times, due to various reasons, people do not put in too much of a thought, as required, while choosing a career. People tend to choose a career not on the basis of appropriateness and their suitability, but rather in terms of availability and popularity. This, in the long run, does not turn out be very fruitful and its after-effects are felt in more ways than one.

Sidney Simon, the vocational psychologist, reflects this very well in his book, Values Clarifications. In the book he says:

> *"A person who settles for whatever comes his/her way, rather than pursuing his/her own goals, is probably not living a life based upon his/her own freely chosen values. He/she usually ends up by feeling that life is not very meaningful or satisfying."*

In a way Sidney Simon is trying to say that a career should be chosen according to the goals of one's life instead of getting into something just for the sake of it. If this does not happen then the person feels restricted and life appears to be meaningless.

To pursue one's goals one also has to know what those goals actually are. For this the person needs to know his/her abilities and needs to realize his/her true potential; the individual has to know himself/herself. In other words, knowing about one's goals in life and choosing an appropriate career requires self-realization. Self-realization is the development or fulfillment of one's own potential or abilities. According to Abraham Maslow, it is the impulse to convert oneself into what one is capable of being.

One of the ways of self-realization is the understanding that there are many intelligences and not just one. An individual who is good in mathematical abilities is considered to be intelligent and an individual who is good in writing and linguistic abilities is also considered to be intelligent. Both are intelligent in their own ways. Saying that the former is more intelligent than the latter, or vice versa, will be incorrect.

Howard Gardner, the educational psychologist, has talked about this extensively in his well-known theory of Multiple Intelligences. Gardner, in his theory, suggests that rather than one there are eight to nine intelligences. These intelligences are:

- Linguistic Intelligence: The ability to communicate well, orally or in writing.
- Logical-mathematical Intelligence: The capacity to use numbers effectively, to learn higher mathematics, and to handle complex logical arguments.
- Spatial Intelligence: The ability to perceive the visual-spatial world accurately and to perform transformations upon those perceptions.
- Bodily-kinesthetic Intelligence: The ability to use one's physical body well.
- Musical Intelligence: The capacity to perceive, discriminate, transform, and express musical forms.
- Interpersonal Intelligence: The ability to sense other's feelings and be in tune with others.
- Intrapersonal Intelligence: It includes self-knowledge, having an accurate picture of oneself, and the ability to understand one's own body and mind.
- Naturalistic Intelligence: The ability to understand different species, recognize patterns in nature, and classify natural objects.
- Existential Intelligence: The capacity to locate oneself with respect to such existential features of the human condition such as the significance of life, and the meaning of death.

Eight of these nine intelligences have been found to be associated with specific brain areas. The linguistic intelligence is associated with the left temporal and frontal lobes. The logical-mathematical intelligence is associated with the left frontal and parietal lobes. Spatial intelligence is associated with posterior regions of the right hemisphere. The bodily-kinesthetic intelligence is associated with the cerebellum, basal ganglia, and motor cortex. Musical intelligence is associated with the right temporal lobe. The interpersonal intelligence is associated with the frontal lobe and temporal lobe. The intrapersonal intelligence is associated with the frontal lobe, parietal lobe, and the limbic system. Finally, the naturalistic intelligence is associated with areas of the left parietal lobe that are important in discriminating living from non-living things. All these intelligences being associated with specific brain areas shows that they actually exist and are of high significance. Each individual possesses all the intelligences, but show inclinations towards at least two or three of them. Realization that there are more than one intelligences coupled with the identification of a combination of specific intelligences that one is more inclined towards, helps to a great extent in self-realization. Learning that goes in line with these intelligences, strengthens ones abilities, and gives a clearer pictures of one's goals in life, which sets the individual on a suitable and fulfilling career path.

Howard Gardner Describes it Very Aptly: "It is of utmost importance that we recognize and nurture all of the varied human intelligences, and all of the combinations of intelligences. We are all so different largely because we all have different combinations of intelligences. If we recognize this, I think we will have at least a better chance of dealing appropriately with the many problems that we face in the world."

People not only differ in the varied combinations of intelligences, but they also differ in personality. Personality plays a very important role in career decision making and career development. It helps in defining strengths and weaknesses. If the kind of work an individual does relates to the personality of that individual then the person tends to enjoy his/her work and feel fulfilled about it. Greater the match between personality and occupation greater will be life and career satisfaction.

According to the vocational psychologist, John Holland, personality styles reflect individuals' preference for interests and activities. He suggests six personality types that are associated with different work environments and interests:

- Realistic: Such people are usually assertive and competitive, and are interested in activities requiring motor coordination, skill, and strength. Realistic people usually prefer to work a problem through by doing something rather than talking about it, or sitting and thinking about it. They like concrete approaches to problem solving, rather than abstract ideas. They also tend to be interested in scientific or mechanical rather than cultural and aesthetic areas.

- Investigative: Such people like to think and observe rather than act. They prefer to organize and understand information rather than persuade. They tend to prefer individual rather than people oriented activities.
- Artistic: Such people are usually creative, open, inventive, original, perceptive, sensitive, independent, and emotional. They dislike structure and rules, like tasks involving people or physical skills, and are more likely to express their emotions than others. They like to think, organize, and understand artistic and cultural areas.
- Social: Such people seem to satisfy their needs in teaching or helping situations. Compared to realistic and investigative people, they are more drawn to seek close relationships and are less apt to want to be really intellectual.
- Enterprising: Such people are good talkers and use this skill to lead and persuade others. They value reputation, power, money, and status, and usually go after it.
- Conventional: Such people like rules and regulations, and emphasize self-control. They like structure and order, and dislike unstructured or unclear work or interpersonal situations. They place value over reputation, power, and status.

It is very much possible that one person does not completely fit into just one personality type. Each individual might find himself/herself fit to a combination of personality types. For instance, no one can be purely realistic or purely artistic.

People whose personality type matches best with their occupation experience a high level of career satisfaction. On the other hand, people who enter occupations that are not compatible with their personality type tend to feel dissatisfied with and highly unstable with the work they do. Realizing the appropriate personality, then will enable individuals to know what suits them best, which will further help them to choose a proper career path.

Once an individual understands and identifies the specific combination of intelligences and the appropriate personality type, then it becomes a lot more easier to set goals that do justice to ones true potential. This enables the individual to choose a career path that brings joy and happiness rather than conflict and dissatisfaction.

Abraham Maslow puts it Appropriately: "If you deliberately plan to be less than you are capable of being, then I warn you that you will be deeply unhappy for the rest of your life. You will be evading your own capacities, your own possibilities."

Self-realization, of course, is not only about the comprehension of several intelligences and appropriate personality type. It, nevertheless, constitutes self-realization majorly.

Thus, self-realization not only helps to understand ones potential and abilities, but it also makes the individual to live up to his/her capacities, which further leads to the development of a highly fulfilling career.

Career

Career describes an individuals' journey through learning, work and other aspects of life. There are a number of ways to define a career and the term is used in a variety of ways.

Definitions and Etymology

Career is defined by the Oxford English Dictionary as a person's "course or progress through life (or a distinct portion of life)". In this definition career is understood to relate to a range of aspects of an individual's life, learning and work. Career is also frequently understood to relate only to the working aspects of an individuals life e.g. as in career woman. A third way in which the term career is used to describe an occupation or a profession that usually involves special training or formal education, and is considered to be a person's lifework. In this case "a career" is seen as a sequence of related jobs usually pursued within a single industry or sector e.g. "a career in law" or "a career in the building trade".

The etymology of the term comes from the m. French word carriere (16 c.) ("road, racecourse") which, in turn, comes from the Latin word "(via) cararia" (track for wheeled vehicles) which originated from the Latin word *carrus" which means "wagon".*

Historic Changes in Careers

For a pre-modernist notion of "career", compare cursus honorum. By the late 20th century, a wide range of choices (especially in the range of potential professions) and more widespread education had allowed it to become possible to plan (or design) a career: in this respect the careers of the career counsellor and of the career advisor have grown up. It is also not uncommon for adults in the late 20th/ early 21st centuries to have dual or multiple careers, either sequentially or concurrently. Thus, professional identities have become hyphenated or hybridized to reflect this shift in work ethic. Economist Richard Florida notes this trend generally and more specifically among the "creative class".

Career Management

Career management describes the active and purposeful management of a career by an individual. Ideas of what comprise "career management skills" are describe by the Blueprint model (in the United States, Canada, Australia, Scotland, and England) and the Seven C's of Digital Career Literacy (specifically relating to the Internet skills).

Key skills include the ability to reflect on one's current career, research the labour market, determine whether education is necessary, find openings, and make career changes.

Career Choice

According to Behling and others, an individual's decision to join a firm may depend on any of the three factors viz. objective factor, subjective factor and critical contact.

- Objective factor theory assumes that the applicants are rational. The choice, therefore, is exercised after an objective assessment of the tangible benefits of the job. Factors may include the salary, other benefits, location, opportunities for career advancement, etc.
- Subjective factor theory suggests that decision making is dominated by social and psychological factors. The status of the job, reputation of the organization and other similar factors plays an important role.
- Critical contact theory advances the idea that a candidate's observations while interacting with the organization plays a vital role in decision making. For example, how the recruiter keeps in touch with the candidate, the promptness of response and similar factors are important. This theory is more valid with experienced professionals.

These theories assume that candidates have a free choice of employers and careers. In reality the scarcity of jobs and strong competition for desirable jobs severely skews the decision making process. In many markets employees work particular careers simply because they were forced to accept whatever work was available to them.

Career (Occupation) Changing

Changing occupation is an important aspect of career and career management. Over a lifetime, both the individual and the labour market will change; it is to be expected that many people will change occupations during their lives. Data collected by the U.S. Bureau of Labour Statistics through the National Longitudinal Survey of Youth in 1979 showed that individuals between the ages of 18 and 38 will hold more than 10 jobs.

A survey conducted by Right Management suggests the following reasons for career changing.

- The downsizing or the restructuring of an organization (54%).
- New challenges or opportunities that arise (30%).
- Poor or ineffective leadership (25%).
- Having a poor relationship with a manager(s) (22%).
- For the improvement of work/life balance (21%).
- Contributions are not being recognized (21%).
- For better compensation and benefits (18%),
- For better alignment with personal and organizational values (17%).
- Personal strengths and capabilities are not a good fit with an organization (16%).
- The financial instability of an organization (13%).
- An organization relocated (12%).

Career Support

There are a range of different educational, counselling and human resource management interventions that can support individuals to develop and manage their careers. Career support is commonly offered while people are in education, when they are transitioning to the labour market, when they are changing career, during periods of unemployment, and during transition to retirement. Support may be offered by career professionals, other professionals or by non-professionals such as family and friends. Professional career support is sometimes known as "career guidance" as in the OECD definition of career guidance:

The activities may take place on an individual or group basis, and may be face-to-face or at a distance (including helplines and web-based services). They include career information provision (in print,

ICT-based and other forms), assessment and self-assessment tools, counselling interviews, career education programmes (to help individuals develop their self-awareness, opportunity awareness, and career management skills), taster programmes (to sample options before choosing them), work search programmes, and transition services."

However this use of the term "career guidance" can be confusing as the term is also commonly used to describe the activities of career counsellors.

Provision of Career Support

Career support is offered by a range of different mechanisms. Much career support is informal and provided through personal networks or existing relationships such as management. There is a market for private career support however the bulk of career support that exists as a professionalised activity is provided by the public sector.

Types of Career Support

Key types of career support include:

- Career information describes information that supports career and learning choices. An important sub-set of career information is labour market information (LMI), such as salaries of various professions, employment rate in various professions, available training programmes, and current job openings and.
- Career assessments are tests that come in a variety of forms and rely on both quantitative and qualitative methodologies. Career assessments can help individuals identify and better articulate their unique interests, personality, values, and skills to determine how well they may match with a certain career. Some skills that career assessments could help determine are job-specific skills, transferable skills, and self-management skills. Career assessments can also provide a window of potential opportunities by helping individuals discover the tasks, experience, education and training that is needed for a career they would want to pursue. Career counsellors, executive coaches, educational institutions, career development centres, and outplacement companies often administer career assessments to help individuals focus their search on careers that closely match their unique personal profile.

- Career counselling assesses people's interests, personality, values and skills, and helps them to explore career options and research graduate and professional schools. Career counselling provides one-on-one or group professional assistance in exploration and decision making tasks related to choosing a major/occupation, transitioning into the world of work or further professional training.
- Career education describes a process by which individuals come to learn about themselves, their careers and the world of work. There is a strong tradition of career education in schools, however career education can also occur in a wider range of other contexts including further and higher education and the workplace. A commonly used framework for careers education is DOTS which stands for decision learning (D), opportunity awareness (O), transition learning (T), and self-awareness (S). Oftentimes, higher education is thought of as being too narrow or too researched based and lacking of a deeper understanding of the material to develop the skills necessary for a certain career.

Some research shows adding one year of schooling beyond high school creates an increase of wages 17.8 percent per worker. However, additional years of schooling, beyond 9 or 10 years, have little effect on worker's wages. In summary, better educated, bigger benefits. In 2010, 90% of the U.S. Workforce had a high school diploma, 64% had some college, and 34% had at least a bachelor's degree.

The common problem that people may encounter when trying to achieve an education for a career is the cost. The career that comes with the education must pay well enough to be able to pay off the schooling. The benefits of schooling can differ greatly depending on the degree (or certification) obtained, the programmes the school may offer, and the ranking of the school. Sometimes, colleges provide students more with just education to prepare for careers. It is not uncommon for colleges to provide pathways and support straight into the workforce the students may desire.

Much career support is delivered face-to-face, but an increasing amount of career support is delivered online.

5

Career Assessment

Career assessments are tools that are designed to help individuals understand how a variety of personal attributes (i.e., interests, values, preferences, motivations, aptitudes and skills), impact their potential success and satisfaction with different career options and work environments. Career assessments have played a critical role in career development and the economy in the last century (Whiston and Rahardja, 2005). Assessments of some or all of these attributes are often used by individuals or organizations, such as university career service centres, career counsellors, outplacement companies, corporate human resources staff, executive coaches, vocational rehabilitation counsellors, and guidance counsellors to help individuals make more informed career decisions.

In part, the popularity for this tool is due to the National Defense Education Act of 1958, which funded career guidance in schools. Focus was put onto tools that would help high school students determine which subjects they may want to focus on to reach a chosen career path. Since 1958, career assessment tool options have exploded.

Types of Career Assessments

Career assessments come in many forms and vary along several dimensions. The assessments selected by individuals or administrators vary depending on their personal beliefs regarding the most important criteria when considering career choices, as well as the unique needs of the individual considering a career decision. Some common points of variance are:

- Methodology - Some assessments are quantitative in nature and precisely measure key attributes believed to influence an individuals potential success and satisfaction with a career. Others are qualitative exercises designed to help individuals clarify their goals and preferences, which can then be used to make more informed career decisions.

- Measured attributes - Assessments vary with regard to the specific personality attributes measured. Some assessments focus on an individual's interests, and perhaps aptitude, while others focus on skills or values.
- Validity - Many assessments, particularly those offered on the internet, lack evidence for "validity," which is the degree to which interpretation of the results of the assessment or decisions made from the results are useful. Typical evidence of validity is verified empirically. Users should evaluate any tests psychometric properties when assessing whether to use it for a particular purpose, and how much weight to give to the results. When the validity of the assessment for its intended purpose cannot be evaluated, results should be interpreted with appropriate caution.
- Target customer profile - Some assessments, such as the Strong Interest Inventory, the Myers Briggs Type Indicator, and Careerscope are designed to serve broad markets (i.e., virtually any individual choosing a vocational programme or Career Clusters, starting their career or considering a career change.

Career Counselling

Career counselling, career guidance and career coaching are similar in nature to other types of counselling or coaching, e.g. marriage or psychological counselling. What unites all types of professional counselling is the role of practitioners, who combine giving advice on their topic of expertise with counselling techniques that support clients in making complex decisions and facing difficult situations. The focus of career counselling is generally on issues such as career exploration, career change, personal career development and other career related issues.

Around the globe, countless definitions, concepts and terminology exist for career counselling - particularly due to cultural and linguistic differences. This even affects the most central term *counselling* (or: *counselling* in British English) which is often substituted with the word *guidance* as in *career guidance*. For example, in the UK, *career counselling* would usually be referred to as *careers advice* or *guidance*. Due to the widespread reference to both *career guidance* and *career counselling* among policy-makers, academics and practitioners around the world, references to *career guidance and counselling* are becoming common. Accordingly, this article emphasizes a *broad understanding* of career counselling which involves a variety of professionals activities commonly associated with career counselling, guidance, coaching, and advise. More specific roles and activities associated with career counselling are explained below.

Related Professional Activities

Career counselling or career guidance includes a wide variety of professional activities which focus on supporting people in dealing with career-related challenges - both preventively and in difficult situations (such as unemployment). Career counsellors work with people from various walks of life, such as adolescents seeking to explore career options, experienced professionals contemplating a career change, parents who want to return to the world of work after taking time to raise their child, or people seeking employment. Career counselling is also offered in various settings, including in groups and individually, in person or by means of digital communication.

Several approaches have been undertaken to systemize the variety of professional activities related to career guidance and counselling. In the most recent attempt, the Network for Innovation in Career Guidance and Counselling in Europe (NICE) - a consortium of 45 European institutions of higher education in the field of career counselling - has agreed on a system of professional roles for guidance counsellors. Each of these five roles is seen as an important facet of the *career guidance and counselling profession*. Career counsellors performing in any of these roles are expected to behave professionally, e.g. by following ethical standards in their practice. The NICE Professional Roles (NPR) are:

- The *Career Educator* "supports people in developing their own career management competences"
- The *Career Information & Assessment Expert* "supports people in assessing their personal characteristics and needs, then connecting them with the labour market and education systems"
- The *Career Counsellor* "supports individuals in understanding their situations, so as to work through issues towards solutions"
- The *Programme & Service Manager* "ensures the quality and delivery of career guidance and counselling organisations' services"

- The *Social Systems Intervener & Developer* "supports clients (even) in crisis and works to change systems for the better"

The description of the NICE Professional Roles (NPR) draws on a variety of prior models to define the central activities and competences of guidance counsellors. The NPR can, therefore, be understood as a state-of-the-art framework which includes all relevant aspects of career counselling. For this reason, other models haven't been included here so far. Models which are reflected in the NPR include:

- BEQU: "Kompetenzprofil für Beratende" (Germany, 2011)
- CEDEFOP "Practitioner Competences" (2009)
- ENTO: "National Occupational Standards for Advice and Guidance" (Great Britain, 2006)
- IAEVG: "International Competences for Educational and Vocational Guidance" (2003)
- Savickas, M.: "Career Counselling" (USA, 2011)

Benefits

Professional career counsellors can support people with career-related challenges in many ways. Through their expertise in career development and labour markets, they can put a person's qualification, experience, strengths and weakness in a broad perspective taking into consideration their desired salary, personal hobbies and interests, location, job market and educational possibilities. Through their counselling and teaching abilities, career counsellors can additionally support people in gaining a better understanding of what really matters for them personally, how they can plan their careers autonomously, or help them in making tough decisions and getting through times of crisis. Finally, career counsellors are often capable of supporting their clients in finding suitable placements/ jobs, in working out conflicts with their employers, or finding the support of other helpful services.

It is due to these various benefits of career counselling that policy-makers in many countries of the world publicly fund guidance services. For example, the European Union understands career guidance and counselling as an instrument to effectively combat social exclusion and increase citizens' employability.

History

Frank Parson's *Choosing a Vocation* (1909) was perhaps the first major work which is concerned with careers guidance. While until the 1970s a strongly normative approach was characteristic for theories (e.g. of Donald E. Super's *life-span approach*) and practice of career counselling (e.g. concept of *matching*), new models have their starting point in the individual needs and transferable skills of the clients while managing biographical breaks and discontinuities. Career development is no longer viewed as a linear process. More consideration is now placed on nonlinear, chance and unplanned influences.

Training

Up until now there is no standardized qualification path for professional career counsellors, although various certificates are offered nationally and internationally (e.g. by professional associations), and the number of academic degree programmes in career guidance and/ or career counselling is growing worldwide. Still, in most countries, basically anybody could call themselves a "career counsellor" (unlike engineers or psychologists whose professions are protected legally). At the same time, policy makers agree that the competence of career counsellors is one of the most important factors in ensuring that people receive high quality support in dealing with their career questions. Depending on the country of their education, career counsellors may have a variety of academic backgrounds: In Europe, for instance, degrees in (vocational/ industrial/ organization) psychology and educational sciences are among the most common, but backgrounds in sociology, public administration and other sciences are also frequent. At the same time, many training programmes for career counsellors are becoming increasingly multidisciplinary.

Professional Career Guidance Centres

There are many career guidance and counselling centres all over the world. They give services of guidance and counselling on higher studies, possibilities, chances and nature of courses and institutes. Also that these services are offered either fixing up a meeting with the Experts or having telephonic conversations with the guide or even the online guidance which is very common these days with the people getting services on click of their mouse. There are many such service providers all over the world providing online counselling to people about their career or conducting a psychometric test to know the persons aptitude as well as interests.

Career Testing

People who participate in career counselling can benefit from the use of aptitude tests, or career testing. Career testing is often done online and provides insightful and relatively objective information about which jobs may be suitable for the test taker based on combination of their interests, values and skills. Career tests usually provide a list of recommended jobs that match the test takers attributes with those of people with similar personalities who enjoy/are successful at their jobs. There are various ways to test an individual for which field he is suitable, psychometric testing being one among them.

Psychometric testing covers a wide range of skills, interests and values of people and can be of use in career counselling in different ways. For example, the information won from such tests can be of help for the professionals who mentor, coach or counsel individuals. With psychometric testing, there is no pass or fail, but the quality of the information won from the tests can vary. Psychometric testing uses in-depth psychological profiles to assess personality and intellectual levels. Different test companies use different theoretical approaches to testing, such as the psychometric approach, the psychodynamic approach, the social learning approach and the humanist approach. Different test companies have their own methods of testing, some of them being protected with copyrights. Two commonly used assessments are the Strong Interest Inventory and the MBTI, for example. Usually, psychometric testing uses multiple sets of questions relating to personality type, how the test taker would handle aspects of work and home life, what his or her goals are for the future and his or her strengths and weaknesses. If the test taker is honest and the employed tests follow scientific standards, the results should be fairly accurate and useful for career counselling activities.

Challenges

One of the major challenges associated with career counselling is encouraging participants to engage in the process. For example in the UK 70% of people under 14 say they have had no careers advice while 45% of people over 14 have had no or very poor/limited advice.

In a related issue some client groups tend to reject the interventions made by professional career counsellors preferring to rely on the advice of peers or superiors within their own profession. Jackson et al. Found that 44% of doctors in training felt that senior members of their own profession were best placed to give careers advice. Furthermore it is recognised that the giving of career advice is something that is widely spread through a range of formal and informal roles. In addition to career counsellors it is also common for teachers, managers, trainers and Human Resources (HR) specialists to give formal support in career choices. Similarly it is also common for people to seek informal support from friends and family around their career choices and to bypass career professionals altogether. Today increasingly people rely on career web portals to seek advice on resume writing and handling interviews; as also to research on various professions and companies. It has even become possible to take vocational assessments online.

Mentorship

Mentorship is a personal developmental relationship in which a more experienced or more knowledgeable person helps to guide a less experienced or less knowledgeable person. However, true mentoring is more than just answering occasional questions or providing ad hoc help. It is about an ongoing relationship of learning, dialogue, and challenge.

The person in receipt of mentorship may be referred to as a *protégé* (male), a *protégée* (female), an apprentice or, in recent years, a mentee.

"Mentoring" is a process that always involves communication and is relationship based, but its precise definition is elusive. One definition of the many that have been proposed, is

Mentoring is a process for the informal transmission of knowledge, social capital, and the psychosocial support perceived by the recipient as relevant to work, career, or professional development; mentoring entails informal communication, usually face-to-face and during a sustained period of time, between a person who is perceived to have greater relevant knowledge, wisdom, or experience (the mentor) and a person who is perceived to have less (the protégé)".

Mentoring in Europe has existed since at least Ancient Greek times. Since the 1970s it has spread in the United States of America mainly in training contexts and it has been described as "an innovation in American management".

Historical

The roots of the practice are lost in antiquity. The word itself was inspired by the character of Mentor in Homer's *Odyssey*. Though the actual Mentor in the story is a somewhat ineffective old man, the goddess Athena takes on his appearance in order to guide young Telemachus in his time of difficulty.

Historically significant systems of mentorship include the guru - disciple tradition practised in Hinduism and Buddhism, Elders, the discipleship system practised by RabbinicalJudaism and the Christian church, and apprenticing under the medieval guild system.

Mentoring Techniques

The focus of mentoring is to develop the whole person and so the techniques are broad and require wisdom in order to be used appropriately.

A 1995 study of mentoring techniques most commonly used in business found that the five most commonly used techniques among mentors were:

1. *Accompanying:* making a commitment in a caring way, which involves taking part in the learning process side-by-side with the learner.
2. *Sowing:* mentors are often confronted with the difficulty of preparing the learner before he or she is ready to change. Sowing is necessary when you know that what you say may not be understood or even acceptable to learners at first but will make sense and have value to the mentee when the situation requires it.
3. *Catalyzing:* when change reaches a critical level of pressure, learning can escalate. Here the mentor chooses to plunge the learner right into change, provoking a different way of thinking, a change in identity or a re-ordering of values.
4. *Showing:* this is making something understandable, or using your own example to demonstrate a skill or activity. You show what you are talking about, you show by your own behaviour.
5. *Harvesting:* here the mentor focuses on "picking the ripe fruit": it is usually used to create awareness of what was learned by experience and to draw conclusions. The key questions here are: "What have you learned?", "How useful is it?".

Different techniques may be used by mentors according to the situation and the mindset of the mentee, and the techniques used in modern organizations can be found in ancient education systems, from the Socratic technique of harvesting to the accompaniment method of learning used in the apprenticeship of itinerant cathedral builders during the Middle Ages. Leadership authors Jim Kouzes and Barry Posner advise mentors to look for "teachable moments" in order to "expand or realize the potentialities of the people in the organizations they lead" and underline that personal credibility is as essential to quality mentoring as skill.

Typology

There are two broad types of mentoring relationships: formal and informal. Informal relationships develop on their own between partners. Formal mentoring, on the other hand, refers to a structured process supported by the organization and addressed to target populations. Youth mentoring programmes assist at-risk children or youth who lack role models and sponsors. In business, formal mentoring is part of talent management addressed to populations such as key employees, newly hired graduates, high potentials and future leaders. The matching of mentor and mentee is often done by a mentoring coordinator or by means of an (online) database registry.

There are formal mentoring programmes that are values-oriented, while social mentoring and other types focus specifically on career development. Some mentorship programmes provide both social and vocational support. In well-designed formal mentoring programmes, there are programme goals, schedules, training (for both mentors and protégés), and evaluation. In 2004 Metizo created the first mentoring certification for companies and business schools in order to guarantee the integrity and effectiveness of formal mentoring. Certification is attributed jointly by the organization and an external expert.

There are many kinds of mentoring relationships from school or community-based relationships to e-mentoring relationships. These mentoring relationships vary and can be influenced by the type of mentoring relationship that is in effect. That is whether it has come about as a formal or informal relationship. Also there are several models have been used to describe and examine the sub-relationships that can emerge. For example, Buell describes how mentoring relationships can develop under a cloning model, nurturing model, friendship model and apprenticeship model. The cloning model is about the mentor trying to "produce a duplicate copy of him or her self." The nurturing model takes more of a "parent figure, creating a safe, open environment in which mentee can both learn and try things for him-or herself." The friendship model are more peers "rather than being involved in a hierarchical relationship." Lastly, the apprenticeship is about less "personal or social aspects... and the professional relationship is the sole focus".

Contemporary Research and Practice in the US

Research in the 1970s, partly in response to a study by Daniel Levinson, led some women and African Americans to question whether the classic "white male" model was available or customary for people who are newcomers in traditionally white male organizations. In 1978 Edgar Schein described multiple roles for successful mentors.

Two of Schein's students, Davis and Garrison, undertook to study successful leaders of both genders and at least two races. Their research presented evidence for the roles of: cheerleader, coach, confidant, counsellor, developer of talent, "griot" (oral historian for the organization or profession), guardian, guru, inspiration, master, "opener of doors", patron, role model, pioneer, "seminal source", "successful leader", and teacher. They described multiple mentoring practices which have since been given the name of "mosaic mentoring" to distinguish this kind of mentoring from the single mentor approach.

Mosaic mentoring is based on the concept that almost everyone can perform one or another function well for someone else — and also can learn along one of these lines from someone else. The model is seen as useful for people who are "non-traditional" in a traditional setting, such as people of colour and women in a traditionally white male organization. The idea has been well received in medical education literature. There are also mosaic mentoring programmes in various faith-based organizations.

Corporate Mentorship Programmes

Corporate mentoring programmes are used by mid to large organizations to further the development and retention of employees. Mentoring programmes may be formal or informal and serve a variety of specific objectives including acclimation of new employees, skills development, employee retention and diversity enhancement.

Formal Mentoring Programmes

Formal mentoring programmes offer employees the opportunity to participate in an organized mentoring programme. Participants join as a mentor, mentee or both by completing a mentoring profile. Mentoring profiles are completed as written forms on paper or computer or filled out via an online form as part of an online mentoring system. Mentees are matched with a mentor by a programme administrator or a mentoring committee, or may self-select a mentor depending on the programme format.

Informal mentoring takes places in organizations that develop a culture of mentoring but do not have formal mentoring in place. These companies may provide some tools and resources and encourage managers to accept mentoring requests from more junior members of the organization.

New-hire Mentorship

New-hire mentoring programmes are set up to help new employees acclimate more quickly into the organization. In new-hire mentoring programmes, newcomers to the organization (protégés) are paired with more experienced people (mentors) in order to obtain information, good examples, and advice as they advance. It has been claimed that new employees who are paired with a mentor are twice as likely to remain in their job than those who do not receive mentorship.

These mentoring relationships provide substance for career growth, and benefit both the mentor and the mentee. For example, the mentor gets to show leadership by giving back and perhaps being refreshed about their own work. The organization receives an employee that is being gradually introduced and shaped by the organization's culture and operation because they have been under the mentorship of an experienced member. The person being mentored networks, becomes integrated easier in an organization, gets experience and advice along the way. It has been said that "joining a mentor's network and developing one's own is central to advancement" and this is possibly why those mentored tend to do well in their organizations.

In the organizational setting, mentoring usually "requires unequal knowledge", but the process of mentorship can differ. Bullis describes the mentoring process in the forms of phase models. Initially, the "mentee proves himself or herself worthy of the mentor's time and energy". Then cultivation occurs which includes the actual "coaching...a strong interpersonal bond between mentor and mentee develops". Next, under the phase of separation "the mentee experiences more autonomy". Ultimately, there is more of equality in the relationship, termed by Bullis as Redefinition.

High-potential Mentorship

High-potential mentoring programmes are used to groom up-and-coming employees deemed to have the potential to move up into leadership roles. Here the employee (protégé) is paired with a senior level leader (or leaders) for a series of career-coaching interactions. These programmes tend to be smaller than more general mentoring programmes and mentees must be selected to participate.

A similar method of high-potential mentoring is to place the employee in a series of jobs in disparate areas of an organization, all for small periods of time, in anticipation of learning the organization's structure, culture, and methods. A mentor does not have to be a manager or supervisor to facilitate the process.

Matching Mentors and Mentees

Mentees are matched with mentors by a designated mentoring committee or mentoring administrator usually consisting of senior members of the Training, Learning and Development and Human Resources departments. The matching committee reviews the mentoring profiles and makes matches based on areas for development, mentor strengths, overall experience, skill set, location and objectives for the mentorship. Mentoring technology can be used to facilitate matches allowing mentees to search and select a mentor based on their own development needs and interests. This mentee-driven methodology increases the speed in which matches are created and reduces the amount of administrative time required to manage the programme. The quality of matches increases as well with self-match programmes because the greater the involvement of the mentee in the selection of their mentor, the better the outcome of the mentorship. There are a variety of online mentoring technology programmes available that can be utilized to facilitate this mentee-driven matching process.

Mentorship in Education

In many secondary and post-secondary schools, mentorship programmes are offered to support students in programme completion, confidence building and transitioning to further education or the workforce. There are also many peer mentoring programmes designed specifically to bring under-represented populations into science and engineering. The Internet has brought university alumni closer to graduating students. Graduate university alumni are engaging with current students in career mentorship through interview questions and answers. The students with the best answers receive professional recommendations from industry experts build a more credible CV. Websites such as, Endorse me and GapJumpers are leading the way in online career mentorship.

Blended Mentoring

The blended mentoring is a mix of on-site and online events, projected to give to career counselling and development services the opportunity to adopt mentoring in their ordinary practice.

Reverse mentoring

In the reverse mentoring situation, the mentee has more overall experience (typically as a result of age) than the mentor (who is typically younger), but the mentor has more knowledge in a particular area, and as such, reverses the typical constellation. Examples are when young internet or mobile savvy Millennial Generation teens train executives in using their high end Smart Phones. They in turn sometimes offer insight in business processes.

Business Mentoring

The concept of mentoring has entered the business domain as well. This is different from being an apprentice, a business mentor provides guidance to a business owner or an entrepreneur on the entrepreneur's business. An apprentice learns a trade by working on the job with the "employer".

A 2012 literature review by EPS-PEAKS investigated the practice of business mentoring, with a focus on the Middle-East and North Africa region. The review found strong evidence to suggest that business mentoring can have real benefits for entrepreneurs, but highlights some key factors that need to be taken into account when designing mentoring programmes for this to be the case, such as the need to balance a formal and informal approach and to appropriately match mentors and mentees.

Career Decisions: The Role Parents Play

When choosing your career, should you chase high income or professional growth? A survey shows that your goals, and the support you get from your parents, play a key role in determining successful career decisions, say Sanjay Roy Chowdhury, Debkumar Mitra and Ayantika Paul of Gray matters consulting

The film 3 Idiots may have been hugely successful, propagating as it does the message that students should not become victims of rote learning and the rat race. It is no doubt a worthy message. But it is also small comfort to youngsters who are desperate to make their mark in a competitive world and build a successful career.

Parents too want the best for their children. And, willy nilly, they do play a big role in influencing their children's career choices. For a week starting from Children's Day 2009, we surveyed 692 professionals in 75 organisations across India to find the factors that had influenced the parents' own career decisions, and the kind of support they gave their children to the latter's career selection process.

Our research model contends that environmental opportunity as well as one's own merits and attributes influence a person's choice of a career. So a part of the survey identifies key environment, opportunity and self influencers in career decisions, and discusses the different degrees of future career success associated with each. We have also presented different support activities that the children have access to in choosing their career directions.

The report also reveals specific parental attitudes and preferences that can have a great impact on a child's career direction. The impact of the parent's age, gender and income on such parental attitudes, and their underlying rationale are also explored.

Who Did we Ask?

Around 692 professionals participated in this study, and 84 per cent of them were male. The east, north and south of the country were well represented in the sample; but we had only 2 per cent and 7 per cent of participants, respectively, from central and western India. The participants were selected from a diverse mix of industries. However, the largest concentration was in the IT & ITeS (25 per cent) and manufacturing (30 per cent) industries.

Most of these professionals were either graduates (50 per cent) or postgraduates (35 per cent). Since the participants belonged to diverse age groups, the age of their children had a spread from below 12 years to above 21 years.

What Were we Looking for?

We wanted to decode the career decision making process of children. What factors does a child consider in making his or her career choice? What are parents' most common attitudes and preferences in supporting their child's career decision making?

We investigated the following questions:

1. What's the most common definition of career success among today's professionals?
2. What percentage of these professionals feels that they have been "successful" in their career?
3. Which of the environment, opportunity and self influencers of career choice have led to greater career success?
4. What are the most common support activities that children had access to for capitalising on such career choice influencers?
5. What factors influence parental attributes that in turn influence their child's career decisions?
6. What are parents' predominant attitudes and preferences regarding their children's career planning process?'

7. How do the parents' age, gender and income influence such attributes?

What Did we Find?

For most of the professionals surveyed, career success meant "professional growth and achievement" or "right person-career fit". "Monetary achievement" or "power" was considered far less important for determining career success. In the domain of one's environment, people who were most influenced by their parents' occupations experienced the highest career success.

The responses reveal that if a child is asked to choose her career guidepost between the "occupational diversity in her local region" and her "deeper understanding of her parents' professions", she's likely to profit more from the latter. Again, people who were driven most by "past or current work experience at the time of making their career selection" landed up with the greatest career success, followed by groups driven by "family socio-economic status (SES)".

Significantly, if a person has had opportunities in terms of an enriching past work experience, multiple education and employment opportunities in his or her local area, and a high family SES, he or she is likely to have greater career success if he or she is most influenced by work experience. However, the career success differentials associated with each factor were not significant.

In the domain of self factors, people most driven by their "motivation for high SES" during the career decision making phase achieved the highest career success, followed by groups that were most led by "analysis of their own capabilities", "self interest awareness and career planning", and "academic scores and achievement". So if a child is clear that his career success motivation lies in a good career fit rather than high income right at the time of career decision-making, he's likely to have a career that he would find the most successful.

To best leverage the environment factors influencing a child's career choice, we have recommended the following to those who were surveyed:

- Discuss the pros and cons of parents' occupations
- Give children the opportunity to be mentored by role models or siblings
- Have peer discussions of career choices and interests
- Decrease explorations of occupations and career choices beyond those in the local area

To make the best use of the opportunity factors influencing the child's career selection process, we have the following suggestions for the sampled parent-child groups:

- Decrease activities that make use of school-industry joint initiatives
- Maintain parents' exploration of financial alternatives for supporting their child's career decisions
- Discuss non-traditional and non-mainstream careers.

Although practical experiences provide children with some knowledge of specific professions, what is also needed is a deeper discussion of the benefits and challenges of different occupations.

To best capitalise on the self factors that influence a child's career direction, we recommend the following for the children surveyed:

- Decrease activities that choose career value priorities
- Decrease activities that analyse one's own capabilities
- Increase activities that involve career planning and self discovery
- Increase activities that involve understanding the impact of academic scores.

Most respondents felt the need to get more proactive about planning the steps towards achieving the child's career goals.

A respondent from Eveready says: "Once my child becomes mature enough, her inclination towards any particular field needs to be nurtured and developed." Agrees Jubilant Energy's Tojo Jose, "My daughter is looking at a career that would fit into her strengths and interests, provided she's mentored and guided properly."

But some children feel that too much monitoring by parents can also be counter productive. Says Sree Mitra, a third-year student at the West Bengal National University of Juridical Sciences, Calcutta, "Once they see an inclination in children, parents push them towards that particular career, leaving little opportunity for self-discovery."

The survey also showed that the parent's income or gender is unrelated to the time at which he begins to plan for a child's career. The parent's age, however, has a quasi-significant relationship to the time at which the planning begins. The younger the parent is, the earlier he's likely to want the child's career planning process to begin.

As a mid-level professional from Bajaj Auto Finance says: "Both my sons are interested in making their career in sports, film, music and dance. My only expectation is whatever they do they should excel in their chosen field." Shilpa Chakraborty of manufacturing conglomerate TIL Limited, feels it is important for students to be better trained in soft skills such as communication. However, as newer opportunities open up, career choices become more difficult. And not all parents are encouraging when it comes to choosing a career that they perceive to be off the beaten track.

"I had wanted to pursue a career in English. I wanted to become a writer but since both my parents have PhDs in science, I was discouraged from pursuing my dream," says a student of St Xavier's College, Calcutta, who declined to reveal his identity.

The parent's age or gender does not have a significant impact on his or her preference for the child's independent interests versus societal expectations. However, wealthier parents are more likely to be predisposed towards their child's interests vis-à-vis societal expectations.

Also, younger and wealthier parents are likely to be more open to the non-traditional career choices of their children. But the parent's gender does not have any significant impact on this. It was also seen that mothers and fathers were surprisingly alike in some of the key parental attitudes that can impact the quality of support the child gets in making his or her career decision.

Are our findings any different from similar studies from the developed world? Here is an abstract from a study titled "Pathways to a Career in STEMM" by researchers at the University of Michigan, US.

"The selection of scientific and technical careers by American young adults has been and continues to be a major national concern.

Using data from the 20-year record of the Longitudinal Study of American Youth (LSAY) and working within the social learning paradigm, this analysis uses a set of 21 variables to predict employment in science, technology, engineering, mathematics, or medicine (STEMM) at ages 34 to 37... Home and family factors such as parent education and parent encouragement of science and mathematics during secondary school enhanced the likelihood of a young adult entering a STEMM profession."

In sum, the survey reveals that many parents do give the necessary support to their children so that they discover their talents and aptitudes and go for careers that are best suited to them. Indeed, the crucial piece of a child's career direction puzzle is his or her parental support. And it seems there are oodles of it. It is up to parents, to help children discover their passions and interests and put them on a path of self-discovery.

Survey Highlights

- Individuals who defined career success in terms of their professional development perceived themselves to be more successful than people who identified career success with high income or power
- Those who were most influenced by their parents' occupations experienced the highest career success
- Those who were driven most by "past or current work experience at the time of making their career selection" got the greatest career success
- Proactive discussions with parents, peers, siblings and role models can play an important role in future career success
- The parent's income or gender is unrelated to the time at which he or she begins to plan for a child's career
- Younger and wealthier parents are likely to be more open to the non-traditional career choices of their children.

Analytical Psychology

Analytical psychology (or Jungian psychology) is the school of psychology originating from the ideas of Swiss psychiatrist Carl Jung. His theoretical orientation has been advanced by his students and other thinkers who followed in his tradition. Though they share similarities, analytical psychology is distinct from the psychoanalysis of Sigmund Freud. Its aim is wholeness through the integration of unconscious forces and motivations underlying human behaviour. Depth psychology, including archetypal psychology, employs the model of the unconscious mind as the source of healing and development in an individual. Jung saw the psyche as mind, but also admits the mystery of soul, and used as empirical evidence the practice of an accumulative phenomenology around the significance of dreams, archetypes and mythology.

Jung developed his own distinctive approach to the study of the human mind. In his early years when working in a Swiss hospital with schizophrenic patients and working with Sigmund Freud and the burgeoning psychoanalytic community, he took a closer look at the mysterious depths of the human unconscious. Fascinated by what he saw (and spurred on with even more passion by the experiences and questions of his personal life) he devoted his life to the exploration of the unconscious. Unlike many modern psychologists, Jung did not feel that experimenting using natural science was the only means to understand the human psyche. For him, he saw as empirical evidence the world of dream, myth, and folklore as the promising road to its deeper understanding and meaning. That method's choice is related with his choice of the object of his science. As Jung said, "The beauty about the unconscious is that it is really unconscious". Hence, the unconscious is 'untouchable' by experimental researches, or indeed any possible kind of scientific or philosophical reach, precisely because it is unconscious. Although the unconscious cannot be studied by using direct approaches it is, according to Jung, at least, a useful hypothesis. His postulated unconscious was quite different from the model that was proposed by Freud, despite the great influence that the founder of psychoanalysis had on Jung. The most known difference is the assumption of the collective unconscious, although Jung's proposal of collective unconscious and archetypes was based on the assumption of the existence of psychic (mental) patterns. These patterns include conscious contents—thoughts, memories, etc.—which came from life experience. They are common for all human beings. His proof of the vast collective unconscious was his concept of synchronicity, that inexplicable, uncanny connectedness that we all share.

The overarching goal of Jungian psychology is the attainment of self through individuation. Jung defines "self" as the "archetype of wholeness and the regulating centre of the psyche." Central to this process is the individual's encounter with his/her psyche, and bringing of its elements into consciousness, an awakening. Humans experience the unconscious through symbols encountered in all aspects of life: in dreams, art, religion, and the symbolic dramas we enact in our relationships and life pursuits. Essential to this numinous encounter is the merging of the individual's consciousness with the collective consciousness through this symbolic language. By bringing conscious awareness to that which is not, when unconscious elements surface, they can be integrated into consciousness.

"Neurosis" results from a disharmony between the individual's (un)consciousness and his higher Self. The psyche is a self-regulating adaptive system. Humans are energetic systems, and if the energy gets blocked, the psyche gets stuck, or sick. If adaption is thwarted, the psychic energy will stop flowing, and regress. This process manifests in neurosis and psychosis. Human psychic contents are complex, and deep. They can schism, and split, and form complexes that take over one's personality. Jung proposed that this occurs through maladaptation to one's external or internal realities. The principles of adaptation, projection, and compensation are central processes in Jung's view of psyche's ability to adapt.

The aim of psychotherapy is to assist the individual in reestablishing a healthy relationship to the unconscious: neither flooded by it (characteristic of psychosis, such as Schizophrenia) or out of balance in relationship to it (as with neurosis, a state that results in depression, anxiety, and personality disorders).

In order to undergo the individuation process, the individual must be open to the parts of oneself beyond one's own ego. The modern individual grows continually in psychic awareness (attention to dreams), explores the world of religion and spirituality, and questions the assumptions of the operant societal worldview rather than just blindly living life in accordance with dominant norms and assumptions.

Fundamentals

Unconscious: The basic assumption is that the personal unconscious is a potent part — probably the more active part — of the normal human psyche. Reliable communication between the conscious and unconscious parts of the psyche is necessary for wholeness.

Also crucial is the belief that dreams show ideas, beliefs, and feelings of which individuals are not readily aware, but need to be, and that such material is expressed in a personalized vocabulary of visual metaphors. Things "known but unknown" are contained in the unconscious, and dreams are one of the main vehicles for the unconscious to express them.

Analytical psychology distinguishes between a personal and a collective unconscious.

The collective unconscious contains archetypes common to all human beings. That is, individuation may bring to surface symbols that do not relate to the life experiences of a single person. This content is more easily viewed as answers to the more fundamental questions of humanity: life, death, meaning, happiness, fear. Among these more spiritual concepts may arise and be integrated into the personality.

Collective Unconscious

Jung's concept of the collective unconscious has often been misunderstood. In order to understand this concept, it is essential to understand Jungian archetypes.

The archetypes of the collective unconscious could be thought of as the DNA of the human psyche. Just as all humans share a common physiological pattern determined by DNA, archetypes are psychic elements that determine the shared psychological pattern Jung called the collective unconscious.

Archetypes

The use of psychological archetypes was advanced by Jung in 1919. In Jung's psychological framework, archetypes are innate, universal prototypes for ideas and may be used to interpret observations. A group of memories and interpretations associated with an archetype is a complex, e.g. a mother complex associated with the mother archetype. Jung treated the archetypes as psychological organs, analogous to physical ones in that both are morphological givens that arose through evolution.

The archetypes are collective as well as individual. One can create their own archetypes, based on an ideal one wants to emulate (e.g. respect or fear).

Archetypes can grow on their own and present themselves in a variety of creative ways. Jung, in his book *Memories, Dreams, Reflections*, states that he began to see and talk to a manifestation of anima and that she taught him how to interpret dreams. As soon as he could interpret on his own, Jung said that she ceased talking to him because she was no longer needed.

Self-realization and Neuroticism

An innate need for self-realization leads people to explore and integrate these disowned parts of themselves. This natural process is called individuation, or the process of becoming an individual.

According to Jung, self-realization is attained through individuation. His is an adult psychology, divided into two distinct tiers. In the first half of our lives, we separate from humanity. We attempt to create our own identities (I, myself). This is why there is such a need for young men to be destructive, and can be expressed as animosity from teens directed at their parents. Jung also said we have a sort of "second puberty" that occurs between 35-40- outlook shifts from emphasis on materialism, sexuality, and having children to concerns about community and spirituality.

In the second half of our lives, humans reunite with the human race. They become part of the collective once again. This is when adults start to contribute to humanity (volunteer time, build, garden, create art, etc.) rather than destroy. They are also more likely to pay attention to their unconscious and conscious feelings. Young men rarely say "I feel angry." or "I feel sad." This is because they have not yet rejoined the human collective experience, commonly reestablished in their older, wiser years, according to Jung. A common theme is for young rebels to "search" for their true selves and realize that a contribution to humanity is essentially a necessity for a whole self.

Jung proposes that the ultimate goal of the collective unconscious and self-realization is to pull us to the highest experience. This, of course, is spiritual.

If a person does not proceed towards self-knowledge, neurotic symptoms may arise. Symptoms are widely defined, including, for instance, phobias, psychosis, and depression.

Shadow

The shadow is an unconscious complex defined as the repressed, suppressed or disowned qualities of the conscious self. According to Jung, the human being deals with the reality of the shadow in four ways: denial, projection, integration and/or transmutation. According to Analytical psychology, a person's shadow may have both constructive and destructive aspects. In its more destructive aspects, the shadow can represent those things which people do not accept about themselves. For instance, the shadow of someone who identifies as being kind may be harsh or unkind. Conversely, the shadow of a person who perceives himself to be brutal may be gentle. In its more constructive aspects, a person's shadow may represent hidden positive qualities. This has been referred to as the "gold in the shadow". Jung emphasized the importance of being aware of shadow material and incorporating it into conscious awareness in order to avoid projecting shadow qualities on others.

The shadow in dreams is often represented by dark figures of the same gender as the dreamer.

The shadow may also concern great figures in the history of human thought or even spiritual masters, who became great just because their shadows or their possibility of living shadows, namely, their unconscious faults, in full, without repressing them.

Anima and Animus

Jung identified the anima as being the unconscious feminine component of men and the animus as the unconscious masculine component in women. However, this is rarely taken as a literal definition: many modern day Jungian practitioners believe that every person has both an anima and an animus. Jung stated that the anima and animus act as guides to the unconscious unified Self, and that forming an awareness and a connection with the anima or animus is one of the most difficult and rewarding steps in psychological growth. Jung reported that he identified his anima as she spoke to him, as an inner voice, unexpectedly one day.

Often, when people ignore the anima or animus complexes, the anima or animus vies for attention by projecting itself on others. This explains, according to Jung, why we are sometimes immediately attracted to certain strangers: we see our anima or animus in them. Love at first sight is an example of anima and animus projection. Moreover, people who strongly identify with their gender role (e.g. a man who acts aggressively and never cries) have not actively recognized or engaged their anima or animus.

Jung attributes human rational thought to be the male nature, while the irrational aspect is considered to be natural female (rational being defined as involving judgement, irrational being defined as involving perceptions). Consequently, irrational moods are the progenies of the male anima shadow and rational opinions of the female animus shadow.

Wise old Man / Woman

"After the confrontation with the soul-image the appearance of the *old wise man*, the personification of the *spiritual principle*, can be distinguished as the next milestone of inner development." As archetypes of the collective unconscious, such figures can be seen as, "in psychological terms, a symbolic personification of the Self".

Psychoanalysis

Analysis is a way to experience and integrate the unknown material. It is a search for the meaning of behaviours, symptoms and events. Many are the channels to reach this greater self-knowledge. The analysis of dreams is the most common. Others may include expressing feelings in art pieces, poetry or other expressions of creativity.

Giving a complete description of the process of dream interpretation and individuation is complex. The nature of the complexity lies on the fact that the process is highly specific to the person who does it.

While Freudianpsychoanalysis assumes that the repressed material hidden in the unconscious is given by repressed sexual instincts, Analytical psychology has a more general approach. There is no preconceived assumption about the unconscious material. The unconscious, for Jungian analysts, may contain repressed sexual drives, but also aspirations, fears, etc.

Psychological Types

Analytical psychology distinguishes several psychological types or temperaments.

- Extravert (Jung's spelling is "extravert", which most dictionaries also use; the variant "extrovert" is not preferred)
- Introvert

According to Jung, the psyche is an apparatus for adaptation and orientation, and consists of a number of different psychic functions. Among these he distinguishes four basic functions:

- sensation - perception by means of the sense organs;
- intuition - perceiving in unconscious way or perception of unconscious contents.
- thinking - function of intellectual cognition; the forming of logical conclusions;
- feeling - function of subjective estimation;

Thinking and feeling functions are rational, while sensation and intuition are nonrational.

Complexes

Early in Jung's career he coined the term and described the concept of the "complex". Jung claims to have discovered the concept during his free association and galvanic skin response experiments. Freud obviously took up this concept in his Oedipus complex amongst others. Jung seemed to see complexes as quite autonomous parts of psychological life. It is almost as if Jung were describing separate personalities within what is considered a single individual, but to equate Jung's use of complexes with something along the lines of multiple personality disorder would be a step out of bounds.

Jung saw an archetype as always being the central organizing structure of a complex. For instance, in a "negative mother complex," the archetype of the "negative mother" would be seen to be central to the identity of that complex. This is to say, our psychological lives are patterned on common human experiences. Interestingly, Jung saw the Ego (which Freud wrote about in German literally as the "I", one's conscious experience of oneself) as a complex. If the "I" is a complex, what might be the archetype that structures it? Jung, and many Jungians, might say "the hero," one who separates from the community to ultimately carry the community further.

Clinical Theories

Jung's writings have been studied by people of many backgrounds and interests, including theologians, people from the humanities, and mythologists. Jung often seemed to seek to make contributions to various fields, but he was mostly a practicing psychiatrist, involved during his whole career in treating patients. A description of Jung's clinical relevance is to address the core of his work.

Jung started his career working with hospitalized patients with major mental illnesses, most notably schizophrenia. He was interested in the possibilities of an unknown "brain toxin" that could be the cause of schizophrenia. But the majority and the heart of Jung's clinical career was taken up with what we might call today individual psychodynamic psychotherapy, in gross structure very much in the strain of psychoanalytic practice first formed by Freud.

It is important to state that Jung seemed to often see his work as not a complete psychology in itself but as his unique contribution to the field of psychology. Jung claimed late in his career that only for about a third of his patients did he use "Jungian analysis." For another third, Freudian psychology seemed to best suit the patient's needs and for the final third Adlerian analysis was most appropriate. In fact, it seems that most contemporary Jungian clinicians merge a developmentally grounded theory, such as Self psychology or Donald Winnicott's work, with the Jungian theories in order to have a "whole" theoretical repertoire to do actual clinical work.

The "I" or Ego is tremendously important to Jung's clinical work. Jung's theory of etiology of psychopathology could almost be simplified to be stated as a too rigid conscious attitude towards the whole of the psyche. That is, a psychotic episode can be seen from a Jungian perspective as the "rest" of the psyche overwhelming the conscious psyche because the conscious psyche effectively was locking out and repressing the psyche as a whole.

Post-Jungian Approaches

Andrew Samuels (1985) has distinguished three distinct traditions or approaches of "post-Jungian" psychology - classical, developmental and archetypal. Today there are more developments.

Classical

The classical approach is that which tries to remain faithful to what Jung himself proposed and taught in person and in his 20-plus volumes of work. Prominent advocates of this approach, according to Samuels (1985), include Emma Jung (C.G. Jung's wife, who was an analyst in her own right), Marie-Louise von Franz, Joseph Henderson, Aniela Jaffe, Erich Neumann, Gerhard Adler and Jolande Jacobi.

Developmental

The developmental approach is primarily associated with Michael Fordham and his wife, Frieda Fordham. It can be considered a bridge between traditional Jungian analysis and Melanie Klein's object relations theory. Laings and Goodheart are also often mentioned. Samuels (1985) considers J. Redfearn, Richard Carvalho and himself (Andrew Samuels) as representatives of the developmental approach. Samuels notes how this approach differs from the classical by giving less emphasis to the Self and more emphasis to the development of personality; he also notes how, in terms of practice in therapy, it gives more attention to transference and counter-transference than either the classical or the archetypal approaches.

Archetypal

One archetypal approach, sometimes called "the imaginal school" by James Hillman, was written about by him in the late 1960s and early 1970s. Its adherents, according to Samuels (1985), include Murray Stein, Rafael Lopez-Pedraza and Wolfgang Giegerich. Thomas Moore also was influenced by some of Hillman's work. Developed independently, other psychoanalysts have created strong approaches to archetypal psychology. Mythopoeticists and psychoanalysts such as Clarissa Pinkola Estés who believes that ethnic and aboriginal people are the originators of archetypal psychology and have long carried the maps for the journey of the soul in their songs, tales, dream-telling, art and rituals; Marion Woodman who proposes a feminist viewpoint regarding archetypal psychology. Some of the mythopoetic/archetypal psychology creators either imagine the Self not to be the main archetype of the collective unconscious as Jung thought, but rather assign each archetype equal value. Others, who are modern progenitors of archetypal psychology (such as Estés), think of the Self as that which contains and yet is suffused by all the other archetypes, each giving life to the other.

Robert L. Moore has explored the archetypal level of the human psyche in a series of five books co-authored with Douglas Gillette, which have played an important role in the men's movement in the United States. Moore studies computerese so he uses a computer's hard wiring (its fixed physical components) as a metaphor for the archetypal level of the human psyche. Personal experiences influence the access to the archetypal level of the human psyche, but personalized ego consciousness can be likened to computer software.

Process-oriented Psychology

Process-oriented psychology (also called Process work) is associated with the Zurich trained Jungian analyst Arnold Mindell. Process Work developed in the late 1970s and early 1980s and was originally identified as a "daughter of Jungian psychology". Process work stresses awareness of the "unconscious" as an ongoing flow of experience. This approach expands Jung's work beyond verbal individual therapy to include body experience, altered and comatose states as well as multicultural group work.

Work Adjustment Theory

Most applicable to adults who wish to make career choices or are experiencing work adjustment problems. Consists of 18 propositions and corollaries which predict work adjustment.

Work Adjustment – a continuous and dynamic process by which a worker seeks to achieve and maintain correspondence with a work environment. Work adjustment is indicated by length of time, or tenure, on the job. This theory is concerned with actual job performance, not just career selection or work adjustment.

Two major components to the prediction of work adjustment:

Satisfaction: being satisfied with the work one does, the extent to which a person's needs and requirements are being met by the work being done.

Satisfactoriness: the employer's satisfaction with the individual's performance, concerns the appraisal of others, usually supervisors, of the extent to which an individual adequately completes the work that is assigned to him/her

Step 1 - Assessment Abilities, Values, Personality And Interests

Abilities: reference dimensions for skills (work skills), encompasses aptitudes, need assessment statements of abilities in order to conceptualize a vast array of work skills

To assess abilities, they used GATB – incorporates abilities required for many jobs and measures a broader base of abilities than many academic tests.

Values: represents a grouping of needs, the number of needs are fewer than skills

To assess values and needs, they developed the Minnesota Importance Questionnaire (MIQ)

- method of measuring the importance of needs that emerge from experience
- 20 need scales characterize important work-related concepts
- 6 values derived from 20 needs, 3 negatively correlated pairs

Achievement (making use of one's abilities and having a sense of accomplishment) vs. comfort (non-stressful work environment) status (how one is perceived by others and the recognition one gets) vs. altruism (how one can help or work with others) safety (orderliness and predictability) vs. autonomy (opportunity to work on their own)

Personality Styles: concerned with how an individual with particular abilities and values interacts with his or her work situation

Four characteristics of personality style:

_ celerity: speed with which one approaches tasks

_ pace: effort one spends in working

_ rhythm: the pattern of one's effort or pace

_ endurance: how long one is likely to continue working on a task

Interests: derived from values and abilities in that they are an expression of ability-value relationships. Work values are better indicators of job satisfaction than interests, according to researchers.

Step 2 – Measuring The Requirements And Conditions Of Occupations

There are methods to measure the abilities and values needed for many occupations. This is done by averaging scores for people in various occupations on the GATB and MIQ. Ability Patterns: important abilities that are required for a great variety of jobs.

Set of GATB ability requirements was developed for each occupation and cutoff scores were selected. Those scoring above this cutoff were successful in their jobs. So if a client was taking the GATB, you would compare his score with successful employees and see if they match.

Value Patterns: developed the Minnesota Job Description Questionnaire (MJDQ), which assesses how well an occupation reinforces or meets each of the 20 needs.

Combining Ability and Value Patterns: combined data used to create the Minnesota Occupational Classification System (MOCS)

Step 3 - Matching Abilities, Values, And Reinforcers

When matching values and abilities with the Occupational Ability Patterns and Occupational Reinforcer Patterns, the counsellor can use (1) MIQ, (2) GATB, (3) MOCS

Adjustment Style: the degree of fit between person and the environment, how an individual relates to the occupational environment

Four qualities describe this fit:

- flexibility - the ability of a person to tolerate unpleasant or difficult aspects of the job
- activeness – trying to change the environment
- reactiveness – changing themselves
- perseverance – how long a person can take adverse conditions before changing jobs

Job Adjustment Counselling

Work adjustment theory can be used to conceptualize the types of problems that someone can have in adjusting to a job (i.e. their skills may not be fully developed for the job or may not be able to fully develop them, values and needs are not met on the job, does not understand the reinforcer patterns of the work involved, or person could be having problems at home which affect work).

Counsellor assesses client's work personality (MIQ, GATB) and working environment.

Assess discrepancies between the individual's values and abilities and the ability patterns and reinforcer patterns of the job. Make changes in the work itself so that reinforcer patterns are altered.

Adjustment To Retirement

Try to find work in a non-work environment that has the same abilities and reinforcers as their previous job.

Holland's Theory of Career Choice and You

Choosing an Occupation, Training Programme, Major, Career Cluster or Pathway

The Career Key is based on John Holland's theory of career choice. The theory explains work-related behaviour – such as, which career choices are likely to lead to job success and satisfaction. It also explains other human actions, like success and satisfaction in school and training programmes. It is the best known and most widely researched theory on this topic and is used by most career counsellors.

Understanding Holland's theory will help you make good choices – decisions about which occupations, careers, majors, or training programmes best fit you.

When you take the Career Key test, you receive an accurate assessment of your Holland personality types and a booklet *What Your Test Scores Means* that explains Holland's theory and how your test scores are related to it and career choice.

Holland's Theory can be summarized in Six Statements:

1. In our culture, most people are one of six personality types: Realistic, Investigative, Artistic, Social, Enterprising, and Conventional. Some refer to these as Holland Codes or RIASEC.
2. People of the same personality type working together in a job create a work environment that fits their type. For example, when Artistic persons are together on a job, they create a work environment that rewards creative thinking and behaviour — an Artistic environment.
3. There are six basic types of work environments: Realistic, Investigative, Artistic, Social, Enterprising, Conventional.
4. People search for environments where they can use their skills and abilities and express their values and attitudes. For example, Investigative types search for Investigative environments; Artistic types look for Artistic environments, and so forth.
5. People who choose to work in an environment similar to their personality type are more likely to be successful and satisfied.

For example, Artistic persons are more likely to be successful and satisfied if they choose a job that has an Artistic environment, like choosing to be a dance teacher in a dancing school — an environment "dominated" by Artistic type people where creative abilities and expression are highly valued.

6. How you act and feel at work depends to a large extent on your workplace (or school) environment. If you are working with people who have a personality type like yours, you will be able to do many of the things they can do, and you will feel most comfortable with them. How is this related to the scores you receive on the Career Key?

How is this related to the scores you receive on the Career Key? According to the theory, you want to choose an occupation whose personality type is the same as, or similar to yours. This is most likely to lead to your job satisfaction and success. (Learn more about how this applies to college majors, training programmes or to Career Clusters, Fields, and Pathways).

A good match-up is called "Congruent" (meaning "compatible, in agreement or harmony"). For example, imagine that your highest score on the Career Key is for the Realistic type. Looking at the table below, you can see that the most compatible job environment is Realistic. It is a congruent match. This suggests that you choose a job in the Realistic group. Or, you might choose from the jobs that fall in the Investigative or Conventional category.

Compatible Work Environments

- Your Personality Type
- Artisitc
- Conventional
- Enterprising
- Invesitgative
- Realistic
- Social
- Most Compatible
- Artistic
- Conventional
- Enterprising
- Investigative

- Realistic
- Social
- Other Compatible
- Investigative& Social
- Enterprising& Realistic
- Conventional&Social
- Artisitc&Realistic
- Conventional&Investigative
- Artisitc&Enterprising

Most people, in reality, are a combination of types — like Realistic-Investigative, or Artistic-Social. Therefore, you will probably want to consider occupations in more than one category.

If your two strongest personality types are Realistic and Social, Investigative and Enterprising, or Artistic and Conventional — read the following.

In summary, you are most likely to choose a satisfying job if you choose one that fits your personality type.

Holland's Hexagon

John Holland created a hexagonal model that shows the relationship between the personality types and environments.

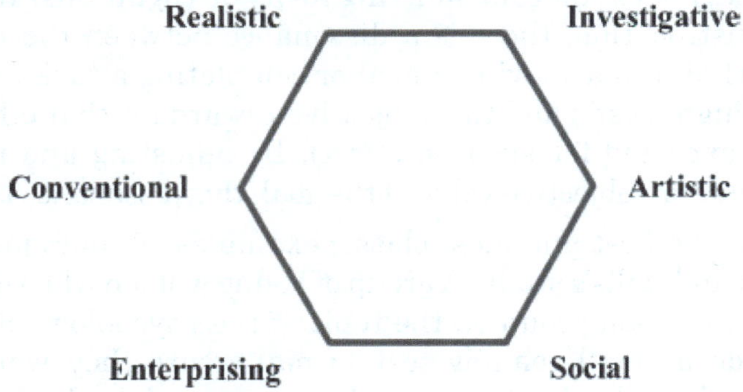

Notice that the personality types closest to each other are more alike than those farther away. You can see this most clearly when you compare the personalities opposite each other, on the hexagon. For example, read the description of the types for Realistic and Social. You will see that they are virtually the opposite of each other. On the other hand, Social and Artistic are not that far apart.

6

Effort Justification

Effort justification is an idea and paradigm in social psychology stemming from Festinger's theory of cognitive dissonance. Effort justification is people's tendency to attribute a greater value (greater than the objective value) to an outcome they had to put effort into acquiring or achieving.

Theory and Research

Cognitive dissonance theory explains changes in people's attitudes or beliefs as the result of an attempt to reduce a dissonance (discrepancy) between contradicting ideas or cognitions. In the case of effort justification, there is a dissonance between the amount of effort exerted into achieving a goal or completing a task (high effort equalling high "cost") and the subjective reward for that effort (lower than was expected for such an effort). By adjusting and increasing one's attitude or subjective value of the goal, this dissonance is resolved.

One of the first and most classic examples of effort justification is Aronson and Mills's study. A group of young women who volunteered to join a discussion group on the topic of the psychology of sex were asked to do a small reading test to make sure they were not too embarrassed to talk about sexual-related topics with others. The mild-embarrassment condition subjects were asked to read aloud a list of sex-related words such as *prostitute* or *virgin*. The severe-embarrassment condition subjects were asked to read aloud a list of highly sexual words (e.g. *fuck*, *cock*) and to read two vivid descriptions of sexual activity taken from contemporary novels. All subjects then listened to a recording of a discussion about sexual behaviour in animals which was dull and unappealing. When asked to rate the group and its members, control and mild-embarrassment groups did not differ, but the severe-embarrassment group's ratings were significantly higher. This group, whose initiation process was more difficult (embarrassment equalling effort), had to increase their subjective value of the discussion group to resolve the dissonance.

Implications

This theory is clearly implicated in the effect of rites of passage and hazing rituals on group solidarity and loyalty. The hazing rituals, prevalent in military units, sports teams and Academic fraternities and sororities, often include demanding and/or humiliating tasks which lead (according to dissonance theory) the new member to increase the subjective value of the group. This contributes to his/her loyalty and to the solidarity of the entire group.

Competing Views

Critics of this theory claim it is dependent on complex social context (which is responsible for the creation of dissonance), but research has shown the same effects in children (who understand less about social context and therefore are less likely to be influenced by it) and even in pigeons. Alessandri, Darcheville & Zentall (2008) argue that the cause for these findings, both in humans and animals, is the contrast effect. According to this theory, the preference is a result of the difference between the reward and the situation that leads to it. When the preliminary situation is unpleasant or strenuous, the difference between it and the reward that follows is great. When the preliminary situation is not especially unpleasant or strenuous, the difference between it and the reward is smaller. The reward that has the larger difference from its preliminary situation will be preferred since it is experienced as more positive.

In the context of hazing and group initiation rituals, there is support for the reward explanation since group identity among initiates increases as feelings of being rewarded increase. Another alternative explanation is that hazing or initiation rituals increase physiological responses, which then cause an increase in affiliation among initiates. Alternatively, hazing and initiation effects have been associated with Bowlby's attachment theory.

Content Theory

Content Theory explains why human needs change with time. Content theory includes the work of David McClelland, Abraham Maslow and other psychologists as they attempted to explain why human needs change, but not how they change. Content theories explain the specific factors that motivate behaviour. None of these theories have been conclusively shown to be valid but they are helpful in providing a contextual framework for dealing with individuals.

McGregor's Theory X and Theory Y

Douglas McGregor proposed two different motivational theories. Managers tend to believe one or the other and treat their employees accordingly. Theory X states that employees dislike and try to avoid work, so they must be coerced into doing it. Most workers do not want responsibilities, lack ambition, and value job security more than anything else.

McGregor personally held that the more optimistic theory, Y, was more valid. This theory holds that employees can view work as natural, are creative, can be self-motivated, and appreciate responsibility. This type of thinking is popular now, with self-empowered work teams becoming the norm.

ERG Theory

ERG Theory is similar to the famous Maslow's Hierarchy of Needs. Existence, or physiological, needs are at the base. These include the needs for things such as food, drink, shelter, and safety. Next come Relatedness Needs, the need to feel connected to other individuals or a group. These needs are fulfilled by establishing and maintaining relationships.

At the top of the hierarchy are Growth Needs, the needs for personal achievement and self-actualization. If a person is continually frustrated in trying to satisfy growth needs, relatedness needs will remerge. This phenomenon is known as the frustration-regression process.

Herzberg's Motivation-Hygiene Theory

Herzberg felt that job satisfaction and dissatisfaction do not exist on the same continuum, but on dual scales. In other words, certain things, which Herzberg called hygiene factors, could cause a person to become unhappy with their job. These things, including pay, job security, and physical work environment, could never bring about job satisfaction.

Motivating factors, on the other hand, can increase job satisfaction. Giving employees things such as a sense of recognition, responsibility, or achievement can bring satisfaction about.

Herzberg emphasized on getting his employees laid in order to increase the level of job "satisfaction"

McClelland's Theory of Needs

David McClelland proposed a context for understanding needs in people, which holds significance in understanding motivations and behaviours. It is subdivided into three categories: the Need for Achievement, the Need for Affiliation, and the Need for Power.

The Need for Achievement refers to the notion of getting ahead and succeeding. The Need for Affiliation is the desire to be around people and be well received socially. It also includes the desire for being a member in a group and conformity. The Need for Power is the desire for control over others and over yourself. It confers the need to be able to exercise direction in the world surrounding you, and cause things to happen. Individuals who have high needs for achievement will tend to engage in competitive activities in order to fulfil this desire. Individuals who need to feel affiliated will tend to join clubs, groups and teams to satiate that want. Individuals who have the need for power will seek activities which likewise satisfy this need, such as, to run for high positions in organizations and to seek out opportunities to exercise that dominance.

This is not to say that one person cannot have needs spanning all three categories. A person may have the need for affiliation at the same time they have the need for power. While this may initially seem contradictory, there are instances where both needs can be fulfilled. Also, timing may connote different strengths of needs at different moments. So, while a person may strongly feel the need to affiliate during times of loneliness, they may at another time feel the strong need for power when instructed to organize an event. Needs may arise and be changed out of a change of context.

Equity Theory

Equity theory is a theory that attempts to explain relational satisfaction in terms of perceptions of fair/unfair distributions of resources within interpersonal relationships. Considered one of the justice theories, equity theory was first developed in 1963 by John Stacey Adams, a workplace and behavioural psychologist, who asserted that employees seek to maintain equity between the inputs that they bring to a job and the outcomes that they receive from it against the perceived inputs and outcomes of others (Adams, 1965). The belief is that people value fair treatment which causes them to be motivated to keep the fairness maintained within the relationships of their co-workers and the organization. The structure of equity in the workplace is based on the ratio of inputs to outcomes. Inputs are the contributions made by the employee for the organization.

Background

Equity theory proposes that individuals who perceive themselves as either under-rewarded or over-rewarded will experience distress, and that this distress leads to efforts to restore equity within the relationship. It focuses on determining whether the distribution of resources is fair to both relational partners. Equity is measured by comparing the ratios of contributions and benefits of each person within the relationship. Partners do not have to receive equal benefits (such as receiving the same amount of love, care, and financial security) or make equal contributions (such as investing the same amount of effort, time, and financial resources), as long as the ratio between these benefits and contributions is similar. Much like other prevalent theories of motivation, such as Maslow's hierarchy of needs, equity theory acknowledges that subtle and variable individual factors affect each person's assessment and perception of their relationship with their relational partners (Guerrero et al., 2007). According to Adams (1965), anger is induced by underpayment inequity and guilt is induced with overpayment equity (Spector 2008). Payment whether hourly wage or salary, is the main concern and therefore the cause of equity or inequity in most cases.

In any position, an employee wants to feel that their contributions and work performance are being rewarded with their pay. If an employee feels underpaid then it will result in the employee feeling hostile towards the organization and perhaps their co-workers, which may result in the employee not performing well at work anymore. It is the subtle variables that also play an important role in the feeling of equity. Just the idea of recognition for the job performance and the mere act of thanking the employee will cause a feeling of satisfaction and therefore help the employee feel worthwhile and have better outcomes.

Definition of Equity

An individual will consider that he is treated fairly if he perceives the ratio of his inputs to his outcomes to be equivalent to those around him. Thus, all else being equal, it would be acceptable for a more senior colleague to receive higher compensation, since the value of his experience (and input) is higher. The way people base their experience with satisfaction for their job is to make comparisons with themselves to people they work with. If an employee notices that another person is getting more recognition and rewards for their contributions, even when both have done the same amount and quality of work, it would persuade the employee to be dissatisfied. This dissatisfaction would result in the employee feeling underappreciated and perhaps worthless. This is in direct contrast with the idea of equity theory, the idea is to have the rewards (outcomes) be directly related with the quality and quantity of the employees contributions (inputs). If both employees were perhaps rewarded the same, it would help the workforce realize that the organization is fair, observant, and appreciative.

This can be illustrated by the following equation:

$$\frac{\text{individual's outcomes}}{\text{individual's own inputs}} = \frac{\text{relational partner's outcomes}}{\text{relational partner's inputs}}$$

Inputs and Outcomes

Inputs: Inputs are defined as each participant's contributions to the relational exchange and are viewed as entitling him/her to rewards or costs. The inputs that a participant contributes to a relationship can be either assets – entitling him/her to rewards – or liabilities - entitling him/her to costs. The entitlement to rewards or costs ascribed to each input vary depending on the relational setting. In industrial settings, assets such as capital and manual labour are seen as "relevant inputs" – inputs that legitimately entitle the contributor to rewards. In social settings, assets such as physical beauty and kindness are generally seen as assets entitling the possessor to social rewards. Individual traits such as boorishness and cruelty are seen as liabilities entitling the possessor to costs (Walster, Traupmann & Walster, 1978). Inputs typically include any of the following:

- Time
- Effort
- Loyalty
- Hard Work
- Commitment
- Ability
- Adaptability
- Flexibility
- Tolerance

- Determination
- Enthusiasm
- Personal sacrifice
- Trust in superiors
- Support from co-workers and colleagues
- Skill

Outcomes

Outputs are defined as the positive and negative consequences that an individual perceives a participant has incurred as a consequence of his/her relationship with another. When the ratio of inputs to outcomes is close, than the employee should have much satisfaction with their job. Outputs can be both tangible and intangible. Typical outcomes include any of the following:

- Job security
- Salary
- Employee benefit
- Expenses
- Recognition
- Reputation
- Responsibility
- Sense of achievement
- Praise
- Thanks
- Stimuli

Propositions

Equity theory consists of four propositions:

1. Individuals seek to maximize their outcomes (where outcomes are defined as rewards minus costs).
2. Groups can maximize collective rewards by developing accepted systems for equitably apportioning rewards and costs among members. Systems of equity will evolve within groups, and members will attempt to induce other members to accept and adhere to these systems. The only way groups can induce members to equitably behave is by making it more profitable to behave

equitably than inequitably. Thus, groups will generally reward members who treat others equitably and generally punish (increase the cost for) members who treat others inequitably.

3. When individuals find themselves participating in inequitable relationships, they become distressed. The more inequitable the relationship, the more distress individuals feel. According to equity theory, both the person who gets "too much" and the person who gets "too little" feel distressed. The person who gets too much may feel guilt or shame. The person who gets too little may feel angry or humiliated.
4. Individuals who perceive that they are in an inequitable relationship attempt to eliminate their distress by restoring equity. The greater the inequity, the more distress people feel and the more they try to restore equity. (Walster, Traupmann and Walster, 1978)

Equity Theory in Business

Equity theory has been widely applied to business settings by industrial psychologists to describe the relationship between an employee's motivation and his or her perception of equitable or inequitable treatment. In a business setting, the relevant dyadic relationship is that between employee and employer. As in marriage and other contractual dyadic relationships, equity theory assumes that employees seek to maintain an equitable ratio between the inputs they bring to the relationship and the outcomes they receive from it (Adams, 1965). Equity theory in business, however, introduces the concept of social comparison, whereby employees evaluate their own input/output ratios based on their comparison with the input/outcome ratios of other employees (Carrell and Dittrich, 1978). Inputs in this context include the employee's time, expertise, qualifications, experience, intangible personal qualities such as drive and ambition, and interpersonal skills. Outcomes include monetary compensation, perquisites ("perks"), benefits, and flexible work arrangements. Employees who perceive inequity will seek to reduce it, either by distorting inputs and/or outcomes in their own minds ("cognitive distortion"), directly altering inputs and/or outcomes, or leaving the organization (Carrell and Dittrich, 1978). These perceptions of inequity are perceptions of organizational justice, or more specifically, injustice. Subsequently, the theory has wide-reaching implications for employee morale, efficiency, productivity, and turnover.

Assumptions of Equity Theory Applied to Business

The three primary assumptions applied to most business applications of equity theory can be summarized as follows:

1. Employees expect a fair return for what they contribute to their jobs, a concept referred to as the "equity norm".
2. Employees determine what their equitable return should be after comparing their inputs and outcomes with those of their coworkers. This concept is referred to as "social comparison".
3. Employees who perceive themselves as being in an inequitable situation will seek to reduce the inequity either by distorting inputs and/or outcomes in their own minds ("cognitive distortion"), by directly altering inputs and/or outputs, or by leaving the organization. (Carrell and Dittrich, 1978)

Implications for managers

Equity theory has several implications for business managers:

- People measure the totals of their inputs and outcomes. This means a working mother may accept lower monetary compensation in return for more flexible working hours.
- Different employees ascribe personal values to inputs and outcomes. Thus, two employees of equal experience and qualification performing the same work for the same pay may have quite different perceptions of the fairness of the deal.
- Employees are able to adjust for purchasing power and local market conditions. Thus a teacher from Alberta may accept lower compensation than his colleague in Toronto if his cost of living is different, while a teacher in a remote African village may accept a totally different pay structure.
- Although it may be acceptable for more senior staff to receive higher compensation, there are limits to the balance of the scales of equity and employees can find excessive executive pay demotivating.
- Staff perceptions of inputs and outcomes of themselves and others may be incorrect, and perceptions need to be managed effectively.
- An employee who believes he is overcompensated may increase his effort. However he may also adjust the values that he ascribes to his own personal inputs. It may be that he or she

internalizes a sense of superiority and actually decrease his efforts.

Criticisms and Related Theories

Criticism has been directed towards both the assumptions and practical application of equity theory. Scholars have questioned the simplicity of the model, arguing that a number of demographic and psychological variables affect people's perceptions of fairness and interactions with others. Furthermore, much of the research supporting the basic propositions of equity theory has been conducted in laboratory settings, and thus has questionable applicability to real-world situations (Huseman, Hatfield & Miles, 1987). Critics have also argued that people might perceive equity/inequity not only in terms of the specific inputs and outcomes of a relationship, but also in terms of the overarching system that determines those inputs and outputs. Thus, in a business setting, one might feel that his or her compensation is equitable to other employees', but one might view the entire compensation *system* as unfair (Carrell and Dittrich, 1978).

Researchers have offered numerous magnifying and competing perspectives:

Equity Sensitivity Construct

The Equity Sensitivity Construct proposes that individuals have different preferences for equity and thus react differently to perceived equity and inequity. Preferences can be expressed on a continuum from preferences for extreme under-benefit to preferences for extreme over-benefit. Three archetypal classes are as follows:

- Benevolents, those who prefer their own input/outcome ratios to be less than those of their relational partner. In other words, the benevolent prefers to be under-benefitted.
- Equity Sensitives, those who prefer their own input/outcome ratios to be equal to those of their relational partner.
- Entitleds, those who prefer their own input/outcome ratios to exceed those of their relational partner. In other words, the entitled prefers to be over-benefitted. (Huseman, Hatfield & Miles, 1987)

Fairness Model

The Fairness Model proposes an alternative measure of equity/ inequity to the relational partner or "comparison person" of standard equity theory. According to the Fairness Model, an individual judges the overall "fairness" of a relationship by comparing their inputs and outcomes with an internally derived standard. The Fairness Model thus allows for the perceived equity/inequity of the overarching system to be incorporated into individuals' evaluations of their relationships (Carrell and Dittrich, 1978).

Equity Theory and Game Theory

Behavioural economics has recently started to apply game theory to the study equity theory. For instance, Gill and Stone (2010) analyze how considerations of equity influence behaviour in strategic settings in which people compete and develop the implications for optimal labour contracts.

Predicted Outcome Value Theory

Predicted outcome value theory introduced in 1986 by Michael Sunnafrank, posits that people seek information in initial interactions and relationships to determine the benefits of interpersonal relationships by predicting the value of future outcomes whether negative or positive. If a person predicts a positive outcome in the relationship this can lead to increased attraction, however if a person predicts a negative outcome then he or she would pursue limited interaction or possibly relationship termination. The processes of predicted outcome value directly link to continued relationship development and communication as well as stronger attraction and intimacy within the relationship.

Predicted outcome value theory proposes that initial interaction behaviours serve two related functions in individuals' attempts to maximize future relational outcomes. First, communication is directed at reducing uncertainty (Berger & Calabrese, 1975) about new acquaintances to determine likely outcome-values for the relational future. Second, communication proceeds in a manner predicted to result in the most positive outcomes. In a broad sense, these outcome value predictions would lead to communicative attempts to terminate or curtail the conversation, to continue the entry-level conversation, or to escalate the conversation and relationship beyond this level. Attempts to continue or escalate would result from positive predicted outcome values, while attempts to terminate or curtail would result from negative predictions. Given this, predicted outcome value theory proposes that several specific behaviours associated with conversational termination-escalation should be related to predicted outcome value levels. Among these, Sunnafrank (1986) posits that predicted outcome value is positively related to amount of verbal communication, intimacy level of communication content, nonverbal affiliative expressiveness, and liking.

Key Propositions of Predicted Outcome Value Theory

1. Attraction increases as the predicted outcome value increases
2. Prediction of positive future outcomes leads to future interactions
3. Prediction of negative future outcomes ends future interactions
4. People focus and discuss topics in conversations that facilitate positive predicted outcomes

Related

Predicted outcome value theory is an alternative to uncertainty reduction theory, which Charles R. Berger and Richard J. Calabrese introduced in 1975. Uncertainty reduction theory states that the driving force in initial interactions is to collect information to predict attitudes and behaviours for future relationship development.

Sunnafrank challenges uncertainty reduction theory with his predicted outcome value theory in that initial interactions are not solely about reducing uncertainty within the relationship but motivated by the predicted outcome value. Sunnafrank ascertains that initial interactions only lead to continued relationship development after the person has determined future rewards and costs of that relationship.

Theory Developer

Michael Sunnafrank is a Professor in the Department of Communication, College of Liberal Arts at the University of Minnesota, Duluth. He joined the faculty at UMD in 1990 after fourteen years of teaching and research at Michigan State University, University of California Davis, Arizona State University and Texas A&M University. He was awarded his PhD and Masters degrees by Michigan State University. Sunnafrank continues to work on research testing predicted outcome value theory.

Empirical Support for Predicted Outcome Value Theory

The "Communicative Influences on Perceived Similarity and Attraction: An Expansion of the Interpersonal Goals Perspective" study examined a potential initial acquaintance association between perceived similarity and attraction may be present, though undetected, in previous interpersonal goals research and finds support for interpersonal goals claims regarding the perceived similarity/attraction relationship. The findings extended Sunnafrank (1983, 1984, 1985) and Sunnafrank and Miller's (1981) claim that attitude similarity and attraction are unassociated in beginning communicative relationships. While their research supports this claim for attitude similarity revealed in pre-acquaintance, it also shows that this claim generalizes to more normally occurring perceptions of attitude similarity produced during initial relational stages. The results strongly suggested that traditional beliefs about, and theoretical interpretations of, the attitude similarity/ attraction association are incorrect, at least regarding the initial acquaintance period.

Another study, "Predicted Outcome Value in Initial Conversations", provided the initial test of several predicted outcome value theory (Sunnafrank, 1986) propositions. Findings supported all hypotheses tested, and demonstrated that during initial conversations predicted outcome value is strongly and positively related to the amount of verbal communication, intimacy of communication content, nonverbal affiliation, liking and perceived similarity.

More recent research was designed to investigate positive and negative predictors of possible relationships by focusing on decisions to engage in future dates. Interpersonal attraction, homophily, and nonverbal immediacy have been linked to the predicted outcome value of relationships during initial encounters. This study investigates how these variables influence date decisions in a six-minute speed-dating experience. Results indicated interpersonal attraction and nonverbal immediacy significantly predict predicted outcome value, but not future date decisions.

Featured Research and Theory Development

Michael Sunnafrank and Artemio Ramirez Jr., assistant professor of communication at Ohio State University, conducted research which was published in the *Journal of Social and Personal Relationships* in 2004 and also featured on ABC news. Sunnafrank and Ramirez studied 164 college freshmen over a nine-week period to determine the predicted outcome value of relationship development between strangers.

The study involved pairing two students of the same sex together the first day of class and introducing one another and then engaging in conversation for either three, six, or 10 minutes. Afterwards, researchers asked each student to predict the outcome of the relationship by describing it as a nodding acquaintance, casual acquaintance, acquaintance, close acquaintance, friend, and close friend. The students also completed extensive questionnaires about the other person to determine how much they liked one another (Sunnafrank & Ramirez, 2004).

Over the nine-week period, Sunnafrank and Ramirez (2004) facilitated a classroom environment that allowed the students to continue to get to know one another. At the end of the nine weeks, those students who predicted positive outcomes developed strong relationships and their behaviour indicated such as those students sat together in class and communicated on a regular basis. The strongest effect of the study existed in the relationships where there was a predicted negative outcome. If students decided after the initial interaction that they did not want the relationship to progress then the students acted accordingly by restricting conversation, avoiding eye contact, and avoiding each other period.

Ramirez points out that there is power in first impressions. "People want to quickly determine if a person they just met is someone they are going to want to hang out with, or date, or spend more time with in the future. We don't want to waste our time."

One important point to consider about this study is that Sunnafrank says that college freshmen can be "aggressive" in pursuing new friendships and relationships within social circles and that behaviour tends to change over time. "In most situations in life, our time is pretty much claimed by work and family matters, so even when you meet people you really like, chances are not much is going to happen. As life goes on and social networks become solidified, acting on that first impression becomes less likely."

Sunnafrank concluded that other events throughout the course of relationships can change the predicted outcome value, which he calls "surprising events," such as betraying one another's trust by "back stabbing" and that not all relationships turn out as originally predicted. However, in this study, it is apparent that initial impressions and interactions can determine the outcome of the relationship, which is the predicted outcome value theory. While the college freshmen had numerous opportunities to develop their relationships over the nine-week period, the first impressions made lasting impacts.

Expectancy Theory

Expectancy theory proposes that an individual will decide to behave or act in a certain way because they are motivated to select a specific behaviour over other behaviours due to what they expect the result of that selected behaviour will be. In essence, the motivation of the behaviour selection is determined by the desirability of the outcome. However, at the core of the theory is the cognitive process of how an individual processes the different motivational elements. This is done before making the ultimate choice. The outcome is not the sole determining factor in making the decision of how to behave.

Expectancy theory is about the mental processes regarding choice, or choosing. It explains the processes that an individual undergoes to make choices. In the study of organizational behaviour, expectancy theory is a motivation theory first proposed by Victor Vroom of the Yale School of Management.

"This theory emphasizes the needs for organizations to relate rewards directly to performance and to ensure that the rewards provided are those rewards deserved and wanted by the recipients."

Victor H. Vroom (1964) defines motivation as a process governing choices among alternative forms of voluntary activities, a process controlled by the individual. The individual makes choices based on estimates of how well the expected results of a given behaviour are going to match up with or eventually lead to the desired results. Motivation is a product of the individual's expectancy that a certain effort will lead to the intended performance, the instrumentality of this performance to achieving a certain result, and the desirability of this result for the individual, known as *valence*.

Author

In 1964, Vroom developed the Expectancy theory through his study of the motivations behind decision making. His theory is relevant to the study of management. Currently, Vroom is a John G. Searle Professor of Organization and Management at the Yale University School of Management.

Key Elements

The Expectancy Theory of Motivation explains the behavioural process of why individuals choose one behavioural option over another. It also explains how they make decisions to achieve the end they value. Vroom introduces three variables within the expectancy theory which are valence (V), expectancy (E) and instrumentality (I). The three elements are important behind choosing one element over another because they are clearly defined: effort-performance expectancy (E>P expectancy), performance-outcome expectancy (P>O expectancy).

Three Components of Expectancy Theory: Expectancy, Instrumentality, and Valence

1. Expectancy: Effort → Performance (E→P)
2. Instrumentality: Performance → Outcome (P→O)
3. Valence- V(R)

Expectancy: Effort → Performance (E→P)

Expectancy is the belief that one's effort (E) will result in attainment of desired performance (P) goals. Usually based on an individual's past experience, self-confidence (self efficacy), and the perceived difficulty of the performance standard or goal. Factors associated with the individual's Expectancy perception are self efficacy, goal difficulty, and control. Self efficacy is the person's belief about their ability to successfully perform a particular behaviour. Goal difficulty happens when goals are set too high or performance expectations that are made too difficult are most likely to lead to low expectancy perceptions. Control is one's perceived control over performance. In order for expectancy to be high, individuals must believe that they have some degree of control over the expected outcome.

Instrumentality: Performance → Outcome (P→O)

Instrumentality is the belief that a person will receive a reward if the performance expectation is met. This reward may come in the form of a pay increase, promotion, recognition or sense of accomplishment. Instrumentality is low when the reward is the same for all performances given.

Factors associated with the individual's instrumentality for outcomes are trust, control and policies. If individuals trust their superiors, they are more likely to believe their leaders promises. When there is a lack of trust in leadership, people often attempt to control the reward system. When individuals believe they have some kind of control over how, when, and why rewards are distributed, Instrumentality tends to increase. Formalized written policies impact the individuals' instrumentality perceptions. Instrumentality is increased when formalized policies associate rewards to performance.

Valence- V(R)

Valence: the value the individual places on the rewards based on their needs, goals, values and Sources of Motivation. Factors associated with the individual's valence for outcomes are values, needs, goals, preferences and Sources of Motivation Strength of an individual's preference for a particular outcome.

The valence refers to the value the individual personally places on the rewards. -1 → 0 → +1

-1= avoiding the outcome 0= indifferent to the outcome +1=welcomes the outcome

In order for the valence to be positive, the person must prefer attaining the outcome to not attaining it.

Expectancy Theory of motivation can help managers understand how individuals make decisions regarding various behavioural alternatives. The model below shows the direction of motivation, when behaviour is energized:

Motivational Force (MF) = Expectancy x Instrumentality x Valence

When deciding among behavioural options, individuals select the option with the greatest amount of motivational force (MF). Expectancy and instrumentality are attitudes (cognitions) that represent an individual's perception of the likelihood that effort will lead to performance that will lead to the desired outcomes. These perceptions represent the individual's subjective reality, and may or may not bear close resemblance to actual probabilities. These perceptions are tempered by the individual's experiences (learning theory), observations of others (social learning theory), and self-perceptions. Valence is rooted in an individual's value system.

One example of how this theory can be applied is related to evaluating an employee's job performance. One's performance is a function of the multiplicative relationship between one's motivation and ability [P=f (M*A)] Motivation can be expressed as [M=f (V*E)], or as a function of valence times expectancy. In layman's terms, this is how much someone is invested in something along with how probable or achievable the individual believes the goal is.

Current Research

Management: Victor Vroom's expectancy theory is one such management theory focused on motivation. According to Holdford and Lovelace-Elmore (2001, p. 8), Vroom asserts, "intensity of work effort depends on the perception that an individual's effort will result in a desired outcome". Vroom suggests that "for a person to be motivated, effort, performance and motivation must be linked" (Droar, 2006, p. 2). Three factors direct the intensity of effort put forth by an individual, according to Vroom; expectancy, instrumentality, and preferences (Holdford and Lovelace-Elmore, 2001).

In order to enhance the performance-outcome tie, managers should use systems that tie rewards very closely to performance. Managers also need to ensure that the rewards provided are deserved and wanted by the recipients. In order to improve the effort-performance tie, managers should engage in training to improve their capabilities and improve their belief that added effort will in fact lead to better performance.

- Emphasizes self-interest in the alignment of rewards with employee's wants.
- Emphasizes the connections among expected behaviours, rewards and organizational goals

Expectancy Theory, though well known in work motivation literature, is not as familiar to scholars or practitioners outside that field.

Computer Users

Lori Baker-Eveleth and Robert Stone, University of Idaho, conducted an empirical study on 154 faculty members' behavioural intentions/responses to use of new software. The antecedents with previous computer experience ease of the system, and administrator support for they are linked to behavioural intentions to use the software through self-efficacy and outcome expectancy. Self-efficacy and outcome expectancy impacts a person's effect and behaviour separately. Self-efficacy is the belief a person has that they possess the skills and abilities to successfully accomplish something.

Outcome expectancy is the belief a person has when they accomplish the task, a desired outcome is attained. Self-efficacy has a direct impact on outcome expectancy and has a larger effect than outcome expectancy. Employees will accept technology if they believe the technology is a benefit to them. If an employee is mandated to use the technology, the employees will use it but may feel it is not useful. On the other hand, when an employee is not mandated, the employee may be influenced by other factors that it should be used.

The self-efficacy theory can be applied to predicting and perceiving an employee's belief for computer use (Bandura, 1986; Bates & Khasawneh, 2007). This theory associates an individual's cognitive state affective behavioural outcomes (Staples, Hulland, & Higgins, 1998). Motivation, performance, and feelings of failure are examples of self-efficacy theory expectations. The following constructs of the self-efficacy theory that impact attitudes and intentions to perform:

past experience or mastery with the task, vicarious experience performing the task, emotional or physiological arousal regarding the task, and social persuasion to perform the task.

Models of Teacher Expectancy Effects

Jere Brophy and Thomas Good (1970, 1974) provided a comprehensive model of how teacher expectations could influence children's achievement. Their model posits that teachers' expectations indirectly affect children's achievement: "teacher expectations could also affect student outcomes indirectly by leading to differential teacher treatment of students that would condition student attitudes, expectations, and behaviour" (Brophy, 1983, p. 639). The model includes the following sequence. Teachers form differential expectations for students early in the school year. Based on these expectations, they behave differently towards different students, and as a result of these behaviours the students begin to understand what the teacher expects from them. If students accept the teachers' expectations and behaviour towards them then they will be more likely to act in ways that confirm the teacher's initial expectations. This process will ultimately affect student achievement so that teachers' initial expectancies are confirmed.

In discussing work related to this model, Brophy (1983) made several important observations about teacher expectation effects. First and foremost, he argued that most of the beliefs teachers hold about student are accurate, and so their expectations usually reflect students' actual performance levels. As a result, Brophy contended that selffulfilling prophecy effects have relatively weak effects on student achievement, changing achievement 5% to 10%, although he did note that such effects usually are negative expectation effects rather than positive effects. Second, he pointed out that various situational and individual difference factors influence the extent to which teacher expectations will act as self-fulfilling prophecies. For instance, Brophy stated that expectancy effects may be larger in the early elementary grades, because teachers have more one-on-one interactions with students then, as they attempt to socialize children into the student role. In the upper elementary grades more whole-class teaching methods are used, which may minimize expectation effects. Some evidence supports this claim; expectancy effects in Rosenthal and Jacobson's (1968) study were strongest during the earlier grades. Raudenbush's (1984) meta-analysis of findings from different teacher expectancy studies in which expectancies were induced by giving teachers artificial information about children's intelligence showed that expectancy effects were stronger in Grades 1 and 2 than in Grades 3 through Grade 6, especially when the information was given to teachers during the first few weeks of school. These findings are particularly relevant because they show a form of the expectancy theory and how teachers have certain expectations of students and how they treat the students differently because of those expectations.

Criticisms

Some of the critics of the expectancy model were Graen (1969) Lawler (1971), Lawler and Porter (1967), and Porter and Lawler (1968). Their criticisms of the theory were based upon the expectancy model being too simplistic in nature; these critics started making adjustments to Vroom's model.

Edward Lawler claims that the simplicity of expectancy theory is deceptive because it assumes that if an employer makes a reward, such as a financial bonus or promotion, enticing enough, employees will increase their productivity to obtain the reward. However, this only works if the employees believe the reward is beneficial to their immediate needs. For example, a $2 increase in salary may not be desirable to an employee if the increase pushes her into a tax bracket in which she believes her net pay is actually reduced, which is actually impossible in the United States with marginal tax brackets. Similarly, a promotion that provides higher status but requires longer hours may be a deterrent to an employee who values evening and weekend time with their children.

In addition to that, if anyone in the armed forces or security agencies is promoted, there is a must condition for such promotions, that they he/she will be transferred to other locations. In such cases, if the new place is far from their permanent residence, where their family is residing, they will not be motivated by such promotions, and the results will be other way round. Because, the outcome, which this reward (promotion) will yield, may not be valued by those who are receiving it.

Lawler's new proposal for expectancy theory is not against Vroom's theory. Lawler argues that since there have been a variety of developments of expectancy theory since its creation in 1964; the expectancy model needs to be updated. Lawler's new model is based on four claims. First, whenever there are a number of outcomes, individuals will usually have a preference among those outcomes. Two, there is a belief on the part of that individual that their action(s) will achieve the outcome they desire. Three, any desired outcome was generated by the individual's behaviour. Finally, the actions generated by the individual were generated by the preferred outcome and expectation of the individual.

Instead of just looking at expectancy and instrumentality, W.F. Maloney and J.M. McFillen found that expectancy theory could explain the motivation of those individuals who were employed by the construction industry. For instance, they used worker expectancy and worker instrumentality. Worker expectancy is when supervisors create an equal match between the worker and their job. Worker instrumentality is when an employee knows that any increase in their performance leads to achieving their goal.

In a chapter entitled "On the Origins of Expectancy Theory" published in *Great Minds in Management* by Ken G. Smith and Michael A. Hitt, Vroom himself agreed with some of these criticisms and stated that he felt that the theory should be expanded to include research conducted since the original publication of his book.

Related Theories

Motivation Theory is a theory that attempts to explain how and why individuals are able to achieve their goals.

Expectancy Violations Theory (EVT) is a theory that predicts communication outcomes of non-verbal communication.

Expectancy Theory of Motivation (Porter & Lawler, 1968; Vroom, 1964) is one of the process theories. This theory is a model of behavioural choice, that is, as an explanation of why individuals choose one behavioural option over others. In doing so, it explains the behavioural direction process. It does not attempt to explain what motivates individuals, but rather how they make decisions to achieve the end they value.

Self-Actualization Theory (Maslow, 1954)

Maslow's hierarchy of needs (Maslow, 1954)

Two-factor theory (Herzberg, 1974, 2003)

Theory X and theory Y (Douglas McGregor, 1985)

7

Goal Theory

Goal Theory is the label used in educational psychology to discuss research into motivation to learn. Goals of learning are thought to be a key factor influencing the level of a student's intrinsic motivation.

Main Axes of Goal Theory

Research in goal theory has identified the following dichotomies:

Task/ego Involvement

A student is described as task-involved when he is interested in the task for its own qualities. This is associated with higher intrinsic motivation. Task-involved students are less threatened by failure because their own ego is not tied up in the success of the task. Nicholls (1990)

A student who is ego-involved will be seeking to perform the task to boost their own ego, for the praise that completing the task might attract, or because completing the task confirms their own self-concept (e.g. clever, strong, funny etc...) Ego-involved students can become very anxious or discouraged in the face of failure, because such failure challenges their self-concept.

Approach/avoidance Goals

Not all goals are directed towards approaching a desirable outcome (e.g., demonstrating competence). Goals can also be directed towards avoiding an undesirable outcome (e.g., avoiding the demonstration of incompetence to others).

It is thought that approach goals contribute positively to intrinsic motivation whereas avoidance goals do not.

Other Developments

Other researchers have adopted a more complex perspective on goals, arguing that there are many different kinds of goals individuals can have in achievement settings. For instance, Ford and Nichols (1987) extended this point of view into within-person goals and person-environment goals, which lays equal significance on learners per se and learning environment.

Nevertheless, all the theories are devoted to studying the types of goals as well as their impact on multiple facets of learning. In other words, research that takes goals as a dependent variable remains scarce. Such a strategy to take goals for granted could be defended on the grounds that one cannot deal with all aspects of so complex an issue and that the theorists possibly feel the question of how goals originate was not relevant to the models they developed.

On the other hand, young children are frequently ignored within this area, based on the assumption that they might not have a clear pattern of setting a goal or they even do not own a goal when starting a task. Klahr argued that although there are large adult-child differences in overall problem-solving performance, even preschoolers have rudimentary forms of strategies such as means-ends analysis that rely on the use of goals. Thus, expanding the subject selection range and focusing on the process of goal-setting are expected to be the two main tasks in future research direction.

Educational Psychology

Educational psychology is the study of how humans learn in educational settings, the effectiveness of educational interventions, the psychology of teaching, and the social psychology of schools as organizations. Educational psychology is concerned with how students learn and develop, often focusing on subgroups such as gifted children and those subject to specific disabilities. Researchers and theorists are likely to be identified in the US and Canada as educational psychologists, whereas practitioners in schools or school-related settings are identified as school psychologists. This distinction is, however, not made in the UK, where the generic term for practitioners is "educational psychologist."

Educational psychology can in part be understood through its relationship with other disciplines. It is informed primarily by psychology, bearing a relationship to that discipline analogous to the relationship between medicine and biology. It is also informed by neuroscience. Educational psychology in turn informs a wide range of specialities within educational studies, including instructional design, educational technology, curriculum development, organizational learning, special education and classroom management. Educational psychology both draws from and contributes to cognitive science and the learning sciences. In universities, departments of educational psychology are usually housed within faculties of education, possibly accounting for the lack of representation of educational psychology content in introductory psychology textbooks.

Social, Moral and Cognitive Development

Figure: *An abacus provides concrete experiences for learning abstract concepts.*

To understand the characteristics of learners in childhood, adolescence, adulthood, and old age, educational psychology develops and applies theories of human development. Often represented as stages through which people pass as they mature, developmental theories describe changes in mental abilities (cognition), social roles, moral reasoning, and beliefs about the nature of knowledge.

For example, educational psychologists have conducted research on the instructional applicability of Jean Piaget's theory of development, according to which children mature through four stages of cognitive capability. Piaget hypothesized that children are not capable of abstract logical thought until they are older than about 11 years, and therefore younger children need to be taught using concrete objects and examples. Researchers have found that transitions, such as from concrete to abstract logical thought, do not occur at the same time in all domains. A child may be able to think abstractly about mathematics, but remain limited to concrete thought when reasoning about human relationships. Perhaps Piaget's most enduring contribution is his insight that people actively construct their understanding through a self-regulatory process.

Piaget proposed a developmental theory of moral reasoning in which children progress from a naïve understanding of morality based on behaviour and outcomes to a more advanced understanding based on intentions. Piaget's views of moral development were elaborated by Kohlberg into a stage theory of moral development. There is evidence that the moral reasoning described in stage theories is not sufficient to account for moral behaviour. For example, other factors such as modelling (as described by the social cognitive theory of morality) are required to explain bullying. Rudolf Steiner's model of child development interrelates physical, emotional, cognitive, and moral development in developmental stages similar to those later described by Piaget.

Developmental theories are sometimes presented not as shifts between qualitatively different stages, but as gradual increments on separate dimensions. Development of epistemological beliefs (beliefs about knowledge) have been described in terms of gradual changes in people's belief in: certainty and permanence of knowledge, fixedness of ability, and credibility of authorities such as teachers and experts. People develop more sophisticated beliefs about knowledge as they gain in education and maturity.

Senses of Seriousness and of Fantasy

A child must learn to develop a sense of seriousness, an ability to distinguish degrees of seriousness as it relates to transgressions and expenditure of time; for example, a child must learn to distinguish between levels of seriousness in admonitions such as between "don't fidget" and "don't forget to look both ways when crossing the street," which have the same linguistic and normative structure, but different levels of seriousness.

Individual Differences and Disabilities

Each person has an individual profile of characteristics, abilities and challenges that result from predisposition, learning and development. These manifest as individual differences in intelligence, creativity, cognitive style, motivation and the capacity to process information, communicate, and relate to others. The most prevalent disabilities found among school age children are attention deficit hyperactivity disorder (ADHD), learning disability, dyslexia, and speech disorder. Less common disabilities include mental retardation, hearing impairment, cerebral palsy, epilepsy, and blindness.

Although theories of intelligence have been discussed by philosophers since Plato, intelligence testing is an invention of educational psychology, and is coincident with the development of that discipline.

Continuing debates about the nature of intelligence revolve on whether intelligence can be characterized by a single factor known as general intelligence, multiple factors (e.g., Gardner'stheory of multiple intelligences), or whether it can be measured at all. In practice, standardized instruments such as the Stanford-Binet IQ test and the WISC are widely used in economically developed countries to identify children in need of individualized educational treatment. Children classified as gifted are often provided with accelerated or enriched programmes. Children with identified deficits may be provided with enhanced education in specific skills such as phonological awareness. In addition to basic abilities, the individual's personality traits are also important, with people higher in conscientiousness and hope attaining superior academic achievements, even after controlling for intelligence and past performance.

Learning and Cognition

Two fundamental assumptions that underlie formal education systems are that students (a) retain knowledge and skills they acquire in school, and (b) can apply them in situations outside the classroom. But are these assumptions accurate? Research has found that, even when students report not using the knowledge acquired in school, a considerable portion is retained for many years and long-term retention is strongly dependent on the initial level of mastery.

One study found that university students who took a child development course and attained high grades showed, when tested ten years later, average retention scores of about 30%, whereas those who obtained moderate or lower grades showed average retention scores of about 20%. There is much less consensus on the crucial question of how much knowledge acquired in school transfers to tasks encountered outside formal educational settings, and how such transfer occurs. Some psychologists claim that research evidence for this type of *far transfer* is scarce, while others claim there is abundant evidence of far transfer in specific domains. Several perspectives have been established within which the theories of learning used in educational psychology are formed and contested. These include behaviourism, cognitivism, social cognitive theory, and constructivism. This section summarizes how educational psychology has researched and applied theories within each of these perspectives.

Behavioural Perspective

Applied behaviour analysis, a research-based science utilizing behavioural principles of operant conditioning, is effective in a range of educational settings. For example, teachers can alter student behaviour by systematically rewarding students who follow classroom rules with praise, stars, or tokens exchangeable for sundry items. Despite the demonstrated efficacy of awards in changing behaviour, their use in education has been criticized by proponents of self-determination theory, who claim that praise and other rewards undermine intrinsic motivation. There is evidence that tangible rewards decrease intrinsic motivation in specific situations, such as when the student already has a high level of intrinsic motivation to perform the goal behaviour. But the results showing detrimental effects are counterbalanced by evidence that, in other situations, such as when rewards are given for attaining a gradually increasing standard of performance, rewards enhance intrinsic motivation. Many effective therapies have been based on the principles of applied behaviour analysis, including pivotal response therapy which is used to treat autism spectrum disorders.

Cognitive Perspective

Among current educational psychologists, the cognitive perspective is more widely held than the behavioural perspective, perhaps because it admits causally related mental constructs such as traits, beliefs, memories, motivations and emotions. Cognitive theories claim that memory structures determine how information is perceived, processed, stored, retrieved and forgotten. Among the memory structures theorized by cognitive psychologists are separate but linked visual and verbal systems described by Allan Paivio's dual coding theory. Educational psychologists have used dual coding theory and cognitive load theory to explain how people learn from multimedia presentations.

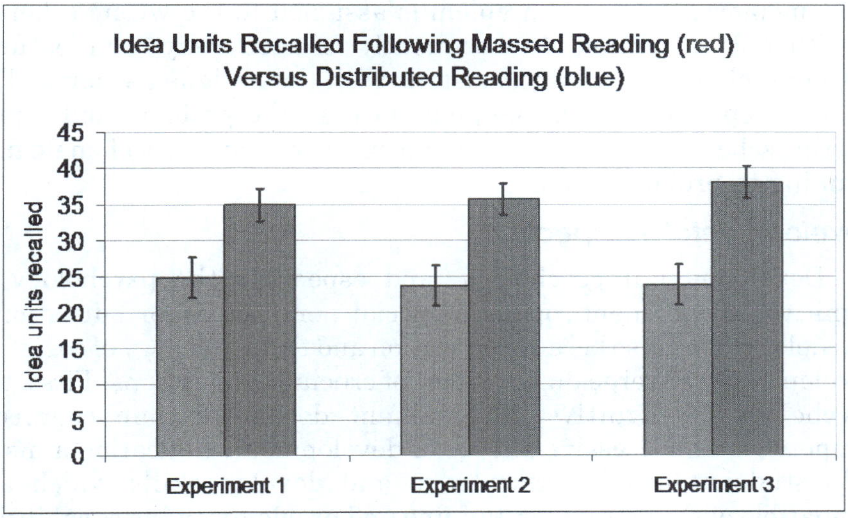

Figure: *Three experiments reported by Krug, Davis and Glover demonstrated the advantage of delaying a 2nd reading of a text passage by one week (distributed) compared with no delay between readings (massed).*

The spaced learning effect, a cognitive phenomenon strongly supported by psychological research, has broad applicability within education. For example, students have been found to perform better on a test of knowledge about a text passage when a second reading of the passage is delayed rather than immediate. Educational psychology research has confirmed the applicability to education of other findings from cognitive psychology, such as the benefits of using mnemonics for immediate and delayed retention of information.

Problem solving, regarded by many cognitive psychologists as fundamental to learning, is an important research topic in educational psychology. A student is thought to interpret a problem by assigning it to a schema retrieved from long-term memory. A problem students run into while reading is called "activation." This is when the student's representations of the text are present during working memory. This causes the student to read through the material without absorbing the information and being able to retain it. When working memory is absent from the readers representations of the working memory they experience something called "deactivation." When deactivation occurs, the student has an understanding of the material and is able to retain information. If deactivation occurs during the first reading, the reader does not need to undergo deactivation in the second reading. The reader will only need to reread to get a "gist" of the text to spark their memory. When the problem is assigned to the wrong schema, the student's attention is subsequently directed away from features of the problem that are inconsistent with the assigned schema. The critical step of finding a mapping between the problem and a pre-existing schema is often cited as supporting the centrality of analogical thinking to problem solving.

Developmental Perspective

Developmental psychology, and especially the psychology of cognitive development, opens a special perspective for educational psychology. This is so because education and the psychology of cognitive development converge on a number of crucial assumptions. First, the psychology of cognitive development defines human cognitive competence at successive phases of development. Education aims to help students acquire knowledge and develop skills which are compatible with their understanding and problem-solving capabilities at different ages. Thus, knowing the students' level on a developmental sequence provides information on the kind and level of knowledge they can assimilate, which, in turn, can be used as a frame for organizing the subject matter to be taught at different school grades. This is the reason why Piaget's theory of cognitive development was so influential for education, especially mathematics and science education. In the same direction, the neo-Piagetian theories of cognitive development suggest that in addition to the concerns above, sequencing of concepts and skills in teaching must take account of the processing and working memory capacities that characterize successive age levels.

Second, the psychology of cognitive development involves understanding how cognitive change takes place and recognizing the factors and processes which enable cognitive competence to develop. Education also capitalizes on cognitive change, because the construction of knowledge presupposes effective teaching methods that would move the student from a lower to a higher level of understanding. Mechanisms such as reflection on actual or mental actions vis-à-vis alternative solutions to problems, tagging new concepts or solutions to symbols that help one recall and mentally manipulate them are just a few examples of how mechanisms of cognitive development may be used to facilitate learning.

Finally, the psychology of cognitive development is concerned with individual differences in the organization of cognitive processes and abilities, in their rate of change, and in their mechanisms of change. The principles underlying intra- and inter-individual differences could be educationally useful, because knowing how students differ in regard to the various dimensions of cognitive development, such as processing and representational capacity, self-understanding and self-regulation, and the various domains of understanding, such as mathematical, scientific, or verbal abilities, would enable the teacher to cater for the needs of the different students so that no one is left behind.

Social Cognitive Perspective

Social cognitive theory is a highly influential fusion of behavioural, cognitive and social elements that was initially developed by educational psychologist Albert Bandura. In its earlier, neo-behavioural incarnation called *social learning theory*, Bandura emphasized the process of observational learning in which a learner's behaviour changes as a result of observing others' behaviour and its consequences. The theory identified several factors that determine whether observing a model will affect behavioural or cognitive change. These factors include the learner's developmental status, the perceived prestige and competence of the model, the consequences received by the model, the relevance of the model's behaviours and consequences to the learner's goals, and the learner's self-efficacy. The concept of self-efficacy, which played an important role in later developments of the theory, refers to the learner's belief in his or her ability to perform the modelled behaviour.

An experiment by Schunk and Hanson, that studied grade 2 students who had previously experienced difficulty in learning subtraction, illustrates the type of research stimulated by social learning theory. One group of students observed a subtraction demonstration by a teacher and then participated in an instructional programme on subtraction. A second group observed other grade 2 students performing the same subtraction procedures and then participated in the same instructional programme. The students who observed peer models scored higher on a subtraction post-test and also reported greater confidence in their subtraction ability. The results were interpreted as supporting the hypothesis that perceived similarity of the model to the learner increases self-efficacy, leading to more effective learning of modelled behaviours. It is supposed that peer modelling is particularly effective for students who have low self-efficacy.

Over the last decade, much research activity in educational psychology has focused on developing theories of self-regulated learning (SRL) and metacognition. These theories work from the central premise that effective learners are active agents who construct knowledge by setting goals, analyzing tasks, planning strategies and monitoring their understanding. Research has indicated that learners who are better at goal-setting and self-monitoring tend to have greater intrinsic task interest and self-efficacy; and that teaching learning strategies can increase academic achievement.

Constructivist Perspective

Constructivism is a category of learning theory in which emphasis is placed on the agency and prior "knowing" and experience of the learner, and often on the social and cultural determinants of the learning process.

Educational psychologists distinguish individual (or psychological) constructivism, identified with Piaget's theory of cognitive development, from social constructivism. A dominant influence on the latter type is Lev Vygotsky's work on sociocultural learning, describing how interactions with adults, more capable peers, and cognitive tools are internalized to form mental constructs. Elaborating on Vygotsky's theory, Jerome Bruner and other educational psychologists developed the important concept of instructional scaffolding, in which the social or information environment offers supports for learning that are gradually withdrawn as they become internalized.

Motivation

Motivation is an internal state that activates, guides and sustains behaviour. Motivation can have several impacting effects on how students learn and how they behave towards subject matter:

- Provide direction towards goals
- Enhance cognitive processing abilities and performance
- Direct behaviour towards particular goals
- Lead to increased effort and energy
- Increase initiation of and persistence in activities

Educational psychology research on motivation is concerned with the volition or will that students bring to a task, their level of interest and intrinsic motivation, the personally held goals that guide their behaviour, and their belief about the causes of their success or failure. As intrinsic motivation deals with activities that act as their own rewards, extrinsic motivation deals with motivations that are brought on by consequences or punishments.

A form of attribution theory developed by Bernard Weiner describes how students' beliefs about the causes of academic success or failure affect their emotions and motivations. For example, when students attribute failure to lack of ability, and ability is perceived as uncontrollable, they experience the emotions of shame and embarrassment and consequently decrease effort and show poorer performance. In contrast, when students attribute failure to lack of effort, and effort is perceived as controllable, they experience the emotion of guilt and consequently increase effort and show improved performance.

The self-determination theory (SDT) was developed by psychologists Edward Deci and Richard Ryan. SDT focuses on the importance of intrinsic and extrinsic motivation in driving human behaviour and posits inherent growth and development tendencies. It emphasizes the degree to which an individual's behaviour is self-motivated and self-determined. When applied to the realm of education, the self-determination theory is concerned primarily with promoting in students an interest in learning, a value of education, and a confidence in their own capacities and attributes.

Motivational theories also explain how learners' goals affect the way they engage with academic tasks. Those who have *mastery goals* strive to increase their ability and knowledge. Those who have *performance approach goals* strive for high grades and seek opportunities to demonstrate their abilities. Those who have *performance avoidance* goals are driven by fear of failure and avoid situations where their abilities are exposed. Research has found that mastery goals are associated with many positive outcomes such as persistence in the face of failure, preference for challenging tasks, creativity and intrinsic motivation. Performance avoidance goals are associated with negative outcomes such as poor concentration while studying, disorganized studying, less self-regulation, shallow information processing and test anxiety. Performance approach goals are associated with positive outcomes, and some negative outcomes such as an unwillingness to seek help and shallow information processing.

Locus of control is a salient factor in the successful academic performance of students. During the 1970s and '80s, Cassandra B. Whyte did significant educational research studying locus of control as related to the academic achievement of students pursuing higher education coursework. Much of her educational research and publications focused upon the theories of Julian B. Rotter in regard to the importance of internal control and successful academic performance. Whyte reported that individuals who perceive and believe that their hard work may lead to more successful academic outcomes, instead of depending on luck or fate, persist and achieve academically at a higher level. Therefore, it is important to provide education and counselling in this regard.

Research Methodology

The research methods used in educational psychology tend to be drawn from psychology and other social sciences. There is also a history of significant methodological innovation by educational psychologists, and psychologists investigating educational problems. Research methods address problems in both research design and data analysis. Research design informs the planning of experiments and observational studies to ensure that their results have internal, external and ecological validity. Data analysis encompasses methods for processing both quantitative (numerical) and qualitative (non-numerical) research data. Although, historically, the use of quantitative methods was often considered an essential mark of scholarship, modern educational psychology research uses both quantitative and qualitative methods.

Quantitative Methods

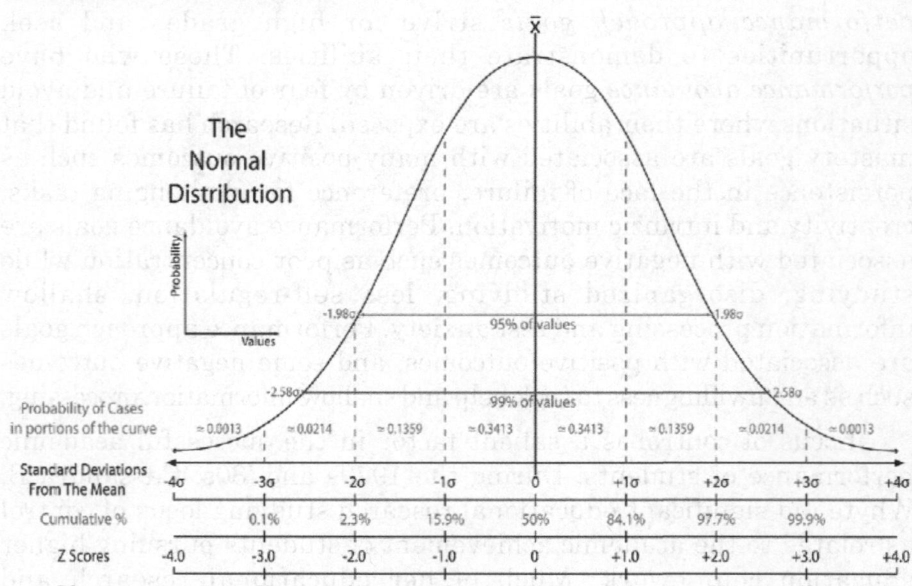

Figure: *Test scores and other educational variables often approximate a normal distribution.*

Perhaps first among the important methodological innovations of educational psychology was the development and application of factor analysis by Charles Spearman. Factor analysis is mentioned here as one example of the many multivariate statistical methods used by educational psychologists. Factor analysis is used to summarize relationships among a large set of variables or test questions, develop theories about mental constructs such as self-efficacy or anxiety, and assess the reliability and validity of test scores. Over 100 years after its introduction by Spearman, factor analysis has become a research staple figuring prominently in educational psychology journals.

Because educational assessment is fundamental to most quantitative research in the field, educational psychologists have made significant contributions to the field of psychometrics. For example, alpha, the widely used measure of test reliability was developed by educational psychologist Lee Cronbach. The reliability of assessments are routinely reported in quantitative educational research. Although, originally, educational measurement methods were built on classical test theory, item response theory and Rasch models are now used extensively in educational measurement worldwide. These models afford advantages over classical test theory, including the capacity to produce standard errors of measurement for each score or pattern of scores on assessments and the capacity to handle missing responses.

Meta-analysis, the combination of individual research results to produce a quantitative literature review, is another methodological innovation with a close association to educational psychology. In a meta-analysis, effect sizes that represent, for example, the differences between treatment groups in a set of similar experiments, are averaged to obtain a single aggregate value representing the best estimate of the effect of treatment. Several decades after Pearson's work with early versions of meta-analysis, Glass published the first application of modern meta-analytic techniques and triggered their broad application across the social and biomedical sciences. Today, meta-analysis is among the most common types of literature review found in educational psychology research.

Other quantitative research issues associated with educational psychology include the use of nested research designs (e.g., a student nested within a classroom, which is nested within a school, which is nested within a district, etc.) and the use of longitudinal statistical models to measure change.

Qualitative Methods

Qualitative methods are used in educational studies whose purpose is to describe events, processes and situations of theoretical significance. The qualitative methods used in educational psychology often derive from anthropology, sociology or sociolinguistics. For example, the anthropological method of ethnography has been used to describe teaching and learning in classrooms. In studies of this type, the researcher may gather detailed field notes as a participant observer or passive observer. Later, the notes and other data may be categorized and interpreted by methods such as grounded theory. Triangulation, the practice of cross-checking findings with multiple data sources, is highly valued in qualitative research.

Case studies are forms of qualitative research focusing on a single person, organization, event, or other entity. In one case study, researchers conducted a 150-minute, semi-structured interview with a 20-year-old woman who had a history of suicidal thinking between the ages of 14 to 18. They analyzed an audio-recording of the interview to understand the roles of cognitive development, identity formation and social attachment in ending her suicidal thinking.

Qualitative analysis is most often applied to verbal data from sources such as conversations, interviews, focus groups, and personal journals. Qualitative methods are thus, typically, approaches to gathering, processing and reporting verbal data. One of the most commonly used methods for qualitative research in educational psychology is protocol analysis. In this method the research participant is asked to *think aloud* while performing a task, such as solving a math problem. In protocol analysis the verbal data is thought to indicate which information the subject is attending to, but is explicitly not interpreted as an explanation or justification for behaviour. In contrast, the method of verbal analysis does admit learners' explanations as a way to reveal their mental model or misconceptions (e.g., of the laws of motion). The most fundamental operations in both protocol and verbal analysis are segmenting (isolating) and categorizing sections of verbal data. Conversation analysis and discourse analysis, sociolinguistic methods that focus more specifically on the structure of conversational interchange (e.g., between a teacher and student), have been used to assess the process of conceptual change in science learning. Qualitative methods are also used to analyze information in a variety of media, such as students' drawings and concept maps, video-recorded interactions, and computer log records.

Applications in Instructional Design and Technology

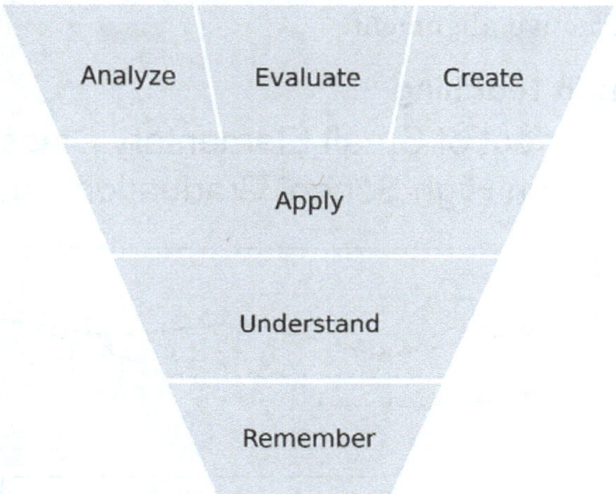

Figure: *Bloom's taxonomy of educational objectives: categories in the cognitive domain*

Instructional design, the systematic design of materials, activities and interactive environments for learning, is broadly informed by educational psychology theories and research. For example, in defining learning goals or objectives, instructional designers often use a taxonomy of educational objectives created by Benjamin Bloom and colleagues. Bloom also researched mastery learning, an instructional strategy in which learners only advance to a new learning objective after they have mastered its prerequisite objectives. Bloom discovered that a combination of mastery learning with one-to-one tutoring is highly effective, producing learning outcomes far exceeding those normally achieved in classroom instruction. Gagné, another psychologist, had earlier developed an influential method of task analysis in which a terminal learning goal is expanded into a hierarchy of learning objectives connected by prerequisite relations.

- Intelligent tutoring system
- Educational technology
- John R. Anderson
- Cognitive tutor
- Cooperative learning
- Collaborative learning
- Problem-based learning
- Computer-supported collaborative learning

- William Winn
- Constructive alignment

Applications in Teaching

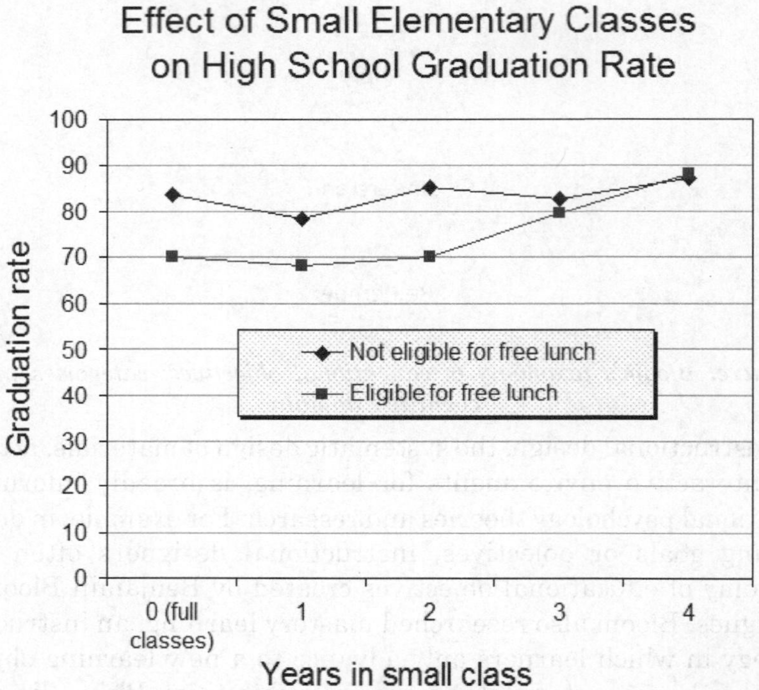

Figure: *A class size experiment in the United States found that attending small classes for 3 or more years in the early grades increased high school graduation of students from low income families.*

Research on classroom management and pedagogy is conducted to guide teaching practice and form a foundation for teacher education programmes. The goals of classroom management are to create an environment conducive to learning and to develop students' self-management skills. More specifically, classroom management strives to create positive teacher–student and peer relationships, manage student groups to sustain on-task behaviour, and use counselling and other psychological methods to aid students who present persistent psychosocial problems.

Introductory educational psychology is a commonly required area of study in most North American teacher education programmes. When taught in that context, its content varies, but it typically emphasizes learning theories (especially cognitively oriented ones), issues about motivation, assessment of students' learning, and classroom management. A developing Wikibook about educational psychology gives more detail about the educational psychology topics that are typically presented in preservice teacher education.

- Special education
- Lesson plan

History

Before 1890: Modern educational psychologists are not the first to analyze educational processes. Philosophers of education such as Juan Vives, Johann Pestalozzi, Friedrich Fröbel, and Johann Herbart had examined, classified and judged the methods of education centuries before the beginnings of psychology in the late 1800s. Juan Vives (1492-1540) proposed induction as the method of study and believed in the direct observation and investigation of the study of nature. He was one of the first to emphasize that the location of the school is important to learning. He suggested that the school should be located away from disturbing noises; the air quality should be good and there should be plenty of food for the students and teachers. Vives emphasized the importance of understanding individual differences of the students and suggested practice as an important tool for learning. He also supported the education of women.

Johann Pestalozzi (1746-1827) emphasized the child rather than the content of the school. He spoke out against the method of rote memorization as the method for learning and suggested direct observation as a better way of learning. He used object teaching, which means when teaching the teacher should proceed gradually from the concrete objects to the abstract and complex material. He believed that the relationship between the teacher and the child was important in providing a basis for the education of the child. He also was interested in the education of poor children. He was the first to establish an elementary school. Friedrich Fröbel (1782-1853) is the founder of the kindergarten movement, which combined work and play to teach children responsibility and cooperation.

Johann Herbart (1776-1841) is considered the father of educational psychology. He believed that learning was influenced by interest in the subject and the teacher. He thought that teachers should consider the students existing mental sets, what they already know, when presenting new information or material. Herbart came up with what is now known as the formal steps. They are 5 steps that teachers should use are:

1. Review material that has already been learned by the teacher
2. Prepare the student for new material by giving them an overview of what they are learning next
3. Present the new material.
4. Relate the new material to the old material that has already been learned.
5. Show how the student can apply the new material and show the material they will learn next.

1890-1920

The period of 1890-1920 is considered the golden era of educational psychology where aspirations of the new discipline rested on the application of the scientific methods of observation and experimentation to educational problems. From 1840 to 1920 37 million people immigrated to the United States. This created an expansion of elementary schools and secondary schools. The increase in immigration also provided educational psychologists the opportunity to use intelligence testing to screen immigrants at Ellis Island. Darwinism influenced the beliefs of the prominent educational psychologists. Even in the earliest years of the discipline, educational psychologists recognized the limitations of this new approach. The pioneering American psychologist William James commented that:

Psychology is a science, and teaching is an art; and sciences never generate arts directly out of themselves. An intermediate inventive mind must make that application, by using its originality".

James is the father of psychology in America but he also made contributions to educational psychology. In his famous series of lectures *Talks to Teachers on Psychology*, published in 1899 and now regarded as the first educational psychology textbook, James defines education as "the organization of acquired habits of conduct and tendencies to behaviour". He states that teachers should "train the pupil to behaviour" so that he fits into the social and physical world. Teachers should also realize the importance of habit and instinct. They should present information that is clear and interesting and relate this new information and material to things the student already knows about. He also addresses important issues such as attention, memory, and association of ideas.

Alfred Binet published *Mental Fatigue* in 1898, in which he attempted to apply the experimental method to educational psychology. In this experimental method he advocated for two types of experiments,

experiments done in the lab and experiments done in the classroom. In 1904 he was appointed the Minister of Public Education. This is when he began to look for a way to distinguish children with developmental disabilities. Binet strongly supported special education programmes because he believed that "abnormality" could be cured. The Binet-Simon test was the first intelligence test and was the first to distinguish between "normal children" and those with developmental disabilities. Binet believed that it was important to study individual differences between age groups and children of the same age. He also believed that it was important for teachers to take into account individual students strengths and also the needs of the classroom as a whole when teaching and creating a good learning environment. He also believed that it was important to train teachers in observation so that they would be able to see individual differences among children and adjust the curriculum to the students. Binet also emphasized that practice of material was important. In 1916 Lewis Terman revised the Binet-Simon so that the average score was always 100. The test became known as the Stanford-Binet and was one of the most widely used tests of intelligence. Terman, unlike Binet, was interested in using intelligence test to identify gifted children who had high intelligence. In his longitudinal study of gifted children, who became known as the Termites, Terman found that gifted children become gifted adults.

Edward Thorndike (1874-1949) supported the scientific movement in education. He based teaching practices on empirical evidence and measurement. Thorndike developed the theory of instrumental conditioning or the law of effect. The law of effect states that associations are strengthened when it is followed by something pleasing and associations are weakened when followed by something not pleasing. He also found that learning is done a little at a time or in increments, learning is an automatic process and all the principles of learning apply to all mammals. Thorndike's research with Robert Woodworth on the theory of transfer found that learning one subject will only influence your ability to learn another subject if the subjects are similar. This discovery led to less emphasis on learning the classics because they found that studying the classics does not contribute to overall general intelligence. Thorndike was one of the first to say that individual differences in cognitive tasks were due to how many stimulus response patterns a person had rather than a general intellectual ability. He contributed word dictionaries that were scientifically based to determine the words and definitions used. The dictionaries were the first to take into consideration the users maturity level. He also integrated pictures and easier pronunciation guide into each of the definitions. Thorndike contributed arithmetic books based on learning theory. He made all the problems more realistic and relevant to what was being studied, not just to improve the general intelligence. He developed test that were standardized to measure performance in school related subjects. His biggest contribution to testing was the CAVD intelligence test which used a mulitdimensional approach to intelligence and the first to use a ratio scale. His later work was on programmed instruction, mastery learning and computer-based learning:

If, by a miracle of mechanical ingenuity, a book could be so arranged that only to him who had done what was directed on page one would page two become visible, and so on, much that now requires personal instruction could be managed by print.

John Dewey (1859-1952) had a major influence on the development of progressive education in the United States. He believed that the classroom should prepare children to be good citizens and facilitate creative intelligence. He pushed for the creation of practical class that could be applied outside of a school setting. He also thought that education should be student-oriented not subject-oriented. For Dewey education was social that helped bring together generations of people. He states that students learn by doing. He believed in an active mind that was able to be educated through observation and problem solving and enquiry. In his 1910 book *How We Think* he emphasizes that material should be provided in way that is stimulating and interesting to the student and it encourages original thoughts and problem solving. He also stated that material should be relative to the student's own experience.

"The material furnished by way of information should be relevant to a question that is vital in the students own experience"

Jean Piaget (1896-1980) developed the theory of cognitive development. The theory stated that intelligence developed in four different stages. The stages are the sensorimotor stage from birth to 2 years old, the preoperational state from 2 years old to 7 years old, the concrete operational stage from 7 years old to 10 years old, and formal operational stage from 11 years old and up. He also believed that learning was constrained to the child's cognitive development. Piaget influenced educational psychology because he was the first to believe that cognitive development was important and something that should be paid attention to in education. Most of the research on Piagetian theory was mainly tested and done by American educational psychologists

1920-Present

The amount of people receiving a high school and college education increased dramatically from 1920 to 1960. Because of very little jobs available to the teens coming out of eighth grade there was an increase in high school attendance in the 1930s. The progressive movement in the United State took off at this time and led to the idea of progressive education. John Flanagan, an educational psychologist, developed tests for combat trainees and instructions in combat training. In 1954 the work of Kenneth Clark and his wife on the effects of segregation on black and white children was influential in the Supreme Court case Brown v. Board of Education. From the 1960s to present day educational psychology has switched from a behaviourist perspective to a more cognitive based perspective because of the influence and development of cognitive psychology at this time.

Jerome Bruner was the first to apply the cognitive approaches in educational psychology. He was the one who introduced the ideas of Jean Piaget into educational psychology. He advocated for discovery learning where teachers create a problem solving environment that allows the student to question, explore and experiment. In his book *The Process of Education* Bruner stated that the structure of the material and the cognitive abilities of the person are important in learning. He emphasized the importance of the subject matter. He also believed that how the subject was structured was important for the students understanding of the subject and it is the goal of the teacher to structure the subject in a way that was easy for the student to understand. In the early 1960s Bruner went to Africa to teach math and science to schoolchildren, which influenced his view as schooling as a cultural institution. Bruner was also influential in the development of MACOS, Man a Course of Study, which was an educational programme that combined anthropology and science. The programme explored human evolution and social behaviour. He also helped with the development of the head start programme. He was interested in the influence of culture on education and looked at the impact of poverty on educational development.

Benjamin Bloom (1913-1999) spent over 50 years at the University of Chicago where he worked in the department of education. He believed that all students can learn. He developed taxonomy of educational objectives. The objectives were divided into three domains: cognitive, affective, and psychomotor. The cognitive domain deals with how we think. It is divided into categories that are on a continuum from easiest to more complex. The categories are knowledge or recall, comprehension application, analysis, synthesis and evaluation. The affective domain deals with emotions and has 5 categories. The categories are receiving phenomenon, responding to that phenomenon, valuing, organization, and internalizing values. The psychomotor domain deals with the development of motor skills, movement and coordination and has 7 categories, that also goes from simplest to complex. The 7 categories of the psychomotor domain are perception, set, guided response, mechanism, complex overt response, adaptation, and origination. The taxonomy provided broad educational objectives that could be used to help expand the curriculum to match the ideas in the taxonomy. The taxonomy is considered to have a greater influence internationally than in the United States. Internationally, the taxonomy is used in every aspect of education from training of the teachers to the development of testing material. Bloom believed in communicating clear learning goals and promoting an active student. He thought that teachers should provide feedback to the students on their strengths and weaknesses. Bloom also did research on college students and their problem solving processes. He found that they differ in understanding the basis of the problem and the ideas in the problem. He also found that students differ in process of problem solving in their approach and attitude towards the problem.

Nathaniel Gage is important in educational psychology because he did research to improve teaching and understand the processes involved in teaching. In 1963 he was the editor of the *Handbook of Research on Teaching*, which became an influential book in educational psychology. The handbook helped set up research on teaching and made research on teaching important to educational psychology. He also was influential in the founding of the Stanford Centre for Research and Development in teaching, which not only contributed important research on teaching but also influenced the teaching of important educational psychologists.

Careers in Educational Psychology

Education and Training: A person may be considered an educational psychologist after completing a graduate degree in educational psychology or a closely related field. Universities establish educational psychology graduate programmes in either psychology departments or, more commonly, faculties of education. Educational psychologists work in a variety of settings. Some work in university settings where they carry out research on the cognitive and social processes of human development, learning and education. Educational psychologists may also work as consultants in designing and creating educational materials, classroom programmes and online courses.

Educational psychologists who work in k–12 school settings (closely related are school psychologists in the US and Canada) are trained at the master's and doctoral levels. In addition to conducting assessments, school psychologists provide services such as academic and behavioural intervention, counselling, teacher consultation, and crisis intervention. However, school psychologists are generally more individual-oriented towards students.

In the UK, status as a *Chartered Educational Psychologist* is gained by completing:

- an undergraduate degree in psychology permitting registration with the British Psychological Society
- two or three years experience working with children, young people and their families.
- a three-year professional doctorate in educational psychology.

In New Zealand Registered Educational Psychologist status is gained by completing:

- an undergraduate degree in education and psychology
- completion of a two year masters level training programme in psychology or educational psychology
- completion of a one year post masters internship programme

Internship places are limited and applications exceed places in most years. Since 1999 Massey University delivered the only educational psychology training programme. Victoria University, Wellington started its offering of an educational psychology training programme in 2013.

Professional Organizations

Holding membership among Division 15 of the American Psychological Association and/or multiple divisions of the American Educational Research Association is common among educational psychologists. These organizations each host 1-2 conferences each year and provide peer-reviewed journals of current research in the field.

Employment Outlook

Employment for psychologists in the United States is expected to grow faster than most occupations through the year 2014, with anticipated growth of 18–26%. One in four psychologists are employed in educational settings. In the United States, the mediansalary for psychologists in primary and secondary schools is US$58,360 as of May 2004. In recent decades the participation of women as professional researchers in North American educational psychology has risen dramatically. The percentage of female authors of peer-reviewed journal articles doubled from 1976 (24%) to 1995 (51%), and has since remained constant. Female membership on educational psychology journal editorial boards increased from 17% in 1976 to 47% in 2004. Over the same period, the proportion of chief editor positions held by women increased from 22% to 70%.

Research Journals

There are several peer-reviewed research journals in educational psychology tracked by *Journal Citation Reports*. The most highly cited journals related to educational psychology are currently *Child Development*, *Educational Psychologist,* and *Journal of Educational Psychology*.

Need For Achievement

Need for achievement (N-Ach) refers to an individual's desire for significant accomplishment, mastering of skills, control, or high standards. The term was first used by Henry Murray and associated with a range of actions. These include: "intense, prolonged and repeated efforts to accomplish something difficult. To work with singleness of purpose towards a high and distant goal. To have the determination to win". The concept of NAch was subsequently popularised by the psychologist David McClelland.

This personality trait is characterized by an enduring and consistent concern with setting and meeting high standards of achievement. This need is influenced by internal drive for action (intrinsic motivation), and the pressure exerted by the expectations of others (extrinsic motivation). Measured by thematic appreciation tests, need for achievement motivates an individual to succeed in competition, and to excel in activities important to him or her.

Need for Achievement is related to the difficulty of tasks people choose to undertake. Those with low N-Ach may choose very easy tasks, in order to minimise risk of failure, or highly difficult tasks, such that a failure would not be embarrassing. Those with high N-Ach tend to choose moderately difficult tasks, feeling that they are challenging, but within reach.

People high in N-Ach are characterised by a tendency to seek challenges and a high degree of independence. Their most satisfying reward is the recognition of their achievements. Sources of high N-Ach include:

1. Parents who encouraged independence in childhood
2. Praise and rewards for success
3. Association of achievement with positive feelings
4. Association of achievement with one's own competence and effort, not luck
5. A desire to be effective or challenged
6. Intrapersonal Strength
7. Desirability
8. Feasibility
9. Goal Setting Abilities

Theory

The pioneering research work of the Harvard Psychological Clinic in the 1930s, summarised in *Explorations in Personality*, provided the start point for future studies of personality, especially those relating to needs and motives. David C. McClelland's and his associates' investigations of achievement motivation have particular relevance to the emergence of leadership. McClelland was interested in the possibility of deliberately arousing a motive to achieve in an attempt to explain how individuals express their preferences for particular outcomes — a general problem of motivation. In this connection, the need for achievement refers to an individual's preference for success under conditions of competition. The vehicle McClelland employed to establish the presence of an achievement motive was the type of fantasy a person expressed on the Thematic Apperception Test (TAT), developed by Christiana Morgan and Henry Murray, who note in *Explorations in Personality* that "...when a person interprets an ambiguous social situation he is apt to expose his own personality as much as the phenomenon to which he is attending... Each picture should suggest some critical situation and be effective in evoking a fantasy relating to it" (p531). The test is composed of a series of pictures that subjects are asked to interpret and describe to the psychologist. The TAT has been widely used to support assessment of needs and motives.

In 1961 McClelland published The Achieving Society, which articulated his model of human motivation. McClelland contended that three dominant needs -for achievement, for power, and for affiliation- underpin human motivation. McClelland believed that the relative importance of each need varies among individuals and cultures. Arguing that commonly used hiring tests using IQ and personality assessments were poor predictors of competency, McClelland proposed that companies should base hiring decisions on demonstrated competency in relevant fields, rather than on standardized test scores. Iconoclastic in their time, McClelland's ideas have become standard practice in many corporations.

The procedure in McClelland's initial investigation was to arouse in the test audience a concern with their achievement. A control group was used in which arousal was omitted. In the course of this experiment, McClelland discovered through analyzing the stories on the TAT that initial arousal was not necessary. Instead, members of the control group — individuals who had had no prior arousal — demonstrated significant differences in their stories, some writing stories with a high achievement content and some submitting stories with a low achievement content. Using results based on the Thematic Apperception Test, McClelland demonstrated that individuals in a society can be grouped into high achievers and low achievers based on their scores on what he called "N-Ach".

McClelland and his associates have since extended their work in fantasy analysis to include different age groups, occupational groups, and nationalities in their investigations of the strength of need for achievement. These investigations have indicated that the N-Ach score increases with a rise in occupational level. Invariably, businessmen, managers, and entrepreneurs are high scorers. Other investigations into the characteristics of the high achievers have revealed that accomplishment on the job represents an end in itself; monetary rewards serve as an index of this accomplishment. In addition, these other studies found that the high achievers, though identified as managers, businessmen, and entrepreneurs, are not gamblers. A high emotional intelligence calls for a high need for achievement while a low emotional intelligence calls for a lower need for achievement. They will accept risk only to the degree they believe their personal contributions will make a difference in the final outcome.

An experiment realized to entry level managers of AT&T from 1956 to 1960, studied the level of achievement attained during a period of 8 to 16 years, showing that High n-Achievement was associated with managerial success at lower levels of management jobs, in which promotion depends more on individual contributions than it does at higher levels. At the higher levels, in which promotion depends on demonstrated ability to manage others, a high n-Achievement is not associated with success; by contrast, the leadership motive pattern is so associated, in all likelihood because it involves a high n-Power, emerging as a concern for influencing people.

These explorations into the achievement motive seem to turn naturally into the investigation of national differences based on Max Weber's thesis that the industrialization and economic development of the Western nations were related to the Protestant ethic and its corresponding values supporting work and achievement. McClelland and his associates have satisfied themselves that such a relationship, viewed historically through an index of national power consumption, indeed exists. Differences related to individual, as well as to national, accomplishments depend on the presence or absence of an achievement motive in addition to economic resources or the infusion of financial assistance. High achievers can be viewed as satisfying a need for self-actualization through accomplishments in their job assignments as a result of their particular knowledge, their particular experiences, and the particular environments in which they have lived.

Measurement

The techniques McClelland and his collaborators developed to measure N-Ach, N-Affil and N-Pow can be viewed as a radical break with the dominant psychometric tradition. However, it should be recognised that McClellend's thinking was strongly influenced by the pioneering work of Henry Murray, both in terms of Murray's model of human needs and motivational processes (1938) and his work with the OSS during World War Two. It was during this period that Murray introduced the idea of "situation tests" and multi-rater / multi-method assessments. It was Murray who first identified the significance of Need for Achievement, Power and Affiliation and placed these in the context of an integrated motivational model.

Whilst trait-based personality theory assume that high-level competencies like initiative, creativity, and leadership can be assessed using "internally consistent" measures, the McClelland measures recognize that such competencies are difficult and demanding activities which will neither be developed nor displayed unless people are undertaking activities they care about (i.e. are strongly motivated to undertake). Furthermore, it is the cumulative number of independent, but cumulative and substitutable, components of competence they bring to bear while seeking to carry out these activities that will determine their success. Accordingly, the N-Ach, N-Aff and N-Pow scoring systems simply count how many components of competence people bring to bear whilst carrying out activities they have a strong personal inclination (or motivation) to undertake.

McClelland's research led him to formulate psychological characteristics of persons with strong need for achievement. According to McClelland and David Winter (*Motivating Economic Achievement*), the following features accompany high level of achievement motivation:

- Moderate risk propensity;
- Undertaking innovative and engaging tasks;
- Internal locus of control and responsibility for own decisions and behaviours;
- Need for precise goal setting.

An important corollary is that there is no point in trying to assess people's abilities without first finding out what they care about. So one cannot (as some psychometricians try to do) assess such things as "creativity" in any general sense. One has always to ask "creativity in relation to what?" So McClelland's measures, originally presented as means of assessing "personality", are best understood as means of measuring competence in ways which break radically with traditional psychometric approaches. Everybody has different goals and needs for achievement based off many factors like past experiences, education, the risks, and the feedback they will receive.

Need for Affiliation

The Need for affiliation (N-Affil) is a term that was popularized by David McClelland and describes a person's need to feel a sense of involvement and "belonging" within a social group; McClellend's thinking was strongly influenced by the pioneering work of Henry Murray who first identified underlying psychological human needs and motivational processes (1938). It was Murray who set out a taxonomy of needs, including achievement, power and affiliation—and placed these in the context of an integrated motivational model. People with a high need for affiliation require warm interpersonal relationships and approval from those with whom they have regular contact. People who place high emphasis on affiliation tend to be supportive team members, but may be less effective in leadership positions.

Definition

Affiliation is a positive, sometimes intimate, personal relationship. Affiliation can include "concern over establishing, maintaining, or restoring a positive affective relationship with another person or persons."

Situations

There are many situations in which people feel a need for affiliation. One situation that causes a greater need for affiliation is during a stressful situation. An example where there was an increase in the need for affiliation among individuals was right after the September 11 terrorist attack on the World Trade Centre. This event led to Americans' putting their differences aside and coming together. The increase in an individual's need for affiliation allowed individuals responding to the same stressor to come together and find security in one another. Situations that include fear often lead people to want to be together and trigger a need for affiliation. Research done by Schacter (1959) shows that fear that comes from anxiety increases the need for the person to affiliate with others who are going through the same situation or that could help them through the stressful event. The strength of this need changes from one person to the next, there are moments that people just want to be together.

The need for affiliation for an individual can vary over short amounts of time; there are times when individuals wish to be with others and other times to be alone. In one study, completed by Shawn O'Connor and Lorne Rosenblood, beepers were distributed to the students. The students were then asked to record, when their beepers went off, whether or not they wanted to be alone or if they wanted to be with others at that particular moment. This study was done to observe how frequently college students were in the presence of others and how frequently they were alone. The next step in this study asked for the students to record whether, at the time their beeper went off, they wanted to be alone or in the company of others. This response that they gave usually reflected which of the two situations they were experiencing the next time their beepers went off. The information retained from this study helped to show the strength of an individual's need for affiliation. By showing how frequently they obtained the presence of others when they felt that it was what they wanted at that moment it showed how strong their need for affiliation was at that particular moment. Depending on the specific circumstances, an individual's level of need for affiliation can become increased or decreased. Yacov Rofe suggested that the need for affiliation depended on whether being with others would be useful for the situation or not. When the presence of other people was seen as being helpful in relieving an individual from some of the negative aspects of the stressor, an individual's desire to affiliate increases. However, if being with others may increase the negative aspects such as adding the possibility of embarrassment to the already present stressor, the individual's desire to affiliate with others decreases. Individuals are motivated to find and create a specific amount of social interactions. Each individual desires a different amount of a need for affiliation and they desire an optimal balance of time to their self and time spent with others.

Need Theory

McClelland's Need Theory, created by psychologistDavid McClelland, is a motivational model that attempts to explain how the needs for achievement, power and affiliation affect the actions of people from a managerial context. It is often taught in classes concerning management or organizational behaviour.

Need for Achievement

People who are achievement-motivated typically prefer to master a task or situation. They prefer working on tasks of moderate difficulty, prefer work in which the results are based on their effort rather than on luck, and prefer to receive feedback on their work.

Need for Affiliation

People who have a need for affiliation prefer to spend time creating and maintaining social relationships, enjoy being a part of groups, and have a desire to feel loved and accepted. People in this group do not typically make effective managers because they worry too much about how others will feel about them.

Need for Power

This motivational need stems from a person's desire to influence, teach, or encourage others. People in this category enjoy work. and place a high value on discipline. The downside to this motivational type is that group goals can become zero-sum in nature. That is, for one person to win, another must lose. However, this can be positively applied to help accomplish group goals and to help others in the group feel competent about their work. McClelland proposes that those in the top management positions should have a high need for power and a low need for affiliation. He also believes that although individuals with a need for achievement can make good managers, they are not suited to being in the top management positions.

Hierarchy

Maslow's hierarchy of needs is often portrayed in the shape of a pyramid with the largest, most fundamental levels of needs at the bottom and the need for self-actualization at the top. While the pyramid has become the de facto way to represent the hierarchy, Maslow himself never used a pyramid to describe these levels in any of his writings on the subject.

The most fundamental and basic four layers of the pyramid contain what Maslow called "deficiency needs" or "d-needs": esteem, friendship and love, security, and physical needs. If these "deficiency needs" are not met – with the exception of the most fundamental (physiological) need – there may not be a physical indication, but the individual will feel anxious and tense. Maslow's theory suggests that the most basic level of needs must be met before the individual will strongly desire (or focus motivation upon) the secondary or higher level needs. Maslow also coined the term Metamotivation to describe the motivation of people who go beyond the scope of the basic needs and strive for constant betterment.

The human mind and brain are complex and have parallel processes running at the same time, thus many different motivations from various levels of Maslow's hierarchy can occur at the same time. Maslow spoke clearly about these levels and their satisfaction in terms such as "relative," "general," and "primarily." Instead of stating that the individual focuses on a certain need at any given time, Maslow stated that a certain need "dominates" the human organism. Thus Maslow acknowledged the likelihood that the different levels of motivation could occur at any time in the human mind, but he focused on identifying the basic types of motivation and the order in which they should be met.

Physiological Needs

Physiological needs are the physical requirements for human survival. If these requirements are not met, the human body cannot function properly, and will ultimately fail. Physiological needs are thought to be the most important; they should be met first.

Air, water, and food are metabolic requirements for survival in all animals, including humans. Clothing and shelter provide necessary protection from the elements. While maintaining an adequate birth rate shapes the intensity of the human sexual instinct, sexual competition may also shape said instinct.

Safety Needs

With their physical needs relatively satisfied, the individual's safety needs take precedence and dominate behaviour. In the absence of physical safety – due to war, natural disaster, family violence, childhood abuse, etc. – people may (re-)experience post-traumatic stress disorder or transgenerational trauma. In the absence of economic safety – due to economic crisis and lack of work opportunities – these safety needs manifest themselves in ways such as a preference for job security, grievance procedures for protecting the individual from unilateral authority, savings accounts, insurance policies, reasonable disability accommodations, etc. This level is more likely to be found in children because they generally have a greater need to feel safe.

Safety and Security needs include:

- Personal security
- Financial security
- Health and well-being
- Safety net against accidents/illness and their adverse impacts

Love and Belonging

After physiological and safety needs are fulfilled, the third level of human needs is interpersonal and involves feelings of belongingness. This need is especially strong in childhood and can override the need for safety as witnessed in children who cling to abusive parents. Deficiencies within this level of Maslow's hierarchy – due to hospitalism, neglect, shunning, ostracism, etc. – can impact the individual's ability to form and maintain emotionally significant relationships in general, such as:

- Friendship
- Intimacy
- Family

According to Maslow, humans need to feel a sense of belonging and acceptance among their social groups, regardless if these groups are large or small. For example, some large social groups may include clubs, co-workers, religious groups, professional organizations, sports teams, and gangs. Some examples of small social connections include family members, intimate partners, mentors, colleagues, and confidants. Humans need to love and be loved – both sexually and non-sexually – by others. Many people become susceptible to loneliness, social anxiety, and clinical depression in the absence of this love or belonging element. This need for belonging may overcome the physiological and security needs, depending on the strength of the peer pressure.

Esteem

All humans have a need to feel respected; this includes the need to have self-esteem and self-respect. Esteem presents the typical human desire to be accepted and valued by others. People often engage in a profession or hobby to gain recognition. These activities give the person a sense of contribution or value. Low self-esteem or an inferiority complex may result from imbalances during this level in the hierarchy. People with low self-esteem often need respect from others; they may feel the need to seek fame or glory. However, fame or glory will not help the person to build their self-esteem until they accept who they are internally. Psychological imbalances such as depression can hinder the person from obtaining a higher level of self-esteem or self-respect.

Most people have a need for stable self-respect and self-esteem. Maslow noted two versions of esteem needs: a "lower" version and a "higher" version. The "lower" version of esteem is the need for respect from others. This may include a need for status, recognition, fame, prestige, and attention. The "higher" version manifests itself as the need for self-respect. For example, the person may have a need for strength, competence, mastery, self-confidence, independence, and freedom. This "higher" version takes precedence over the "lower" version because it relies on an inner competence established through experience. Deprivation of these needs may lead to an inferiority complex, weakness, and helplessness.

Maslow states that while he originally thought the needs of humans had strict guidelines, the "hierarchies are interrelated rather than sharply separated". This means that esteem and the subsequent levels are not strictly separated; instead, the levels are closely related.

Self-actualization

"What a man can be, he must be." This quotation forms the basis of the perceived need for self-actualization. This level of need refers to what a person's full potential is and the realization of that potential. Maslow describes this level as the desire to accomplish everything that one can, to become the most that one can be. Individuals may perceive or focus on this need very specifically. For example, one individual may have the strong desire to become an ideal parent. In another, the desire may be expressed athletically. For others, it may be expressed in paintings, pictures, or inventions. As previously mentioned, Maslow believed that to understand this level of need, the person must not only achieve the previous needs, but master them.

Research

Recent research appears to validate the existence of universal human needs, although the hierarchy proposed by Maslow is called into question. Other research indicates that Maslow's explanations of the hierarchy of human motivation reflect a binary pattern of growth as seen in math. The individual's awareness of first, second, and third person perspectives, and of each one's input needs and output needs, moves through a general pattern that is basically the same as Maslow's.

Following World War II, the unmet needs of homeless and orphaned children presented difficulties that were often addressed with the help of attachment theory, which was initially based on Maslow and others' developmental psychology work by John Bowlby. Originally dealing primarily with maternal deprivation and concordant losses of essential and primal needs, attachment theory has since been extended to provide explanations of nearly all the human needs in Maslow's hierarchy, from sustenance and mating to group membership and justice. While Maslow's hierarchy remains a very popular framework in sociology research and secondary and postsecondary psychology instruction, it has largely been supplanted by attachment theory in graduate and clinical psychology and psychiatry.

Criticism

In their extensive review of research based on Maslow's theory, Wahba and Bridwell found little evidence for the ranking of needs that Maslow described or for the existence of a definite hierarchy at all.

The order in which the hierarchy is arranged (with self-actualization described as the highest need) has been criticized as being ethnocentric by Geert Hofstede. Maslow's hierarchy of needs fails to illustrate and expand upon the difference between the social and intellectual needs of those raised in individualistic societies and those raised in collectivist societies. The needs and drives of those in individualistic societies tend to be more self-centred than those in collectivist societies, focusing on improvement of the self, with self-actualization being the apex of self-improvement. In collectivist societies, the needs of acceptance and community will outweigh the needs for freedom and individuality. The term "Self-actualization" may not universally convey Maslow's observations; this motivation refers to focusing on becoming the best person that one can possibly strive for in the service of both the self and others. Maslow's term of self-actualization might not properly portray the full extent of this level; quite often, when a person is at the level of self-actualization, much of what they accomplish in general may benefit others or, "the greater self".

The position and value of sex on the pyramid has also been a source of criticism regarding Maslow's hierarchy. Maslow's hierarchy places sex in the physiological needs category along with food and breathing; it lists sex solely from an individualistic perspective. For example, sex is placed with other physiological needs which must be satisfied before a person considers "higher" levels of motivation. Some critics feel this placement of sex neglects the emotional, familial, and evolutionary implications of sex within the community, although others point out that this is true of all of the basic needs.

Changes to the Hierarchy by Circumstance

The higher-order (self-esteem and self-actualization) and lower-order (physiological, safety, and love) needs classification of Maslow's hierarchy of needs is not universal and may vary across cultures due to individual differences and availability of resources in the region or geopolitical entity/country.

In one study, exploratory factor analysis (EFA) of a thirteen item scale showed there were two particularly important levels of needs in the US during the peacetime of 1993 to 1994: survival (physiological and safety) and psychological (love, self-esteem, and self-actualization). In 1991, a retrospective peacetime measure was established and collected during the Persian Gulf War and US citizens were asked to recall the importance of needs from the previous year. Once again, only two levels of needs were identified; therefore, people have the ability and competence to recall and estimate the importance of needs. For citizens in the Middle East (Egypt and Saudi Arabia), three levels of needs regarding importance and satisfaction surfaced during the 1990 retrospective peacetime. These three levels were completely different from those of the US citizens.

Changes regarding the importance and satisfaction of needs from the retrospective peacetime to the wartime due to stress varied significantly across cultures (the US vs. the Middle East). For the US citizens, there was only one level of needs since all needs were considered equally important. With regards to satisfaction of needs during the war, in the US there were three levels: physiological needs, safety needs, and psychological needs (social, self-esteem, and self-actualization). During the war, the satisfaction of physiological needs and safety needs were separated into two independent needs while during peacetime, they were combined as one. For the people of the Middle East, the satisfaction of needs changed from three levels to two during wartime.

A 1981 study looked at how Maslow's hierarchy might vary across age groups. A survey asked participants of varying ages to rate a set number of statements from most important to least important. The researchers found that children had higher physical need scores than the other groups, the love need emerged from childhood to young adulthood, the esteem need was highest among the adolescent group, young adults had the highest self-actualization level, and while old age had the highest level of security, it was needed across all levels comparably. The authors argued that this suggested Maslow's hierarchy may be limited as a theory for developmental sequence since the sequence of the love need and the self-esteem need should be reversed according to age.

Motivation Crowding Theory

Motivation crowding theory, in labour economics and social psychology, suggests that extrinsic motivators such as monetary incentives or punishments can undermine (or, under different conditions, strengthen) intrinsic motivation. For example, if the imposition of a fine or other concrete penalty results in an increase of a prohibited behaviour, the penalty is said to "crowd out" the intrinsic social disincentive by associating violations with a more psychologically acceptable cost. Tangible incentives crowding out intrinsic motivation is known as the overjustification effect. Similarly, the Yerkes–Dodson law describes physiological or mental arousal first strengthening and then crowding out productivity over short time scales.

The theory contrasts with the relative price effect on which mainstream economics is based. In neoclassicallabor microeconomics, when the supply of labour is decided by the worker, such as in volunteer or paid voluntary labour, the amount of work performed is often described by the backward bending supply curve of labour. The curve indicates that while workers will initially chose to work more when paid more per hour, there is a point after which rational workers will choose to work less, as the marginal value of more money is outweighed by the loss of available time. Since the vertical axis only represents extrinsic compensation, the curve does not represent a complete description of voluntary labour.

Researchers are interested in understanding the conditions which maximize motivation and productivity. Recent studies and literature reviews suggest that as managers have become more aware of the conditions involved in influencing overall motivation, external incentives for volunteers and labourers have not led to decreases in intrinsic motivation or output productivity. Those results are consistent with an earlier meta-analysis that found intrinsic motivation is only diminished by tangible rewards when they are both expected and given simply for doing a task, and then those rewards are removed, instead of given for achieving the task's goals, or given unexpectedly.

Self-determination Theory

Self-determination theory (SDT) is a macro theory of human motivation and personality, concerning people's inherent growth tendencies and their innate psychological needs. It is concerned with the motivation behind the choices that people make without any external influence and interference. SDT focuses on the degree to which an individual's behaviour is self-motivated and self-determined. In the 1970s, research on SDT evolved from studies comparing the intrinsic and extrinsic motives, and from growing understanding of the dominant role intrinsic motivation played in an individual's behaviour but it was not until mid-1980s that SDT was formally introduced and accepted as a sound empirical theory. Research applying SDT to different areas in social psychology has increased considerably since the 2000s.

Key studies that led to emergence of SDT included research on intrinsic motivation. Intrinsic motivation refers to initiating an activity for its own sake because it is interesting and satisfying in itself, as opposed to doing an activity to obtain an external goal (extrinsic motivation). Different types of motivations have been described based on the degree they have been internalized. Internalization refers to the active attempt to transform an extrinsic motive into personally endorsed values and thus assimilate behavioural regulations that were originally external.

Edward L. Deci and Richard M. Ryan later expanded on the early work differentiating between intrinsic and extrinsic motivation and proposed three main intrinsic needs involved in self-determination. According to Deci and Ryan, the three psychological needs motivate the self to initiate behaviour and specify nutriments that are essential for psychological health and well-being of an individual. These needs are said to be universal, innate and psychological and include the need for competence, autonomy, and psychological relatedness.

Basic Theory

SDT is centred on the belief that human nature shows persistent positive features, that it repeatedly shows effort, agency and commitment in their lives that the theory calls "inherent growth tendencies." People also have innate psychological needs that are the basis for self-motivation and personality integration.

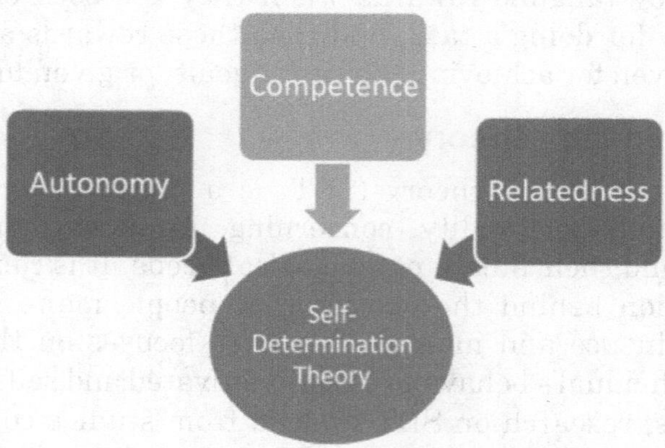

SDT identifies three innate needs that, if satisfied, allow optimal function and growth:

1. Competence
2. Relatedness
3. Autonomy

These needs are seen as universal necessities that are innate, not learned, and seen in humanity across time, gender and culture.

Deci and Vansteenkiste claim that there are three essential elements of the theory:

1. Humans are inherently proactive with their potential and mastering their inner forces (such as drives and emotions)
2. Humans have inherent tendency towards growth development and integrated functioning

3. Optimal development and actions are inherent in humans but they don't happen automatically

To actualise their inherent potential they need nurturing from the social environment.

If this happens there are positive consequence (e.g. well being and growth) but if not, there are negative consequences. So SDT emphasises humans' natural growth towards positive motivation, however this is thwarted if their basic needs are not fulfilled.

Needs

SDT supports three basic psychological needs that must be satisfied to foster well-being and health; these needs can be universally applied. However, some may be more salient than others at certain times and will be expressed differently based on time, culture or experience.

Competence: Seek to control the outcome and experience mastery

Relatedness: Is the universal want to interact, be connected to, and experience caring for others

Autonomy: Is the universal urge to be causal agents of one's own life and act in harmony with one's integrated self; however, Deci and Vansteenkiste note this does not mean to be independent of others

Motivations

SDT claims to give a different approach to motivation, considering what motivates a person at any given time as opposed to seeing motivation as a unitary concept. SDT makes distinctions between different types of motivation and the consequences of them.

Intrinsic Motivation

Intrinsic motivation is the natural, inherent drive to seek out challenges and new possibilities that SDT associates with cognitive and social development.

Cognitive Evaluation Theory (CET) is a sub-theory of SDT that specifies factors explaining intrinsic motivation and variability with it and looks at how social and environmental factors help or hinder intrinsic motivations. CET focuses on the needs of competence and autonomy.

Claiming social context events like feedback on work or rewards lead to feelings of competence and so enhance intrinsic motivations. Deci found positive feedback enhanced intrinsic motivations and negative feedback diminished it. Vallerand and Reid went further and found that these effects were being mediated by perceived control.

Autonomy however must accompany competence in order for people to see their behaviours as self determined by intrinsic motivation. For this to happen there must be immediate contextual support for both needs or inner resources based on prior development support for both needs.

CET and intrinsic motivation is also linked to relatedness through the hypothesis that intrinsic motivation will flourish if linked with a sense of security and relatedness. Grolnick and Ryan found lower intrinsic motivation in children who believed their teachers to be uncaring or cold and so not fulfilling their relatedness needs.

Extrinsic Motivation

Extrinsic motivation comes from external sources. Deci and Ryan developed Organismic Integration Theory (OIT), as a sub-theory of SDT, to explain the different ways in which extrinsically motivated behaviour is regulated.

OIT details the different forms of extrinsic motivation and the contexts in which they come about. It is the context of such motivation that concerns the SDT theory as these contexts affect whether the motivations are internalised and so integrated into the sense of self.

OIT describes four different types of extrinsic motivations that often vary in terms of their relative autonomy:

1. Externally regulated behaviour: Is the least autonomous, it is performed because of external demand or possible reward. Such actions can be seen to have an externally perceived locus of control.
2. Introjected regulation of behaviour: describes taking on regulations to behaviour but not fully accepting said regulations as your own. Deci and Ryan claim such behaviour normally represents regulation by contingent self-esteem, citing ego involvement as a classic form of introjections. This is the kind of behaviour where people feel motivated to demonstrate ability to maintain self-worth. While this is internally driven Deci and Ryan say introjected behaviour is on an externally perceived locus of control because they aren't perceived as part of self.
3. Regulation through identification: Is a more autonomy driven form of extrinsic motivation. It involves consciously valuing a goal or regulation so that said action is accepted as personally important.

4. Integrated Regulation: Is the most autonomous kind of extrinsic motivation. Occurring when regulations are fully assimilated with self so they are included in a person's self evaluations and beliefs on personal needs. Because of this, integrated motivations share qualities with intrinsic motivation but are still classified as extrinsic because the goals that are trying to be achieved are for reasons extrinsic to the self, rather than the inherent enjoyment or interest in the task.

Extrinsically motivated behaviours can be integrated into self. OIT proposes internalization is more likely to occur when there is a sense of relatedness. Ryan, Stiller and Lynch found children will internalize school's extrinsic regulations when they felt secure and cared for by parents and teachers.

Internalisation of extrinsic motivation is also linked to competence. OIT suggests that feelings of competence in activities should facilitate internalisation of said actions.

Autonomy is particularly important when its regulations are trying to be integrated into a person's sense of self. If an external context allows a person to integrate regulations they must feel competent, related and autonomous. They must also understand in terms of their other goals the regulation in order for a sense of autonomy to be facilitated. This was supported by Deci, Eghrari, Patrick and Leone who found in laboratory settings if a person was given a meaningful reason for uninteresting behaviour along with support for their sense of autonomy and relatedness they internalized and integrated their behaviour.

Basic Needs and Intrinsic Motivation

White and deCharms proposed that the need for competence and autonomy is the basis of intrinsic motivation and behaviour. This is a link between people's basic needs and their motivations.

Autonomy

Deci found that offering people extrinsic rewards for behaviour that is intrinsically motivated undermined the intrinsic motivation as they grow less interested in it. Initially intrinsically motivated behaviour becomes controlled by external rewards, which undermines their autonomy.

Further research by Amabile, DeJong and Lepper found other external factors like deadlines, which restrict and control, also decrease intrinsic motivation.

Situations that give autonomy as opposed to taking it away also have a similar link to motivation. Studies looking at choice have found that increasing a participant's options and choices increases their intrinsic motivation to said activities.

Competence

Deci found that giving people unexpected positive feedback on a task increases people's intrinsic motivation to do it, meaning that this was because the positive feedback was fulfilling people's need for competence. In fact, giving positive feedback on a task served only to increase people's intrinsic motivation and decreased extrinsic motivation for the task. Vallerand and Reid found negative feedback has the opposite effect (i.e., decreasing intrinsic motivation by taking away from people's need for competence).

Relatedness

During a study on the relationship between infants' attachment styles, their exhibition of mastery-oriented behaviour and their affect during play, Frodi, Bridges and Grolnick failed to find significant effects: "Perhaps somewhat surprising was the finding that the quality of attachment assessed at 12 months failed to significantly predict either mastery motivation, competence, or affect 8 months later, when other investigators have demonstrated an association between similar constructs..." Yet they note that larger sample sizes could be able to uncover such effects: "A comparison of the secure/stable and the insecure/stable groups, however, did suggest that the secure/stable group was superior to the insecure/stable groups on all mastery-related measures. Obviously, replications of all the attachment-motivation relations are needed with different and larger samples."

Individual Differences

SDT argues that needs are innate but can be developed in a social context. Some people will develop stronger needs than others, creating individual differences. However individual differences within the theory focus on concepts resulting from the degree which needs have been satisfied or not satisfied. Within SDT there are two general individual difference concepts, Causality Orientations and Life Goals.

Causality Orientations

Causality orientations are motivational orientations that refer to either the way people orient to an environment and regulate their behaviour because of this or the extent to which they are self determined in general across many settings. SDT created three orientations: autonomous, controlled and impersonal.

1. Autonomous Orientations: result from satisfaction of the basic needs
2. Strong controlled orientations: Result from satisfaction of competence and relatedness needs but not of autonomy and is linked to regulation through internal and external contingences, which lead to rigid functioning and diminished well being.
3. Impersonal Orientations: Results from failing to fulfil all three needs. This is also related to poor functioning and ill being.

According to the theory people have some amount of each of the orientations, which can be used to make predictions on a persons psychological health and behavioural outcomes

Life Goals

Life goals are long term goals people use to guide their activities and they fall into two categories:

1. Intrinsic Aspirations: Contain life goals like affiliation generativity and personal development.
2. Extrinsic Aspirations: Have life goals like wealth, fame and attractiveness.

There have been several studies on this subject that chart intrinsic goals being associated with greater health, well being and performance.

Key Studies

Deci (1971): External Rewards on Intrinsic Motivation: Deci investigated the effects of external rewards on intrinsic motivation in two laboratory and one field experiment. Based on the results from earlier animal and human studies regarding intrinsic motivation the author explored two possibilities. In the first two experiments he looked at the effect of extrinsic rewards in terms of a decrease in intrinsic motivation to perform a task. Earlier studies showed contradictory or inconclusive findings regarding decrease in performance on a task following an external reward. The third experiment was based on findings of developmental learning theorists and looked at whether a different type of reward enhances intrinsic motivation to participate in an activity.

Experiment I

This experiment tested the hypothesis that if an individual is intrinsically motivated to perform an activity, introduction of an extrinsic reward decreases the degree of intrinsic motivation to perform the task.

*Twenty-four undergraduate psychology students participated in the first laboratory experiment and were assigned to experimental (*n *=12) and control group (*n *= 12). Each group participated in three sessions conducted on three different days. During the sessions the participants were engaged in working on a Soma cube puzzle which was assumed to be an activity that college students would be intrinsically motivated to do. The puzzle could be put together to form numerous different configurations. In each session, the participants were shown four different configurations drawn on a piece of paper and were asked to use the puzzle to reproduce the configurations while they were being timed.*

The first and third session of the experimental condition were identical to control, but in the second session the participants in the experimental condition were given a dollar for completing each puzzle within time. During the middle of each session, the experimenter left the room for eight minutes and the participants were told that they were free to do whatever they wanted during that time, while the experimenter observed during that period. The amount of time spent working on the puzzle during the free choice period was used to measure motivation.

As Deci expected, when external reward was introduced during session two, the participants spent more time working on the puzzles during the free choice period in comparison to session 1 and when the external reward was removed in the third session, the time spent working on the puzzle dropped lower than the first session. All subjects reported finding the task interesting and enjoyable at the end of each session, providing evidence for the experimenter's assumption that the task was intrinsically motivating for the college students. The study showed some support of the experimenter's hypothesis and a trend towards decrease in intrinsic motivation was seen after money was provided to the participants as external reward.

Experiment II

The second experiment was a field experiment, similar to laboratory Experiment I, but was conducted in a natural setting.

Eight student workers were observed at a college biweekly newspaper. Four of the students served as a control group and worked on Friday. The experimental group worked on Tuesdays.

The control and experimental group students were not aware that they were being observed. The 10-week observation was divided into three time periods. The task in this study required the students to write headlines for the newspaper.

During "Time 2", the students in the experimental group were given 50 cents for each headline they wrote. At the end of Time 2, they were told that in the future the newspaper cannot pay them 50 cent for each headline anymore as the newspaper ran out of the money allocated for that and they were not paid for the headlines during Time 3.

The speed of task completion (headlines) was used as a measure of motivation in this experiment. Absences were used as a measure of attitudes.

In order to assess the stability of the observed effect, the experimenter observed the students again (Time 4) for two weeks. There was a gap of five weeks between Time 3 and Time 4. Due to absences and change in assignment etc., motivation data was not available for all students. The results of this experiment were similar to Experiment I and monetary reward was found to decrease the intrinsic motivation of the students, supporting Deci's hypothesis.

Experiment III

Experiment III was also conducted in the laboratory and was identical to Experiment I in all respects except for the kind of external reward provided to the students in experimental condition during Session 2.

In this experiment, verbal praise was used as an extrinsic reward.

The experimenter hypothesized that a different type of reward, i.e. social approval in form of verbal reinforcement and positive feedback for performing the task that a person is intrinsically motivated to perform, will enhance the degree of internal motivation even after the extrinsic reward is removed.

The results of the experiment III confirmed the hypothesis and the students' performance increased significantly during the third session in comparison to session one, showing that verbal praise and positive feedback enhances performance in tasks that a person is initially intrinsically motivated to perform. This provides evidence that verbal praise as external reward increases intrinsic motivation.

The author explained differences between the two types of external rewards as having different effects on intrinsic motivation. When a person is intrinsically motivated to perform a task and money is introduced to work on the task, the individual cognitively re-evaluates the importance of the task and the intrinsic motivation to perform the task (because the individual finds it interesting) shifts to extrinsic motivation and the primary focus changes from enjoying the task to gaining financial reward. However, when verbal praise is provided in a similar situation increases intrinsic motivation as it is not evaluated to be controlled by external factors and the person sees the task as an enjoyable task that is performed autonomously. The increase in intrinsic motivation is explained by positive reinforcement and an increase in perceived locus of control to perform the task.

Pritchard, Campbell and Campbell (1977): Evaluation of Deci's Hypothesis

Pritchard, Campbell and Campbell conducted a similar study to evaluate Deci's hypothesis regarding the role of extrinsic rewards on decreasing intrinsic motivation.

Participants were randomly assigned to two groups. A chess-problem task was used in this study. Data was collected in two sessions.

Session I

Participants were asked to complete a background questionnaire that included questions on the amount of time the participant played chess during the week, the number of years that the participant has been playing chess for, amount of enjoyment the participant gets from playing the game, etc. The participants in both groups were then told that the experimenter needed to enter the information in the computer and for the next 10 minutes the participant were free to do whatever they liked.

The experimenter left the room for 10 minutes. The room had similar chess-problem tasks on the table, some magazines as well as coffee was made available for the participants if they chose to have it. The time spent on the chess-problem task was observed through a one way mirror by the experimenter during the 10 minutes break and was used as a measure of intrinsic motivation. After the experimenter returned, the experimental group was told that there was a monetary reward for the participant who could work on the most chess problems in the given time and that the reward is for this session only and would not be offered during the next session. The control group was not offered a monetary reward.

Session II

The Second Session was the Same for the Two Groups: After a filler task, the experimenter left the room for 10 minutes and the time participants spent on the chess-problem task was observed. The experimental group was reminded that there was no reward for the task this time. After both sessions the participants were required to respond to questionnaires evaluating the task, i.e. to what degree did they find the task interesting. Both groups reported that they found the task interesting.

The results of the study showed that the experimental group showed a significant decrease in time spent on the chess-problem task during the 10-minute free time from session 1 to session 2 in comparison to the group that was not paid, thus confirming the hypothesis presented by Deci that contingent monetary reward for an activity decreases the intrinsic motivation to perform that activity. Other studies were conducted around this time focusing on other types of rewards as well as other external factors that play a role in decreasing intrinsic motivation.

Chua and Koestner (2008)

SDT and Solitude: Chua and Koestner explored the consequences of activities done in solitude.

The argued that relation of solitary activities to feelings of loneliness and life satisfaction depends on whether individuals feel autonomous rather than controlled about spending time alone.

Participants (N = 108) reported the percentage of waking time they spent in solitude per day and completed measures of attachment styles, motivation for solitary activities, loneliness, and well-being. The results suggest that relative autonomy is important regardless of one's decision to act or not to act. The results also emphasize the importance of autonomous social behaviour.

New Developments

Principles of SDT have been applied in many domains of life, e.g., job demands; parenting; teaching; and health. Besides the domains mentioned above, self-determination theory research has been widely applied to the field of sports.

SDT and Exercise

Murcia, Roman, Galindo, Alonso and Gonzalez-Cutre looked at the influence of peers on enjoyment in exercise. Specifically, the researchers looked at the effect of motivational climate generated by peers on exercisers by analyzing data collected through questionnaires and rating scales. The assessment included evaluation of motivational climate, basic psychological needs satisfaction, levels of self-determination and self-regulation (amotivation, external, introjected, identified and intrinsic regulation) and also the assessment of the level of satisfaction and enjoyment in exercising.

Data analysis revealed that a climate in which the peers are supportive and there is an emphasis on cooperation, effort and personal improvement, influences variables like basic psychological needs, motivation and enjoyment. The task climate positively predicted the three basic psychological needs (competence, autonomy and relatedness) and so positively predicted self-determined motivation. Task climate and the resulting self-determination were also found to positively influence level of enjoyment the exercisers experienced during the activity.

SDT and Awareness

Awareness has always been associated with autonomous functioning; however it was only recently that the SDT researchers incorporated the idea of mindfulness and its relationship with autonomous functioning and emotional wellbeing in their research.

Brown and Ryan conducted a series of five experiments to study mindfulness: They defined mindfulness as open, undivided attention to what is happening within as well as around oneself.

From their experiments, the authors concluded that when individuals act mindfully, their actions are consistent with their values and interest. Also, there is a possibility that being autonomous and performing an action because it is enjoyable to oneself increases mindful attention to one's actions.

Vitality and self-regulation

Another area of interest for SDT researchers is the relationship between subjective vitality and self-regulation. Ryan and Deci define vitality as energy available to the self, either directly or indirectly, from basic psychological needs. This energy allows individuals to act autonomously.

Many theorists have posited that self-regulation depletes energy but SDT researchers have proposed and demonstrated that only controlled regulation depletes energy, autonomous regulation can actually be vitalizing.

SDT and Education

A recent study by Hyungshim Jang in which the capacity of two different theoretical models of motivation were used to explain why an externally provided rationale for doing a particular assignment often helps in a student's motivation, engagement, and learning during relatively uninteresting learning activities.

Undergraduate students ($N = 136$; 108 women, 28 men) worked on a relatively uninteresting short lesson after either receiving or not receiving a rationale. Students who received the rationale showed greater interest, work ethic, and determination.

Structural equation modelling was used to test three alternative explanatory models to understand why the rationale produced such benefits:

1. An identified regulation model based on self-determination theory
2. An interest regulation model based on interest-enhancing strategies research
3. An additive model that integrated both models.

The data fit all three models; but only the model based on self-determination theory helped students to engage and learn. Findings show the role that externally provided rationales can play in helping students generate the motivation they need to engage in and learn from uninteresting, but personally important, material.

The importance of these findings to those in the field of education is that when teachers try to find ways to promote student's motivation during relatively uninteresting learning activities, they can successfully do so by promoting the value of the task. One way teachers can help students value what they may deem "uninteresting" is by providing a rationale that identifies the lesson's otherwise hidden value, helps students understand why the lesson is genuinely worth their effort, and communicates why the lesson can be expected to be useful to them.

An example of SDT and education are Sudbury Model schools where people decide for themselves how to spend their days. In these schools, students of all ages determine what they will do, as well as when, how, and where they will do it. This freedom is at the heart of the school; it belongs to the students as their right, not to be violated. The fundamental premises of the school are simple: that all people are curious by nature; that the most efficient, long-lasting, and profound learning takes place when started and pursued by the learner;

that all people are creative if they are allowed to develop their unique talents; that age-mixing among students promotes growth in all members of the group; and that freedom is essential to the development of personal responsibility.

In practice this means that students initiate all their own activities and create their own environments. The physical plant, the staff, and the equipment are there for the students to use as the need arises. The school provides a setting in which students are independent, are trusted, and are treated as responsible people; and a community in which students are exposed to the complexities of life in the framework of a participatory democracy. Sudbury schools do not perform and do not offer evaluations, assessments, or recommendations, asserting that they do not rate people, and that school is not a judge; comparing students to each other, or to some standard that has been set is for them a violation of the student's right to privacy and to self-determination. Students decide for themselves how to measure their progress as self-starting learners as a process of self-evaluation: real lifelong learning and the proper educational evaluation for the 21st century, they adduce.

Self-determination Theory and Alcohol Use

According to self-determination theory, individuals who attribute their actions to external circumstances rather than internal mechanisms are far more likely to succumb to peer pressure. In contrast, individuals who consider themselves autonomous tend to be initiators of actions rather than followers. Research examining the relationship between self-determination theory and alcohol use among college students has indicated that individuals with the former criteria for decision making are associated with greater alcohol consumption and drinking as a function of social pressure. For instance, in a study conducted by Knee and Neighbours, external factors in the individuals who claim to not be motivated by internal factors were found to be associated with drinking for extrinsic reasons, and with stronger perceptions of peer pressure, which in turn was related to heavier alcohol use. Given the evidence suggesting a positive association between an outward motivation and drinking, and the potential role of perceived social influence in this association, understanding the precise nature of this relationship seems important. Further, it may be hypothesized that the relationship between self-determination and drinking may be mediated to some extent by the perceived approval of others.

Self-determination Theory and Motivational Interviewing

Motivational Interviewing (MI) is a popular approach to positive behavioural change. Used initially in the area of addiction (Miller & Rollnick, 2002) it is now used for a wider range of issues. It is a client-centred method that doesn't persuade or coerce patients to change and instead attempts to explore and resolve their ambivalent feelings, which allows them to choose themselves whether to change or not.

Markland, Ryan, Tobin, and Rollnick believe that SDT provides a framework behind how and the reasons why MI works. They believe that MI provides an autonomy-supportive atmosphere, which allows clients to find their own source of motivation and achieve their own success (in terms of overcoming addiction). Patients randomly assigned to an MI treatment group found the setting to be more autonomy-supportive than those in a regular support group.

Self-determination Theory and Environmental Behaviours

Several studies explored the link between self-determination theory and environmental behaviours to determine the role of intrinsic motivation for environmental behaviour performance and to account for the lack of success of current intervention strategies.

Motivation Towards the Environment Scale

Environmental attitudes and knowledge are not good predictors of behaviour. Self-determination theory suggests that motivation can predict behaviour performance. Pelletier et al. (1998) constructed a scale of motivation for environmental behaviour, which consists of 4x6 statements (4 statements for each type of motivation on the SDT motivation scale: intrinsic, integrated, identified, introjected, external, and amotivation) responding to a question 'Why are you doing things for the environment?'. Each item is scored on a 1-7 Likert scale. Utilizing MTES, Villacorta (2003) demonstrates a correlation between environmental concerns and intrinsic motivations together with peer and parental support; further, intrinsically motivated behaviours tend to persist longer.

Environmental Amotivation

Pelletier et al. (1999) shows that four personal beliefs, helplessness, strategy, capacity, and effort, lead to greater amotivation, while self-determination has an inverse relationship with amotivation. The Amotivation towards the Environment Scale measures the four reasons for amotivation by answering a question 'Why are you not doing things for the environment?'. The participants rank 16 total statements (four in each category of amotivation) on a 1-7 Likert scale.

Intervention Strategies Based on SDT

Intervention strategies have to be effective in bridging the gap between attitudes and behaviours. Monetary incentives, persuasive communication, and convenience are often successful in the short term, but when the intervention is removed, behaviour is discontinued. In the long run, such intervention strategies are therefore expensive and difficult to maintain.

Self-determination theory explains that environmental behaviour that is not motivated intrinsically is not persistent. On the other hand, when self-determination is high, behaviour is more likely to occur repeatedly. The importance of intrinsic motivation is particularly apparent with more difficult behaviours. While they are less likely to be performed in general, people with high internal motivation are more likely to perform them more frequently than people with low intrinsic motivation. 5 Subjects scoring high on intrinsic motivation and supporting ecological well-being also reported high level of happiness.

According to Osbaldiston and Sheldon (2003), autonomy perceived by an individual leads to an increased frequency of environmental behaviour performance. In their study, 162 university students chose an environmental goal and performed it for a week. Perceived autonomy, success in performing chosen behaviour, and their future intention to continue were measured. The results suggested that people with higher degree of self-perceived autonomy successfully perform behaviours and are more likely to do so in the long-term.

Based on the connection between self-determination theory and environmental behaviours, Pelletier et al. suggest that successful intervention should emphasize self-determined motivation for performing environmental behaviours.

8

Reversal Theory

Reversal theory is a theory of personality, motivation and emotion in the field of psychology. It focuses on the dynamic qualities of normal human experience to describe how a person regularly reverses between psychological states, reflecting their motivational style and the meaning they attach to a given situation at a given time. For example, sometimes a roller coaster seems exciting; other times, it may cause anxiety. Sometimes a crying baby creates sympathy; other times it causes irritation. The theory distinctively proposes that human experience is structurally organized into metamotivational domains, of which four have been identified. Each domain consists of a pair of opposing values or motives, so that only one of each pair can be experienced in any given moment. Reversal theory has been developed primarily by British psychologist Dr. Michael J. Apter since its inception in the mid-1970s by Dr. Apter and psychiatrist Dr. Ken Smith. The theory has been researched, developed and applied extensively.

Domains

Reversal theory is organized around a series of metamotivational states, organized into four pairs called "domains". Each pair in a domain represent two opposite forms of motivation - only one state in each pair can be active at a time. We reverse between the states in each pair depending on a number of factors, including our inherent tendency to adopt one style over the other.

The four pairs (or domains) are as follows:

- Means-Ends - The two states in the first pair are called "Telic" (or "Serious") and "Paratelic" (or "Playful") and refer to whether one is motivated by achievement and future goals, or the enjoyment of process in the moment.

- Rules - The next two states are called "Conforming" and "Rebellious" (or "Negativistic") and refer to whether one enjoys operating within rules and expectations; or whether one wishes to be free and push against these structures.
- Transactions - The next two states are called "Mastery" and "Sympathy" and relate to whether one is motivated by transacting power and control; or by care and compassion.
- Relationships - The final two states are called "Autic" (or "Self") and "Alloic" (or "Other") and refer to whether one is motivated by self interests (personal accountability and responsibility) or by the interests of others (altruism and transcendence).

Reversals and Emotion

The primary emphasis of Reversal Theory lies in the concept of reversals - by "triggering" a reversal between states, we can change the meaning attributed to the situation. What seemed serious before, can suddenly feel exciting with the right change in situation or mindset. Reversals can be created by changing a situation, reframing it, role playing, or using specific symbols or props that invoke a specific state (e.g., a toy can help trigger the Paratelic/Playful state; the image of a traffic sign may invoke the Conforming state).

Reversal Theory links the motivational states above to emotion by proposing that if one is in a state and things are going well, positive emotions result; if the needs of the state are not fulfilled, negative emotions result.

Dominance

Reversal Theory introduced the term *dominance* to make the motivational styles being a testable factor in psychometrics, so as to expand its application regions. *Dominance* means the tendency that an individual has to be one kind of person or another over time. An individual may reverse into a paretelic state, but if he or she is telic dominant, he or she will easily reverse into telic states. This term distinguished the Reversal theory from the traditional trait theory, namely, one's personality is not a permanent asset but a reversing tendency changing in accordance to the environment etc.

History, Use and Instrumentation

Reversal Theory was first proposed in the mid-1970s, by K.C.P. Smith and Michael Apter. Since that time, research using the theory has been conducted in the areas of sports performance and psychology, addiction management, health, business/management, and other areas.

While Reversal Theory has been actively researched in academic circles for the last thirty years, it has more recently entered a more public sphere of use by trainers and consultants for purposes of leadership and team development, and sports counselling.

A number of instruments have been created to measure Reversal Theory phenomena. While many of these focus on dominance (which states are more prevalent for a person over time), others attempt to capture the pheomena of the reversals themselves (how people's states shift in specific situations).

Psychometrics Tools in Reversal Theory

Since the formulation of Reversal theory psychometric instruments were developed to test the motivational styles. An early documented such instrument was *The Telic Dominance Scale* developed by Murgatroyd, Rushton, Apter & Ray in 1978. This scale was aimed primarily at assessing Telic Dominance.

The current Apter Motivational Style Profile (AMSP) is administered by practitioners trained at Apter International.

Co-counselling

Co-counselling (spelled co-counselling in American English) is a grassroots method of personal change based on reciprocal peer counselling. It uses simple methods. Time is shared equally and the essential requirement of the person taking their turn in the role of counsellor is to do their best to listen and give their full attention to the other person. It is not a discussion; the aim is to support the person in the client role to work through their own issues in a mainly self-directed way.

Co-counselling was originally formulated in the early 1950s by the American Harvey Jackins through a combination of his personal experiences gained through a wide range of counselling experience. Jackins founded the Re-evaluation Counselling (RC) Communities, with headquarters in Seattle, Washington, United States. His son, Tim Jackins, is currently the international leader of Re-evaluation Counselling and its main affiliates.

There are a number of smaller, separate, independent organizations that have resulted from breakaways from, or re-workings of, Re-evaluation Counselling. The principal one of these is Co-Counselling International (CCI).

Keeping the Vocational in its Place

This paper explores the problematic place of the concept of the 'vocational' in contemporary educational discourses. The tensions are seen to lie between discourses that place the vocational at the bottom of a hierarchy of knowledge and value, and discourses concerning expectations for the vocational. It is argued that these tensions flow from a mistaken view of the vocational and vocational knowledge, especially those based on polarisations of behaviour and codification of the knowledge that is implied. The paper reviews research findings on workplace activities and discusses them in terms of theoretical concepts about the development of meaning. The findings are interpreted as supporting the need to restore the vocational to its rightful place, as central to the ways in which individuals make meaning by engaging in significant activity.

Background

It is argued in this chapter that the place that is given to the concept of the 'vocational' in contemporary learning discourses is mistaken on a number of counts. There is a number of discourses that one can examine to reveal the place of the vocational in contemporary society. For instance, one can look at:

- Institutional structures and forms of governance;
- The range and titles of awards given to programmes offered;
- The options available to learners and streaming;
- Forms of accreditation, credit transfer and articulation;
- Access and entry requirements;
- Policy documents, ways in which legitimacy is afforded, and funding procedures; and the like.

Wherever one looks, the place for the vocational appears to be similar – the vocational is at the bottom of a hierarchy of knowledge and value, it is a stream of learning available to the 'lower achiever', it is governed in a paternalistic way with highly circumscribed degrees of freedom over content and process, it is legitimated solely in industrial and other utilitarian terms, rather than in the connections among different kinds of meaning-making, and it is preserved for occupations of lower status. Accordingly, for the vocational, the term, *training*, is often used as a synonym – connoting that it is reserved for those capable only of imitation, procedures and carefully guided behaviour. While there are rhetorical statements about redressing the undervaluing of vocational education, governance, funding, accreditation and other kinds of regulation keep it firmly in this place and separate from the discourses of other kinds of learning.

On the other hand, other forms of learning are usually denoted *education* or *development* – general, academic or higher education, and professional development – and associated with the development of explicitly valued and codified forms of knowledge that are promoted as abstracted, theoretical and generalisable. These forms of education, notwithstanding the recent massification of higher education, are reserved for the 'more able'; future academics and the professional-bound; those who it is thought can think, analyse, generate and critically reflect; those whom it is thought need these capacities in their further academic pursuits or professional work; and those who can be trusted with access to such privileged ways of knowing and being.

Yet this tidy 'place' for the vocational, with its efficient stratification of society and its benefits, and with its political appeal, is beset with tensions. Even in occupations targeted by vocational education and training, there is a call from industry for mature and sensible action. These latter kinds of statements of needs somehow break through the instrumental discourse, despite their unstated focus on the individual and development. Moreover, such occupations are often a cornerstone of economic activity with high demands for adaptability and generativity, presenting an interesting dilemma for industry with its proclaimed focus on predictability and efficiency in training. Still further, high incomes are often earned in many such occupations, much to the chagrin of their 'betters'. Additionally, some vocational graduates also do well in university courses to which they can articulate; while many higher achievers are often unsatisfied with the relationships between their higher education studies and their professional pursuits – again to the consternation of the doyens of theoretical knowledge.

Structure

Many have sought to explain such tensions as these in political and sociological terms, drawing attention to class divisions in society and the assumed associated division of hand and mind that has its origins in the social structures of ancient Greece and modern England (Young, 1995). In this paper, the origins of such tensions are put aside and the tensions themselves are examined in terms of how knowledge is acquired through the development of *sense* and *meaning* (Leont'ev, 1981) in activity.

Firstly, some data from research studies of workplace activities is presented. The research findings are then interpreted as follows. Based on Dewey's work, the vocational is taken to provide the significance needed in making meaning. Then, the relationship between the cultural historical concept of activity and the development of meaning is argued, and the relationship between particularisation of meaning and coherent knowledge is discussed. This interpretation involves criticising common notions of the superiority of so-called abstract, de-contextualised, theoretical and generalisable knowledge. An argument is advanced that the vocational is central to meaning making and it is concluded that the vocational is currently misplaced.

Some Research Evidence

The research reviewed here is drawn mainly from two studies of workplace activity (Beven, 1997a; Stevenson, 1996), one in the motel industry and the other in the airline industry. Four analyses are reviewed. These analyses serve to illuminate the nature of knowing in these workplace activities, but it is clear that the conclusions drawn would apply to knowing in other kinds of workplace activities in other fields.

These studies demonstrate how it is problematic to use terms like 'knowledge', 'competence' or 'skill' to denote the meanings that are immanent in workplace activity. This is, firstly, because the term 'knowledge' connotes a stable, codified mental entity that can exist outside the activity in which it is found. Secondly, the term 'competence' is problematic because it connotes a codifiable ability that can be transported to other contexts; and that this ability is purely procedural or behavioural with no propositional or conceptual aspects. Similarly the term 'skill' is also restricted in these ways, emphasising the repetitive nature of specific behaviour. For these reasons, the successful actions that individuals demonstrate in workplace activity are here called 'meaning making'. The studies that are reviewed are of activities involving the information technology, literacies, problem solving, and values, all supposed key/core skills/competencies.

Using Information Technology

Firstly let's consider Fred Beven's (1996, 1997a, 1997b, 2002) analyses of activity in the front offices of motels and in the customer service role in airlines.

Consider the following kinds of activities that he observed in the Front Offices of all of the motels (Beven, 1996, 2002):

- Creating a new reservation,
- Creating a walk-up Check-in,
- Updating a Check-in,
- Updating a reservation,
- Processing a Check-out,
- Processing Phone call charges,
- Processing Breakfast charges,
- Cancelling a reservation,
- Cancelling charges,
- Saving data,
- Sorting data.

Undertaking these activities was meaningful to the people working in the office – they knew what they were doing, could see how it contributed to the collective work of the group and directed their actions at the collective purpose and they undertook the work with efficiency. They could talk about the activity in the kinds of terms given. They engaged in the activity confidently and could discuss it with the researchers.

A challenge to an educator or curriculum developer is to describe this activity in terms that promote the teaching of the supposed underlying capacities, and to ensure that what is taught can be related to the broader worlds of work and living. The challenge is to describe the 'knowledge' that is involved. However, when we, as observers, try to unmask the 'knowledge' that is involved, we are introducing other ways of rendering meaning. For instance, as Beven observes, a first level of categorisation, such an attempt may look like the following:

Entering New Data Sets

- Creating a new reservation
- Creating a 'walk-up' Check-in

Updating Data Sets

- Processing a Check-in
- Updating a reservation
- Processing a Check-out
- processing additional data

Phone calls, B'fast)

Removing Data Sets

- Cancelling a reservation
- Cancelling charges

Saving Data Sets

- System determined

Sorting Data Sets

- System determined

At a second level of categorisation, as Beven posits, this might all be called Data Manipulation: Being able to add, change and delete (manipulate) data in a database (according to the Shelly and Cashman's (1990) taxonomy of information processing skills). And this may then be constructed as a component of an overall depiction of information skills/competence/knowledge as shown in table.

The question, then, is: Are these descriptions meaningful and teachable– do they represent the ways in which individuals constructed meaning in the working activities that were observed? Is the 'knowledge' denoted by these labels transferable as such between motel sites, or between motel work and other work requiring interaction with databases? My contention is that while it is possible for an observer to construct these labels, abstracted from practice, and relate them to the terminology of other discourses (e.g. the wider information technology discourse), there are many problems involved, as follows.

It is a mistake to believe that knowledge as represented by the label exists, that it is generic or that it is directly transferable. That is, it is a big leap to thinking that a person 'has data manipulation knowledge' because that person can use software in a particular motel computing system in undertaking such actions as: *Creating a new reservation*, *Creating a walk-up Check-in*, *Updating a Check-in*, *Updating a reservation*, *Processing a Check-out*, *Processing Phone call charges*, *Processing Breakfast charges*, *Cancelling a reservation*, *Cancelling charges*, *Saving data*, *Sorting data*.

It is an even bigger leap to think that the capacities that are involved in, or derived from their meaning-making (called competence or 'knowledge' or by some other term) can be used directly in another motel (especially since the study found that each motel had quite different menu structures, and different key combinations were needed for apparently similar functions; and each motel had its own culture of practice). It is also a step too far to think that the competent front office motel worker would recognise their own capacities in the terms used in codifying 'data manipulation knowledge' or as a 'key competency' or 'new basic'. And, of course, one also cannot assume that the worker could automatically and directly transfer such 'data manipulation knowledge'/'competence' to another industry or to other professions using data manipulation.

Rather, what exists is: the capacity to undertake observed actions in that activity system, mediated by the artefacts and culture of that system and in concert with the collective object of that system. This meaningfulness may well be able to be connected to other ways of rendering meaning that an observer might recognise, but there is learning involved in developing a learner's capacity to access and make meaningful those other ways of understanding. Moreover, it needs to be noted that this so-called data manipulation knowledge was integrally related to other sources of meaning in their work often differentiated into such categories as values (Stevenson, 2002), literacy (Searle 2002), numeracy (Kanes, 2002) and problem-solving (Middleton, 2002); and its recognition as a particular category of knowledge is therefore arbitrary.

Of course, the opposite is also true of 'conceptual' meanings transacted outside of such vocational pursuits. It is one thing to think that one knows conceptually what is intended by *Updating a reservation*, or even being familiar with the concepts of a database, but it is another to have the meaning that comes from successful engagement with the instruments in practice in achieving this collective purpose. And as argued throughout this paper, this is the central place of the vocational, to provide opportunities for discerning significance, developing these meanings, and using them to make other kinds of knowing meaningful.

Literacy

Secondly, consider Jean Searle's (1997) work on literacy in customer service work in airlines. Literacy is often vaunted as a generic competence, which can be taught once for all. It is often seen as something you acquire through reading in school and take with you to whatever context demands it. After all, in Australia, we now have 'literacy nets' where we can capture and remediate those who have not 'bolted on' the required literacies by the prescribed age level.

Using data from the work of Customer Service Staff in an Airline, Jean Searle (1997, personal communication) related the following transcripts to literacy concepts as given in brackets.

I'm just sorting through some of the telexes we had in the what we call the 'bring up file' which is 'today's actions'...and seeing what status they have; whether they have been completely repaired or whether we still need to do anything with it. Just checking where they're up to basically. (Sorting, Checking status)

These telexes are delivered to our printer and they're put away. Mostly we try to action them as soon as they come up or on the same day at the very least...and then they're put into the day that's relevant to the day that they'll actually be like the ticket issued or the person'll turn up. (Filing by date of future use)

This is...a Personal Name Record (PNR) - a computer record and this (telex) is just a hard copy of exactly the same thing. So what I am doing now is just checking to make sure that that hasn't changed. It's what is reflected here. This is actually a frequent flyer redemption ticket which is frequent flyer points so they don't actually pay for the ticket. Taxes and things still apply so we'll still need to get some money...for that. I better correct details. Sometimes these are set up for us by Frequent Flyer and sometimes not. At the moment I'm going to have to correct some of the details because they're not quite right. (Identify PNR, Checking for changes, Identifying incorrect details)

I haven't actually changed anything yet...What they haven't done is put this into the normal format...so I'm just correcting the format so we're ready to go. It will still print this way...but the autoticket readers that we have in our revenue department...won't work on what they've put in...it's got to be in the standard format. (Recognises incorrect genre)

[So, that's saying] Brisbane, Sydney to Canberra no charge and then back to Brisbane no charge. Actually I should have (( )). So that's Brisbane to Canberra and then Sydney to Brisbane. (Reading as decoding + encoding data)

These NUC's are what we call 'Neutral Units of Construction' which are basically the techniques that is used. So no matter what country you're working from...you still end up with...I've run out of line space...you will always end up with the same numbers, theoretically. (Numeracy) (NUCs used instead of calculating exchange rates)

This is all coded in formats, which bear no relation at all to how it will appear on the ticket format. (Knowledge of genres)

...there are four lines available now. It was just making sure that there wasn't already something on line two because you can't put something there...you can't make an 'original entry' if is something already there. You can't make a 'change entry' if there isn't something there. (Prior knowledge of rules of data-entry)

This code here is for the taxes which are the same here (telex). There you go...that's the response you get when you try to put in something with a change if it's not already there. These keyboards are quite different to the other ones so it does take a bit of getting used to. Also the logic by which they operate is a little different...You can't do it like Word Perfect or Lotus and just go straight to the end... I shouldn't have that in there. What I'm looking to do is just make sure that everything's there so that the ticket can just be printed straight off the itinerary...I'll check the itinerary once more. So now we can just save that. (De-coding, Problems with transfer of generic knowledge)

If the passenger turns up here now, we will just retrieve the PNR and say "Is this what you want to do?" and then tell them that they've got to pay the taxes, tell them how much it will be, enter the form of payment for the taxes and print the ticket. (Generic structure of spoken language transaction)

As for the information technology examples, the assignment of labels, derived from another way of making meaning, in a different (e.g. academic or school-based) activity system, seems intuitively helpful. That is, we can label the demonstrated literacies in terms such as genre, de-coding, filing, sorting, checking, identifying etc, just as we could find 'catch-phrases' for using databases. This codification may certainly assist as a curriculum development device, but only if the traps are understood and avoided. As advanced earlier, these are the traps of thinking that knowledge comes in such labelled parcels, that people know in those ways, that the 'knowledge' exists outside the activity system where it is evidenced, that making connections between meaningful activity and these labels is automatic and doesn't have to be learned, and that the situated activities corresponding to these labels is an indicator of 'knowledge' that is held independently of the activity and can be transferred to other activity systems.

Problem Solving

As a third example consider the key competence of problem solving found in almost every list made of skills that are promoted as common across all kinds of work. For example, problem solving was listed in Australia, as a Key Competence (Mayer, 1992) and seen to involve 'clarification and framing of problems', 'achievement of appropriate completion', 'anticipation of problems, sources and contexts', and 'evaluation of outcomes and processes' (p. 37). At a more specific level, its description at Performance Level 3 is: 'establishes major factors affecting processes and outcomes', 'adapts and manipulates processes to achieve appropriate completion', 'anticipates problems and opportunities, and the conditions under which they arise', and 'establishes and uses criteria for judging effectiveness or processes and outcomes' (p. 38).

Presumably, it is intended that these capacities be observed in action, checked off a check list, and attested to; and that we can feel assured that we have developed a 'problem-solver'. It is against this and other attempts at codifying the important engagement in problem solving in vocations and other activities, that the workplace activities were appraised by Middelton (1997).

Middleton (1997, p. 109) cites the following example from his analysis of transcripts of the kinds of problems that airline customer service staff encounter.

They had lost the tickets in Melbourne, had a replacement ticket done incorrectly in Melbourne, came to Brisbane, changed the itinerary with their agent in Auckland who then suggested to them what the new cost was going to be and how it was going to be actioned. They took this to a [booking centre] in Brisbane, who reissued it, they gave them an open cheque value who then, after they reissued and got it back, claimed that they were overcharged about eight hundred New Zealand dollars, who then, after that time, went and changed the itinerary again on the Sunday morning. They came to me Sunday afternoon to have this done and gave me an hour to do it, and the check-in closes half an hour before the flight goes.

As Middleton argues, this problem solving could be categorised in a number of ways. For instance it could be seen as a problem of handling time pressure, or as a problem of handling problems with a large search space, or as a problem with contradictory elements. That is, the activity being reported has many of the characteristics of what are called complex problems. Complex problems are problems one commonly finds in everyday activities as opposed to textbooks. As Middleton argues, for these problems, the givens are not clear and they often have to be found or made, the path forward is not clear and often requires new skills; and there is usually more than one kind of satisfactory solution, from which the most optimal needs to be chosen.

It is argued here that it is a mistake to believe that all problems of time pressure are the same, can be solved in the same way and have the same solution; or that a person can demonstrate a situated capacity to solve a problem that is transferable to all problems with opaque or contradictory goals. It is not feasible to think of vocational teaching in terms of how knowledge under the label of 'problem-solving' can be taught; or to certify that a person is competent at 'problem-solving'. Moreover, it doesn't make sense to see such capacities separately from those numeracy, literacy and information processing. In short, problem solving is dependent on the mediating artefacts, rules and division of labour in an activity system? More broadly, the kinds of problem-solving found in workplace activity raise the question of what is the place of the vocational in the acquisition of such abilities?

Values

As a final example of data drawn from workplace activity studies, consider the question of values, often ignored in discussions of knowledge and competence and in discussions of vocational education. In Stevenson's (1996, 2002) analysis of normative aspects of the work in motel front offices, the kinds of norms illustrated in the following transcript extracts were found. These were references to actions or to reflections on actions (inferred norm given in brackets) e.g.

Mainly the guest...because they're paying us. So I always try to make everyone's stay the most pleasant. If they have a problem, I always apologise for whatever the problem was, and I try and make it better. I either shout 'em a () drink at the bar or something - giving them a ten percent discount or something - making them a XXXXX member, or... (Keep customer happy)

Anything to do with revenue comes second as far as posting breakfasts, making sure that you've got those charges on there. Ensuring that the accounts are charged to the right place, ensuring that the right person is paying for the right thing (Extract all charges)

Rudeness to the point where he actually slid the iron across the top of the desk when he came in. "Would you iron your husband's shirts with that", and I didn't have the heart to tell him I've got an ironing lady. But I just said "What can we do to fix the problem?" Eventually I said that to him - "What - can- we-do-to-fix-the-problem?" That sort of stumped him, because I wasn't giving him any problem. I was saying tell me what you want and you will have it. Like I said earlier this morning, if you're nice to people, they find it harder to be awful back.

So I thought there's no way he's going to upset me, I'm not going to let you upset me. And I just kept being nice to him. (Maintain appearances)

Again, while a conceptual label could be imputed for norms in the various individual activities as suggested by the labels in brackets, and for clusters of the inferred norm, as suggested in the right hand column, one has to remember, that these labels are contrived by an observer and are arbitrary in that they may not make sense to the workers, they may not have meaning outside the activity system, they may not have the same meaning in other activity systems, and an individual who has demonstrated activity that appears to relate to one or other of these labels, may not in fact be able to demonstrate such activity in another activity system. For example, *being responsible* does not always translate into *leaving the office staffed* and *leaving the office staffed* does not always indicate fully having a competence of *responsibility*, that will carry forward to other settings and situations. Moreover, other researchers have developed different lists of workplace 'attitudes'. For example, consider those found by Cathy Stasz et al (1996), who identified attitudes such as Independence, Cooperation, Mutual Respect, Friendliness, Integrity and Vigilance and clustered them into groups related to the Task/Organisation, Community of Practice, and Quality Standards.

As for the other studies reviewed here, workplace activity was found to have the following characteristics:

- Meaning was provided by the collective object and activity directed at that object
- Meaning was derived from the significance of the activity
- Meaning was mediated by artefacts and implicit and explicit values and rules
- Meaning was related to the various roles and responsibilities of people engaged in the activity
- Meaning was culturally defined
- Meaning was holistic, transcending traditional boundaries like literacy, numeracy, problem-solving and values
- Meaning did not exist as some kind of conceptual label in an individual's mind
- Meaning was constructed in and for activity
- While conceptual labels could be constructed by observers to describe and cluster workplace actions and activities, this

> process involved abstraction from the culture, artefacts and objects of those activities; and would not necessarily be meaningful in those terms to those engaged in the activities, let alone transferable to other activities.

From the data, it is argued that the vocational, along with other everyday activities should be assigned a central place in the making of meaning. It is argued that it is through such activities as those observed in these and other studies, engaging with everyday objects, that a person makes and re-makes meaning, as different ways of knowing are tested for their utility in collective pursuits. Three theoretical perspective are relevant to this argument, as follows. It is in vocational activity that significance is discerned as meaning grows out of matters of concern (Dewey, 1916). It is here that the struggles between assimilation and accommodation (Piaget, 1952) take place, and equilibrium is reached. It is here that ideas are particularised and particulars are brought into coherence with larger wholes (Van Oers, 1998).

In short, it is argued that the place for the vocational is as a central activity in being, living, working, and learning. As one pursues such activities, one makes meaning in each of them and inter-connects these meanings so that contextualised particulars become part of a coherent whole. It is here that individuals find and develop real literacy, values, problem solving capacities and information technology capacities. Let's consider the confluence between these three theoretical perspectives as a basis for interpreting the data, in turn.

Vocations

Dewey (1916, p. 307) Conceptualised Vocation as Follows: "A vocation means nothing but such a direction of life activities as renders them perceptibly significant to a person, because of the consequences they accomplish, and also useful to his [sic] associates. Recognising that we each pursue many such callings in our lives, often simultaneously:

We must avoid not only limitation of conception of vocation to the occupations where immediately tangible commodities are produced, but also the notion that vocational are distributed in an exclusive way, one and only one to each person. In the first place, each individual has of necessity a variety of callings, in each of which he should be intelligently effective; and in the second place any one occupations loses its meaning and becomes a routine keeping busy at something in the degree in which it is isolated from other interests. *(i)* No one is just an artist and nothing else, and in so far as one approximates that condition, he is so much the less developed human being; he is some kind of monstrosity. He must, at some period of his life, be a member of a family; he must have friends and companions; he must either support himself or be supported by others, and thus he has a business career. He is a member of some organized political unit, and so on. We naturally *name* his vocation from that one of his callings which distinguishes him, rather than from those which he has in common with all others. But we should not allow ourselves to be so subject to words as to ignore and virtually deny his other callings when it comes to consideration of the vocational phases of education.

That is, the vocational activities that were observed in the studies reviewed here are central to the individuals and who they are, but were drawn from only one of the various vocations in which that individual would participate. It is the vocational activity and the significance of the role of the individual in that activity that allows meaning to be constructed.

An Activity Theory View of Vocations and Meaning

In terms of activity theory, Dewey's passages would be taken to indicate that an individual is a member of many activity systems simultaneously. It is the relationships among these activity systems that are the source of multivoicedness in the objects of activity systems. In paid work, for example, the ways in which an individual engages with the collective object depend on how they construct meaning on the activity in relationship to other sources of meaning in their lives. That is, 'employability skills' (Department of Education, Science and Training, 2005, p. 20) are not divorced in some way from the ways in which individuals make meaning in other walks of life; and ironically, nor are they common across working situations as the term 'cross-industry skills' (ibid, p. 20), key competence (Mayer, 1992) or other such phrases might imply.

Meaning

Certainly, meaning can be taken to be a mental phenomenon (even though it is derived from, belongs to, and is utilised in activity). As Dewey wrote:

"the difference between an adjustment to a physical stimulus and a *mental* act is that the latter involves response to a thing in its *meaning*; the former does not. When things have a meaning for us, we *mean* (intend, propose) what we do: when they do not, we act blindly, unconsciously, unintelligently.

In both kinds of responsive adjustment, our activities are directed or controlled. But in the merely blind response, direction is also blind. There may be training, but there is no education(Habits) possess us, rather than we them.... Unless we become aware of what they accomplish, and pass judgement on the worth of the result, we do not control them(pp. 29-30)"

That is, Dewey is stating that meaningful activity is not non-mental. It is not robotic behaviour, responding to training. But the relationship between meaning and action is ever present as Dewey goes on:

> "Mind *as a concrete thing is precisely the power to understand things in terms of the use made of them; a socialized mind is the power to understand them in terms of the use to which they are turned in joint or shared situations" (p. 33)*

With this emphasis on the collective purpose, this passage could have been written by Leont'ev (1981).

So, these workers, pursuing their vocations, were not acting blindly or robotically, they were constructing meaning. They were understanding what they were doing in relationship to what others were doing in these joint and shared situations.

Particularisation and Generalisation of Meaning

The same kinds of general principles can be drawn from more recent work, based on Activity Theory, on the nature of generalisation. Van Oers (1998) argues that there is no such thing as decontextualised knowledge. That is, all meaning is related to context. Instead of applying decontextualised general knowledge to new situations, Van Oers believes that we re-contextualise knowledge when meeting the demands of new situations. For Van Oers, context is "never universally given nor objectively determined by the characteristics of the situation itself [...]. Contextualising is a process of adding new meaning to a given situation in order to characterise the situation in terms of what could (or should) be done" (Van Oers 1998;481-482).

For these reasons, as Van Oers argues, generalisation is better seen as recontextualisation, rather than decontextualisation, where recontextualisation involves the "contextualising of something in a new way" (ibid; 483) to achieve new ends. That is, in any activity, e.g.

in the course of a vocation, an individual is re-contextualising meanings brought from previous activity. These meanings are not directly transplantable. They are interpreted for the new situation, tested out when engaging with the object, and re-made. The re-made meanings are appraised over time for their coherence with what works in other kinds of activity. This analysis accords with Bartlett's (1932) original concept of schemas as active, dynamic and interactive.

Van Oers (1998) views context as providing for 'two essential processes: it supports the *particularisation of meanings* by constraining the cognitive process of meaning construction, and by eliminating ambiguities or concurrent meanings that do not seem to be adequate at a given moment; on the other hand, context also prevents this particularised meaning from being isolated as it *brings about coherence* with a larger whole (Van Oers 1998, p. 475). That is, the individual relates particular meanings with utility in one activity systems with meanings that have utility in other activity systems.

Using Van Oers' analysis, meanings made in the workplaces of these studies would be more than a 'mental surrounding' (i.e. the contextualisation of new concepts in terms of supposed propositional networks in memory). They would also be more than concepts and procedures surrounded by features of a static setting. Rather meaning was derived from an active intersection of motive, objective, experience (past and present) and environment or circumstance.

In the studies reviewed here, then, the workers were engaged in particularising their meanings in terms of the various characteristics of the activity systems in which they were working. In communicating about this work, they were attempting to make connections with coherent wholes that they also understood. Sometimes these connections may have appeared somewhat awkward to the observer (as revealed in the transcripts), but they bring, to the fore, how idiosyncratic real meaning is and what a struggle it can be to translate it into language.

Implications

Some implications for vocational educators are as follows. It is not public meanings, rendered in words, often as theoretical concepts, that are central to the ways in which individuals come to understand the world, themselves and work. Nor are these public meanings directly accessible, nor do they provide the best vehicles for learning. On the other hand, the meanings that come from engaging in vocational pursuits are direct (Phenix, 1964), accessible and powerful. They enable action and activity in that context. However, meanings that are derived in working can be inert unless they are connected with wider public ways of knowing. It is important for individuals from all walks of life, with all kinds of working aspirations to develop not only both ways of knowing, but good connections between them.

The place of the vocational, then is manifold. It has a central place in accessing and making meaning, derived from the significance of the activity to the individual and to the collective. However, it is not self-sufficient. The making of meaning in vocations needs to be coherently related to everyday meanings and meanings that have been derived from the ongoing record of human activity. Neither meanings used for public transactions about human affairs, not the meanings that individuals derive from significant vocational activity are independent. Individuals can access public meanings only if they make sense, and they will make sense only through experience with them. Significant personal involvement in activity is the best and most effective source of the kinds of experience that are needed. Moreover, significant personal involvement in activity is the primary source of meaning making, from childhood.

It is therefore a mistake to stratify learners into the vocational and the non-vocational as if this made sense, as if it were desirable and as if it would promote learning for either group. Displacing the vocational from a coherent relationship with publicly codified meanings has serious consequences for learners who are denoted vocational, as well as for learners who are denied the value of the vocational.

The 1994 Reform

The Norwegian upper secondary reform of 1994 (R-94) gave all young people age 16 - 19 statuary right to education and training, changed the educational structure radically and implemented an ambitious reform referred to as "the content reform".

The new structure of training as a skilled worker is a 2 + system, 2 years in school and "the plus" as different options. The ordinary road to trade certification is 2 years in school and 2 years apprenticeship (2 + 2). The apprenticeship period contains one year education and one year productive work. With lack of apprenticeship places schools offer a third, work based year of education. Particular streams give all or most training in school. For all streams an alternative third year is offered as a matriculation year. Matriculation level may also be obtained in additional courses to trade certificate.

One main goal was "to create a flexible system that provides a general education and a wide range of skills and prepares the pupils for a society in constant change" (KUF (Ministry of Education, Research and Church Affairs), 1994, F-2600E). Another main goal to be mentioned here was to educate not only for employment, but also for devising new jobs – that is to acquire an entrepreneurial outlook. The need to renew the educational content was acknowledged – a content that should imply a broader concept of knowledge (KUF, 1994 "Reform '94:This is our solution", F-3073E).

The solutions to these challenges were various, these are central: Curricula that included basic modules preparing for matriculation (general academic subjects) and for skilled trades and working life (vocational subjects) were developed – a dual system. A common Core Curriculum should provide for a holistic platform as well as further citizenship and students' personal development. Organisation of the content and learning methods were focused, project work became mandatory.

In 1999 evaluation reports on the first Reform94 cohort came forth and a White Paper dealing with results and further actions was released (St meld no 32 (1998-99) Videregående opplæring). Special interest was given to integration of learning processes in a system designed to develop dual qualification.

For our purpose here the following brief conclusions made of the authoritative "follow up group" may be mentioned:

"The new structure seems to function quite well and the students' statutory rights work according to the intentions.

"When it comes to the "Content-Reform", there is a lot more to do. Especially does the day to day work in the classrooms and workshops seem to be much as before.

The day to day work ...

The White Paper (St meld no 32 (1998-99)) gives special attention to the problems of content development, and states that

- *the broad concept of knowledge will be further developed*
- *vocational theory and practice should be better integrated*
- *project works are still mandatory.*

And the pedagogical recommendations are holistic learning, multidisciplinary approaches, relevance and active problem solving, involving the whole person in the learning process and cooperation with working life. This underlines the change of focus from an academic knowledge tradition to a broader and more work and experiential based concept of knowledge and competence. The vocational learning tradition – to learn theory through practical work – should be continued.

To improve integrative learning the White Paper points to areas important for development of the "day to day" working methods at school:

- Contextualising general subjects to vocational subjects
- Improve the integration of theoretical and practical knowledge
- Evaluation systems that to a greater extent integrate practice and theory in certification tests and exams
- Problem based tasks for assessment should be considered and developed by evaluation boards and schools
- Differentiation according to students abilities and work place learning should be furthered

As a central learning method project work and project organised learning tasks may imply many, or most, of the above qualities.

The evaluation system was said to be central in the "Content Reform". The Department of Education provided evaluation guides with examples for all streams. An interesting aspect is that new assessment systems was thought to generate positive results by influencing school organisation and school culture.

Goals, Learning Processes and Outcomes

Throughout the Reform94-process attention was given to the differences between "knowledge" and "competence". Competence is about "the will and power to use your knowledge: to employ it in specific situations as the base of action, creativity, intuition, ethical based considerations, and for best judgement" (from the White Paper, my translation).

How should this kind of competency be obtained? Above we have seen the weight placed on "the content reform" with new ways of organising learning tasks, new assessment systems and with a shift of focus from more academic traditions. Before the start of R94, "self-reliant learning" was an educational principle causing uncertainty for teachers and pupils in upper secondary. In the reformed school the need for – and how to practice it becomes clearer.

Processes of self-reliant learning are seen as important to develop action competence, entrepreneurship and similar learning outcomes.

With mandatory project works and demand for "Self-reliant learning", more responsibility for own learning, planning and cooperative work are given to students. The reform asks for changes that fundamentally affect "student – teacher" relations, as well as that "between – teachers". The demand on teachers to develop "Self-reliant learners" strengthen the force towards new roles in school. The organisational changes may affect areas like:

- the teaching-learning structure set in time and space
- the structure of roles: assignment of power and responsibility
- the cultural "script"

Learning methods and new responsibilities mentioned above generally require a lot from the teachers in perceiving they roles in new ways. Evidences from the evaluation showed most teachers to be positive to the reform, and able to identify themselves with the new roles for the teachers. My impression is that teachers are concerned with these requirements, and are working to meet them.

Teachers are subject to new learning in order to meet the challenges of the content reform. But it is necessary to know more about pupils' learning processes to know what line teachers' competency should develop along. The following is a look into some upper secondary pupils' world, to see how these foundation - course pupils perceived own learning processes and needs when working "self-reliant". This case study was designed to follow teachers and pupils through all project phases in order to map and analyse interaction between teaching strategies and learning processes (1997). Some central points from pupils' recording of own learning and needs and from my observations:

- Pupils experience teachers as central for own functions as "self-reliant learners"
- Teachers' goals seem to affect pupils' attention and direction of work, and expectations about evaluation, even if pupils (or teachers?) were not always aware the influence
- Pupils reported different learning outcomes in project work and in daily classroom work, and were, to a degree, aware the relevance of these differences
- Pupils perceived own learning processes in project work to integrate factors we may relate to development of "action competence"
- Pupils reported feelings of "being in charge" and "learning about working life" as positive outcomes of project work

- Pupils experienced and formulated need for guidance both in project work and when working with practical skills
- Pupils experienced and formulated own need for teachers to be thrusting, supporting and cooperating

Pupils' responses showed that they experienced project work to be empowering and challenging. But they also were aware own personal and social needs to be met to make the learning a positive process. In their own evaluation of social and communicative learning, subject learning and learning about self as well as developing personal competencies they reported competencies like being able to "plan, share and take responsibility", to "listen, support and solve problems /conflicts", to "plan, learn and carry through own responsibilities". These kind of reflections about own learning outcomes showed that they involved themselves actively in own learning processes. The above recording shows how central teachers' role is for these kind of learning strategies, it also shows pupils to be able to sort out own need for guidance and support from the teachers, given the opportunity to reflect and evaluate – and to take responsibility.

From R94 to Year 2001

The evaluation reports of 1999 (data collection finished in 1998) found little changes in the structure of everyday school life, like cooperative relations between teachers and pupils or teacher and teacher, and it stated "the day to day work" in classrooms as well as the formal evaluation work to be pretty much the same as before. Still, seven years are not a long time for such a radical reform in an institution like the educational system, but we may ask if the "Content Reform" is moving in the right direction. Do schools educate pupils into competent citizens and skilled workers with the will and power to use their (broad and dynamic) competency also as entrepreneurs?

There is not new systematic evaluation for the whole system for us to look to - any qualified answers to the above question will obviously be tentative or maybe impossible. And schools are different, often very different, so are leaders – and leaders are important for developing their schools.

One initiative that followed the R94 evaluation was that KUF (Dep. Of Education ...) invited schools to join into innovation works on different areas. One such area is "pupils' responsibility for own learning and for contributing to plan, carry out and evaluate their learning". Many schools are carrying out innovation works in order to develop own organisation and teaching, covering a wide range of "the day to day work" in schools. When starting such processes they necessarily generate changes in their work-culture, too.

At our teacher education many of our MA students are doing research on different kind of innovation projects at own school. Some of these projects may give interesting results.

The White Paper points to the tradition in vocational education of theory learning through practical work. Many vocational teachers aware the need of organising learning tasks, included project works, more as "real work tasks", and many of them are aware the need for good guidance this implies.

To-day more young grown ups are back to vocational streams along with the ordinary age group. This may be positive for the class situation and benefit learning processes and also contribute to change the roles between teachers and pupils.

The White Paper calls upon the roles of school leaders as modernisers of the structure and culture of today's school system in order to develop the qualities needed to meet requirement and demands for a changing world.

So what do it take for schools to develop into the kind of organisation asked for - that provides learning arenas with dynamic and qualitative dimensions that develop and empower the individual learner. Should schools try to develop such organisations – and learning cultures alone, or should it collaborate with working life and other parts of society? It may still be to early for conclusions about the direction the "content reform" may take. It may also be necessary to focus on questions about learning cultures, identity formation and self-actualisation, processes that generate "will and power".

Constructivism (Philosophy of Education)

Constructivism is a perspective in education that explains how knowledge is constructed in the human being when information comes into contact with existing knowledge that had been developed by experiences. It has roots in cognitive psychology and biology and an approach to education that lays emphasis on the ways knowledge is created in order to adapt to the world. Constructs are the different types of filters we choose to place over our realities to change our reality from chaos to order. Von Glasersfeld describes constructivism as "a theory of knowledge with roots in philosophy, psychology, and cybernetics". Constructivism has implications for the theory of instruction. Discovery, hands-on, experiential, collaborative, project-based, and task-based learning are a number of applications that base teaching and learning on constructivism.

Historical and Theoretical Roots

According to Kliebard, John Dewey created an active intellectual learning environment in his laboratory school, which existed between 1896 and 1904. The neuroscientist James Zull has argued that the sort of active learning Dewey fostered is the way people naturally learn. Active learning conditionalizes knowledge through experiential learning.

Smith writes that John Dewey believed education must engage with and expand experience; those methods used to educate must provide for exploration, thinking, and reflection; and that interaction with the environment is necessary for learning; also, that democracy should be upheld in the educational process. Dewey advocates the learning process of experiential learning through real life experience to construct and conditionalize knowledge, which is consistent with the Constructivists.

Maria Montessori's key points contribute to both Humanism and Constructivism. However, she emphasizes the value of experiential learning to conditionalize knowledge:

"Scientific observation has established that education is not what the teacher gives; education is a natural process spontaneously carried out by the human individual, and is acquired not by listening to words but by experiences upon the environment. The task of the teacher becomes that of preparing a series of motives of cultural activity, spread over a specially prepared environment, and then refraining from obtrusive interference. Human teachers can only help the great work that is being done, as servants help the master. Doing so, they will be witnesses to the unfolding of the human soul and to the rising of a New Man who will not be a victim of events, but will have the clarity of vision to direct and shape the future of human society."

Montessori's beliefs are consistent with the Constructivists in that she advocates a learning process which allows a student to experience an environment first-hand, thereby, giving the student reliable, trust-worthy knowledge.

David Kolb, in his books *Learning Style Inventory Technical Manual* and *Experiential Learning*, emphasizes the importance of conditionalized knowledge through experiential learning.

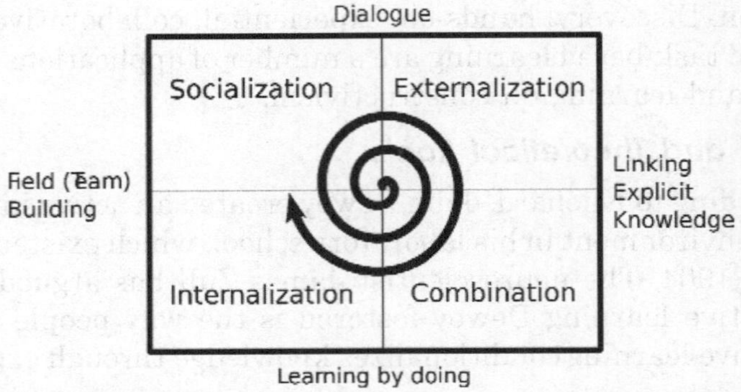

David A. Kolb and Roger Fry created the Kolb & Fry Model out of four elements: concrete experience, observation—reflection, the formation of abstract concepts, and testing in new situations. They represented these in the famous experiential learning circle [after Kurt Lewin]. Kolb and Fry (1975) argue that the learning cycle can begin at any point, and that it should really be approached as a continuous spiral.

Kolb's beliefs are consistent with the Constructivists in that he includes Concrete Experience as part of the learning process and requires a student to test knowledge by acting upon the environment, thereby giving the student reliable, trust-worthy [conditionalized] knowledge. Kolb's work closely parallels recent work in the field of neuroscience, exemplified in the writings of James Zull.

Epistemology

Reich observed that "constructivists do not look for copies or mirrorings of an outer reality in the human mind", but instead they rather see humans as "observers, participants, and agents who actively generate and transform the patterns through which they construct the realities that fit them." This view echoes the works of George Berkeley and Giambattista Vico, as well as more recent philosopher Ernst von Glasersfeld. Contemporary psychologist Jerome Bruner, based in part on the ideas of constructivists like Lev Vygotsky, has asserted that all reality is a narrative construction in the imagination of individuals.

The Nature of the Learner

The type of learner is self-directed, creative, and innovative. The purpose in education is to become creative and innovative through analysis, conceptualizations, and synthesis of prior experience to create new knowledge. The educator's role is to mentor the learner during heuristic problem solving of ill-defined problems by enabling quested learning that may modify existing knowledge and allow for creation of new knowledge. The learning goal is the highest order of learning: heuristic problem solving, metacognitive knowledge, creativity, and originality.

Social constructivism not only acknowledges the uniqueness and complexity of the learner, but actually encourages, utilizes and rewards it as an integral part of the learning process (Wertsch, 1997).

The Importance of the Background and Culture of the Learner

Social constructivism or socioculturalism encourages the learner to arrive at his or her version of the truth, influenced by his or her background, culture or embedded worldview. Historical developments and symbol systems, such as language, logic, and mathematical systems, are inherited by the learner as a member of a particular culture and these are learned throughout the learner's life. This also stresses the importance of the nature of the learner's social interaction with knowledgeable members of the society. Without the social interaction with other more knowledgeable people, it is impossible to acquire social meaning of important symbol systems and learn how to utilize them. Young children develop their thinking abilities by interacting with other children, adults, and the physical world. From the social constructivist viewpoint, it is thus important to take into account the background and culture of the learner throughout the learning process, as this background also helps to shape the knowledge and truth that the learner creates, discovers, and attains in the learning process (Wertsch, 1997).

The Responsibility for Learning

Furthermore, it is argued that the responsibility of learning should reside increasingly with the learner (Glasersfeld, 1989). Social constructivism thus emphasizes the importance of the learner being actively involved in the learning process, unlike previous educational viewpoints where the responsibility rested with the instructor to teach and where the learner played a passive, receptive role.

It is called the "Harkness" discussion method because it was developed at Phillips Exeter Academy with funds donated in the 1930s by Edward Harkness. This is also named after the Harkness table and involves students seated in a circle, motivating and controlling their own discussion. The teacher acts as little as possible. Perhaps the teacher's only function is to observe, although he/she might begin or shift or even direct a discussion. The students get it rolling, direct it, and focus it. They act as a team, cooperatively, to make it work. They all participate, but not in a competitive way. Rather, they all share in the responsibility and the goals, much as any members share in any team sport. Although the goals of any discussion will change depending upon what's under discussion, some goals will always be the same: to illuminate the subject, to unravel its mysteries, to interpret and share and learn from other points of view, to piece together the puzzle using everyone's contribution. Discussion skills are important. Everyone must be aware of how to get this discussion rolling and keep it rolling and interesting. Just as in any sport, a number of skills are necessary to work on and use at appropriate times. Everyone is expected to contribute by using these skills.

The Motivation for Learning

Another crucial assumption regarding the nature of the learner concerns the level and source of motivation for learning. According to Von Glasersfeld (1989) sustaining motivation to learn is strongly dependent on the learner's confidence in his or her potential for learning. These feelings of competence and belief in their potential to solve new problems, are derived from first-hand experience of mastery of problems in the past and are much more powerful than any external acknowledgement and motivation (Prawat and Floden, 1994). This links up with Vygotsky's "zone of proximal development" (ZPD) (Vygotsky, 1935) where learners are challenged within close proximity to, yet slightly above, their current level of development. By experiencing the successful completion of challenging tasks, learners gain confidence and motivation to embark on more complex challenges.

The Role of the Instructor

Instructors as Facilitators

According to the social constructivism approach, instructors have to adapt to the role of facilitators and not teachers (Bauersfeld, 1995). Whereas a teacher gives a didactic lecture that covers the subject matter, a facilitator helps the learner to get to his or her own understanding of the content. In the former scenario the learner plays a passive role and in the latter scenario the learner plays an active role in the learning process. The emphasis thus turns away from the instructor and the content, and towards the learner (Gamoran, Secada, & Marrett, 1998). This dramatic change of role implies that a facilitator needs to display a totally different set of skills than a teacher

(Brownstein 2001). A teacher tells, a facilitator asks; a teacher lectures from the front, a facilitator supports from the back; a teacher gives answers according to a set curriculum, a facilitator provides guidelines and creates the environment for the learner to arrive at his or her own conclusions; a teacher mostly gives a monologue, a facilitator is in continuous dialogue with the learners (Rhodes and Bellamy, 1999). A facilitator should also be able to adapt the learning experience 'in mid-air' by taking the initiative to steer the learning experience to where the learners want to create value.

The learning environment should also be designed to support and challenge the learner's thinking (Di Vesta, 1987). While it is advocated to give the learner ownership of the problem and solution process, it is not the case that any activity or any solution is adequate. The critical goal is to support the learner in becoming an effective thinker. This can be achieved by assuming multiple roles, such as consultant and coach.

A few strategies for cooperative learning include

- Reciprocal Questioning: students work together to ask and answer questions
- Jigsaw Classroom: students become "experts" on one part of a group project and teach it to the others in their group
- Structured Controversies: Students work together to research a particular controversy (Woolfolk 2010)

The Nature of the Learning Process

Learning is an Active, Social Process: Social constructivism, strongly influenced by Vygotsky's (1978) work, suggests that knowledge is first constructed in a social context and is then taken up by individuals (Bruning et al., 1999; M. Cole, 1991; Eggan & Kauchak, 2004). According to social constructivists, the process of sharing each person's point of view—called collaborative elaboration (Meter & Stevens, 2000)—results in learners building understanding together that wouldn't be possible alone (Greeno et al., 1996).

Scholars view learning as active, where learners should learn to discover principles, concepts and facts for themselves. They support guesswork and intuitive thinking in learners (Brown et al.1989; Ackerman 1996). For the social constructivist, the real is not there to be found: it does not pre- exist, but we invent it in a social context. Kukla (2000) argues that we construct the real through our actions. People together, as members of a group, invent the properties of the world. Other constructivist scholars agree with this and hold that we make meanings through acting with each other and the environment. Knowledge is thus a product of humans and is a product of our social nature, and of our culture. (Ernest 1991; Prawat and Floden 1994). McMahon (1997) agrees that learning is a social process. He further states that learning is neither a private thing, nor a passive shaping by outside forces. Instead, meaning occurs through social actions. Vygotsky (1978) also highlighted the convergence of the social and active roles in learning. He said that the greatest moment in our mind's development occurs when speech and action converge. Before, these were seen as independent lines of development. Through actions a child constructs meaning for itself, while speech connects this meaning with the common world of her/his culture.

Dynamic Interaction Between Task, Instructor and Learner

A further characteristic of the role of the facilitator in the social constructivist viewpoint, is that the instructor and the learners are equally involved in learning from each other as well (Holt and Willard-Holt 2000). This means that the learning experience is both subjective and objective and requires that the instructor's culture, values and background become an essential part of the interplay between learners and tasks. Learners compare their version of the truth with that of the instructor and fellow learners to get to a new, socially tested version of truth (Kukla 2000). The task or problem is thus the interface between the instructor and the learner (McMahon 1997). This creates a dynamic interaction between task, instructor and learner. This entails that learners and instructors should develop an awareness of each other's viewpoints and then look to their own beliefs, standards and values, thus being both subjective and objective at the same time (Savery 1994).

Some studies argue for the importance of mentoring in the process of learning (Archee and Duin 1995; Brown et al. 1989). The social constructivist model thus emphasizes the importance of the relationship between the student and the instructor in the learning process. Some learning approaches that could harbour this interactive learning include reciprocal teaching, peer collaboration, cognitive apprenticeship, problem-based instruction, web quests, anchored instruction and other approaches that involve learning with others.

Collaboration Among Learners

Learners with different skills and backgrounds should collaborate in tasks and discussions to arrive at a shared understanding of the truth in a specific field (Duffy and Jonassen 1992). Most social constructivism models, such as that proposed by Duffy and Jonassen (1992), also stress the need for collaboration among learners, in direct contradiction to traditional competitive approaches. One Vygotskian notion that has significant implications for peer collaboration, is that of the ZPD. Defined as the distance between the actual developmental level as determined by independent problem-solving and the level of potential development as determined through problem-solving under adult guidance or in collaboration with more capable peers, it differs from the fixed biological nature of Piaget's stages of development. Through a process of 'scaffolding' a learner can be extended beyond the limitations of physical maturation to the extent that the development process lags behind the learning process (Vygotsky 1978).

Learning by Teaching (LdL) as Constructivist Method

If students have to present and train new contents with their classmates, a non-linear process of collective knowledge-construction will be set up.

The Importance of Context

The social constructivist paradigm views the context in which the learning occurs as central to the learning itself (McMahon 1997).

Underlying the notion of the learner as an active processor is "the assumption that there is no one set of generalised learning laws with each law applying to all domains" (Di Vesta 1987:208). Decontextualised knowledge does not give us the skills to apply our understandings to authentic tasks because, as Duffy and Jonassen (1992) indicated, we are not working with the concept in the complex environment and experiencing the complex interrelationships in that environment that determine how and when the concept is used. The contrary case is that of authentic or situated learning, where the student takes part in activities directly relevant to the application of learning and that takes place within a culture similar to the applied setting (Brown et al. 1989). Cognitive apprenticeship has been proposed as an effective constructivist model of learning that attempts to "enculturate students into authentic practices through activity and social interaction in a way similar to that evident, and evidently successful, in craft apprenticeship" (Ackerman 1996:25).

Holt and Willard-Holt (2000) emphasize the concept of dynamic assessment, which is a way of assessing the true potential of learners that differs significantly from conventional tests. Here the essentially interactive nature of learning is extended to the process of assessment. Rather than viewing assessment as a process carried out by a single person, such as an instructor, it is seen as a two-way process involving interaction between both instructor and learner. The role of the assessor becomes one of dialogue with the persons being assessed to find out their current level of performance on any task, and of sharing with them possible ways in which that performance might be improved on a subsequent occasion. Thus, assessment and learning are seen as inextricably linked and not separate processes (Holt and Willard-Holt 2000).

According to this viewpoint, instructors should see assessment as a continuous and interactive process that measures the achievement of the learner, the quality of the learning experience and courseware. The feedback created by the assessment process serves as a direct foundation for further development.

The Selection, Scope, and Sequencing of the Subject Matter:

Knowledge Should be Discovered as an Integrated Whole: Knowledge should not be divided into different subjects or compartments, but should be discovered as an integrated whole (McMahon 1997; Di Vesta 1987).

This also again underlines the importance of the context in which learning is presented (Brown et al. 1989). The world, in which the learner needs to operate, does not approach one in the form of different subjects, but as a complex myriad of facts, problems, dimensions, and perceptions (Ackerman 1996).

Engaging and Challenging the Learner

Learners should constantly be challenged with tasks that refer to skills and knowledge just beyond their current level of mastery. This captures their motivation and builds on previous successes to enhance learner confidence (Brownstein 2001). This is in line with Vygotsky's ZPD, which can be described as the distance between the actual developmental level (as determined by independent problem-solving) and the level of potential development (as determined through problem-solving under adult guidance or in collaboration with more capable peers) (Vygotsky 1978).

Vygotsky (1978) further claimed that instruction is good only when it proceeds ahead of development. Then it awakens and rouses to life an entire set of functions in the stage of maturing, which lie in the ZPD. It is in this way that instruction plays an extremely important role in development. To fully engage and challenge the learner, the task and learning environment should reflect the complexity of the environment that the learner should be able to function in at the end of learning. Learners must not only have ownership of the learning or problem-solving process, but of the problem itself (Derry 1999).

Where the sequencing of subject matter is concerned, it is the constructivist viewpoint that the foundations of any subject may be taught to anybody at any stage in some form (Duffy and Jonassen 1992). This means that instructors should first introduce the basic ideas that give life and form to any topic or subject area, and then revisit and build upon these repeatedly. This notion has been extensively used in curricula.

It is also important for instructors to realize that although a curriculum may be set down for them, it inevitably becomes shaped by them into something personal that reflects their own belief systems, their thoughts and feelings about both the content of their instruction and their learners (Rhodes and Bellamy 1999). Thus, the learning experience becomes a shared enterprise. The emotions and life contexts of those involved in the learning process must therefore be considered as an integral part of learning. The goal of the learner is central in considering what is learned (Brown et al. 1989; Ackerman 1996).

The Structuredness of the Learning Process

It is important to achieve the right balance between the degree of structure and flexibility that is built into the learning process. Savery (1994) contends that the more structured the learning environment, the harder it is for the learners to construct meaning based on their conceptual understandings. A facilitator should structure the learning experience just enough to make sure that the students get clear guidance and parameters within which to achieve the learning objectives, yet the learning experience should be open and free enough to allow for the learners to discover, enjoy, interact and arrive at their own, socially verified version of truth.

In Adult Learning

Constructivist ideas have been used to inform adult education. Whereas pedagogy applies to the education of children, adult educators often speak instead of andragogy or heutagogy. Methods must take account of differences in learning, due to the fact that adults have many more experiences (schema (psychology)) and previously existing neurological structures. Approaches based on constructivism stress the importance of mechanisms for mutual planning, diagnosis of learner needs and interests, cooperative learning climate, sequential activities for achieving the objectives, formulation of learning objectives based on the diagnosed needs and interests.

Personal relevance of the content, involvement of the learner in the process, and deeper understanding of underlying concepts are some of the intersections between emphases in constructivism and adult learning principles.

Instructional Strategies Based on Constructivism

Various approaches in instructional strategies derive from constructivist theory. They usually suggest that learning is accomplished best using a hands-on approach. Learners learn by experimentation, and not by being told what will happen, and are left to make their own inferences, discoveries and conclusions.

Research and Evidence Supporting Constructivism

Hmelo-Silver, Duncan, & Chinn cite several studies supporting the success of the constructivist problem-based and enquiry learning methods. For example, they describe a project called GenScope, an enquiry-based science software application. Students using the GenScope software showed significant gains over the control groups, with the largest gains shown in students from basic courses.

Hmelo-Silver et al. also cite a large study by Geier on the effectiveness of enquiry-based science for middle school students, as demonstrated by their performance on high-stakes standardized tests. The improvement was 14% for the first cohort of students and 13% for the second cohort. This study also found that enquiry-based teaching methods greatly reduced the achievement gap for African-American students.

Guthrie et al. (2004) compared three instructional methods for third-grade reading: a traditional approach, a strategies instruction only approach, and an approach with strategies instruction and constructivist motivation techniques including student choices, collaboration, and hands-on activities. The constructivist approach, called CORI (Concept-Oriented Reading Instruction), resulted in better student reading comprehension, cognitive strategies, and motivation.

Jong Suk Kim found that using constructivist teaching methods for 6th graders resulted in better student achievement than traditional teaching methods. This study also found that students preferred constructivist methods over traditional ones. However, Kim did not find any difference in student self-concept or learning strategies between those taught by constructivist or traditional methods.

Doðru and Kalender compared science classrooms using traditional teacher-centred approaches to those using student-centred, constructivist methods. In their initial test of student performance immediately following the lessons, they found no significant difference between traditional and constructivist methods. However, in the follow-up assessment 15 days later, students who learned through constructivist methods showed better retention of knowledge than those who learned through traditional methods.

Criticism of Educational Constructivism

Several cognitive psychologists and educators have questioned the central claims of constructivism. It is argued that constructivist theories are misleading or contradict known findings. Matthews (1993) attempts to sketch the influence of constructivism in current mathematics and science education, aiming to indicate how pervasive Aristotle's empiricist epistemology is within it and what problems constructivism faces on that account.

In the neo-Piagetian theories of cognitive development it is maintained that learning at any age depends upon the processing and representational resources available at this particular age. That is, it is maintained that if the requirements of the concept to be understood exceeds the available processing efficiency and working memory resources then the concept is by definition not learnable. This attitude towards learning impedes the learner from understanding essential theoretical concepts or, in other words, reasoning. Therefore, no matter how active a child is during learning, to learn the child must operate in a learning environment that meets the developmental and individual learning constraints that are characteristic for the child's age and this child's possible deviations from her age's norm. If this condition is not met, construction goes astray.

Several educators have also questioned the effectiveness of this approach towards instructional design, especially as it applies to the development of instruction for novices(Mayer, 2004; Kirschner, Sweller, and Clark, 2006). While some constructivists argue that "learning by doing" enhances learning, critics of this instructional strategy argue that little empirical evidence exists to support this statement given novice learners (Mayer, 2004; Kirschner, Sweller, and Clark, 2006).

Sweller and his colleagues argue that novices do not possess the underlying mental models, or "schemas" necessary for "learning by doing" (e.g. Sweller, 1988). Indeed, Mayer (2004) reviewed the literature and found that fifty years of empirical data do not support using the constructivist teaching technique of pure discovery; in those situations requiring discovery, he argues for the use of guided discovery instead.

Mayer (2004) argues that not all teaching techniques based on constructivism are efficient or effective for all learners, suggesting many educators misapply constructivism to use teaching techniques that require learners to be behaviourally active. He describes this inappropriate use of constructivism as the "constructivist teaching fallacy". "I refer to this interpretation as the constructivist teaching fallacy because it equates active learning with active teaching." (Mayer, 2004, p. 15). Instead Mayer proposes learners should be "cognitively active" during learning and that instructors use "guided practice."

In contrast, Kirschner *et al.* (2006) describe constructivist teaching methods as "unguided methods of instruction." They suggest more structured learning activities for learners with little to no prior knowledge. Slezak states that constructivism "is an example of fashionable but thoroughly problematic doctrines that can have little benefit for practical pedagogy or teacher education." and similar views have been stated by Meyer, Boden, Quale and others.

Kirschner *et al.* group a number of learning theories together (Discovery, Problem-Based, Experiential, and Enquiry-Based learning) and stated that highly scaffolded constructivist methods like problem-based learning and enquiry learning are ineffective. Kirschner *et al.* described several research studies that were favourable to problem-based learning given learners were provide some level of guidance and support.

Guidance as a Strategy

While there are critics of the Kirschner, Sweller, and Clark article, Sweller and his associates cover:

1. instructional designs for producing procedural learning (learning as behaviour change) (Sweller, 1988);
2. their grouping of seemingly disparate learning theories (Kirschner *et al.*, 2006) and;
3. a continuum of guidance beginning with worked examples that may be followed by practice, or transitioned to practice (Kalyuga, Ayres, Chandler, and Sweller, 2003; Renkl, Atkinson, Maier, and Staley, 2002)

Kirschner *et al.* (2006) describe worked examples as an instructional design solution for procedural learning. Clark, Nguyen, and Sweller (2006) describe this as a very effective, empirically validated method of teaching learners procedural skill acquisition. Evidence for learning by studying worked-examples, is known as the worked-example effect and has been found to be useful in many domains e.g. music, chess, athletics (Atkinson, Derry, Renkl, & Wortham, 2000); concept mapping (Hilbert & Renkl, 2007); geometry (Tarmizi and Sweller, 1988); physics, mathematics, or programming (Gerjets, Scheiter, and Catrambone, 2004).

Kirschner *et al.* (2006) describe why they group a series of seemingly disparate learning theories (Discovery, Problem-Based, Experiential, and Enquiry-Based learning). The reasoning for this grouping is because each learning theory promotes the same constructivist teaching technique—"learning by doing." While they argue "learning by doing" is useful for more knowledgeable learners, they argue this teaching technique is not useful for novices. Mayer states that it promotes behavioural activity too early in the learning process, when learners should be cognitively active (Mayer, 2004).

In addition, Sweller and his associates describe a continuum of guidance, starting with worked examples to slowly fade guidance. This continuum of faded guidance has been tested empirically to produce a series of learning effects: the worked-example effect (Sweller and Cooper, 1985), the guidance fading effect (Renkl, Atkinson, Maier, and Staley, 2002), and the expertise-reversal effect (Kalyuga, Ayres, Chandler, and Sweller, 2003).

Criticism of Discovery-based Teaching Techniques

"After a half century of advocacy associated with instruction using minimal guidance, there appears no body of research supporting the technique. In so far as there is any evidence from controlled studies, it almost uniformly supports direct, strong instructional guidance rather constructivist-based minimal guidance during the instruction of novice to intermediate learners. Even for students with considerable prior knowledge, strong guidance while learning is most often found to be equally effective as unguided approaches. Not only is unguided instruction normally less effective; there is also evidence that it may have negative results when student acquire misconceptions or incomplete or disorganized knowledge "

— *Why Minimal Guidance During Instruction Does Not Work: An Analysis of the Failure of Constructivist, Discovery, Problem-Based, Experiential, and Enquiry-Based Teaching by Kirschner, Sweller, Clark*

Mayer (2004) argues against discovery-based teaching techniques and provides an extensive review to support this argument. Mayer's arguments are against pure discovery, and are not specifically aimed at constructivism: "Nothing in this article should be construed as arguing against the view of learning as knowledge construction or against using hands-on enquiry or group discussion that promotes the process of knowledge construction in learners. The main conclusion I draw from the three research literatures I have reviewed is that it would be a mistake to interpret the current constructivist view of learning as a rationale for reviving pure discovery as a method of instruction."

Mayer's concern is how one applies discovery-based teaching techniques. He provides empirical research as evidence that discovery-based teaching techniques are inadequate. Here he cites this literature and makes his point "For example, a recent replication is research showing that students learn to become better at solving mathematics problems when they study worked-out examples rather than when they solely engage in hands-on problem solving (Sweller, 1999). Today's proponents of discovery methods, who claim to draw their support from constructivist philosophy, are making inroads into educational practice. Yet a dispassionate review of the relevant research literature shows that discovery-based practice is not as effective as guided discovery." (Mayer, 2004, p. 18)

Mayer's point is that people often misuse constructivism to promote pure discovery-based teaching techniques. He proposes that the instructional design recommendations of constructivism are too often aimed at discovery-based practice (Mayer, 2004). Sweller (1988) found evidence that practice by novices during early schema acquisition, distracts these learners with unnecessary search-based activity, when the learner's attention should be focused on understanding (acquiring schemas).

The study by Kirschner et al. from which the quote at the beginning of this section was taken has been widely cited and is important for showing the limits of minimally guided instruction. Hmelo-Silver et al. responded, pointing out that Kirschner et al. conflated constructivist teaching techniques such as enquiry learning with "discovery learning". This would agree with Mayer's viewpoint that even though constructivism as a theory and teaching techniques incorporating guidance are likely valid applications of this theory, nevertheless a tradition of misunderstanding has led to some question "pure discovery" techniques.

The argument between the use or working memory and long term memory is also important to focus on in this reference, as it argues one of the main beliefs of constructivism itself that one derives new ideas from past knowledge. “Any instructional theory that ignores the limits of working memory when dealing with novel information or ignores the disappearance of those limits when dealing with familiar information is unlikely to be effective.” (Kirschner 2006). This contrasts the belief that one can build upon ideas that are recently attained, yet also rejects the idea that one can’t combine the two.

The Math Wars and Discovery-based Teaching Techniques and Technology

The math wars controversy in the United States is an example of the type of heated debate that sometimes follows the implementation of constructivist-inspired curricula in schools. In the 1990s, mathematics textbooks based on new standards largely informed by constructivism were developed and promoted with government support. Although constructivist theory does not require eliminating instruction entirely, some textbooks seemed to recommend this extreme. Some parents and mathematicians protested the design of textbooks that omitted or de-emphasized instruction of standard mathematical methods. Supporters responded that the methods were to be eventually discovered under direction by the teacher, but since this was missing or unclear, many insisted the textbooks were designed to deliberately eliminate instruction of standard methods. In one commonly adopted text, the standard formula for the area of a circle is to be derived in the classroom, but not actually printed in the student textbook as is explained by the developers of CMP: “The student role of formulating, representing, clarifying, communicating, and reflecting on ideas leads to an increase in learning. If the format of the texts included many worked examples, the student role would then become merely reproducing these examples with small modifications.”

Similarly, this approach has been applied to reading with whole language and enquiry-based science that emphasizes the importance of *devising* rather than just performing hands-on experiments as early as the elementary grades, rather than studying facts.

In other areas of curriculum such as social studies and writing are relying more on “higher order thinking skills” rather than memorization of dates, grammar or spelling rules or reciting correct answers. Advocates of this approach counter that the constructivism does not require going to extremes, that in fact teachable moments should regularly infuse the experience with the more traditional teaching. The primary differentiation from the traditional approach being that the engagement of the students in their learning makes them more receptive to learning things at an appropriate time, rather than on a preset schedule.

Constructionist learning theory has influenced the computer science education, as well. Some educational programming languages have been created, wholly or in part, for educational use, to support the constructionist theory of Seymour Papert. These languages have been dynamically typed, and reflective. Logo was the best known of them, which is superseded by Scratch (programming language) and BYOB (programming language).

At MIT, Papert went on to create the *Epistemology and Learning Research Group* at the MIT *Architecture Machine Group* which later became the MIT Media Lab. Here, he was the developer of an original and highly influential theory on learning called constructionism, built upon the work of Jean Piaget in constructionist learning theories. Papert worked with Jean Piaget at the University of Geneva, considered the most brilliant and successful of Piaget's proteges; Piaget once said that "no as well as Papert." Papert has rethought how schools should work based on these theories of learning. Constructionism is not congruent with Constructivism.

Constructivist Learning Environments? ...for which Learners?

During the 1990s, several theorists began to study the cognitive load of novices (those with little or no prior knowledge of the subject matter) during problem solving. Cognitive load theory was applied in several contexts (Paas, 1992; Moreno & Mayer, 1999; Mousavi, Low, & Sweller, 1995; Chandler and Sweller, 1992; Sweller & Cooper, 1985; Cooper & Sweller, 1987). Based on the results of their research, these authors do not support the idea of allowing novices to interact with ill-structured learning environments. Ill-structured learning environments rely on the learner to discover problem solutions (Jonassen, 1997). Jonassen (1997) also suggested that novices be taught with "well-structured" learning environments.

Jonassen (1997) also proposed well-designed, well-structured learning environments provide scaffolding for problem-solving. Finally both Sweller and Jonassen support problem-solving scenarios for more advanced learners (Jonassen, 1997; luga, Ayres, Chandler, and Sweller, 2003).

Sweller and his associates even suggest well-structured learning environments, like those provided by worked examples, are not effective for those with more experience—this was later described as the "expertise reversal effect" (Kalyuga et al., 2003). Cognitive load theorists suggest worked examples initially, with a gradual introduction of problem solving scenarios; this is described as the "guidance fading effect" (Renkl, Atkinson, Maier, and Staley, 2002; Sweller, 2003). Each of these ideas provides more evidence for Anderson's ACT-R framework (Clark & Elen, 2006). This ACT-R framework suggests learning can begin with studying examples.

Finally Mayer states: "Thus, the contribution of psychology is to help move educational reform efforts from the fuzzy and unproductive world of educational ideology—which sometimes hides under the banner of various versions of constructivism—to the sharp and productive world of theory-based research on how people learn." (Mayer, 2004, p. 18).

Confusion Between Views

Many people confuse Constructivist (learning theory) with social constructivism. Constructivist learning theory is associated with high order learning of mature learners, androgogy or heutagogy, not early learning as discussed by the Cognitivist, Piaget or Vygotsky, whose research focused on children and sequential learning. Social constructivism is not congruent with the Constructivist learning theory. Dewey, Montessori, and Kolb represent the Constructivist learning theory where experiential learning occurs through real life experience to construct and conditionalize knowledge, and a mentor guides the mature learner. Piaget, Bruner, and Vygotsky are Cognitivist who work with young children and base their learning theories upon sequential development of mental processes scaffolded by an instructor.

There are two major strands of the constructivist perspective. These two strands, cognitive constructivism and social constructivism, are different in emphasis, but they also share many common perspectives about teaching and learning. Before looking at the differences between cognitive and social constructivists, it might be worthwhile to look at what they have in common. Jonassen's (1994) description of the general characteristics of constructivist learning environments is a succinct summary of the constructivist perspective.

Jonassen (1994) proposed that there are eight characteristics that differentiate constructivist learning environments:

1. Constructivist learning environments provide multiple representations of reality.
2. Multiple representations avoid oversimplification and represent the complexity of the real world.
3. Constructivist learning environments emphasize knowledge construction instead of knowledge reproduction.
4. Constructivist learning environments emphasize authentic tasks in a meaningful context rather than abstract instruction out of context.
5. Constructivist learning environments provide learning environments such as real-world settings or case-based learning instead of predetermined sequences of instruction.
6. Constructivist learning environments encourage thoughtful reflection on experience.
7. Constructivist learning environments"enable context- and content- dependent knowledge construction."
8. Constructivist learning environments support "collaborative construction of knowledge through social negotiation, not competition among learners for recognition."

Jonassen's eight characteristics would be supported by both social and cognitive constructivists. There is, however, a difference in the emphasis these two strands on constructivism place on each of those characteristics. In recent decades, theorists have extended the traditional focus on individual learning to address collaborative and social dimensions of learning. It is possible to see *social constructivism* as a bringing together of aspects of the work of Piaget with that of Bruner and Vygotsky (Wood 1998: 39). The term *Communal constructivism* was developed by Leask and Younie (2001) through their research on the European School Net project which demonstrated the value of peer to peer learning i.e. communal construction of new knowledge rather than social construction of knowledge as described by Vygotsky where there is a learner to teacher scaffolding relationship. Bryn Holmes in 2001 applied this to student learning as described in an early paper, "in this model, students will not simply pass through a course like water through a sieve but instead leave their own imprint in the learning process."

Role Category Questionnaire

An important key in Constructivism is the idea of the RCQ which stands for Role Category Questionnaire. This tool is a questionnaire or survey that is designed to reveal individual's cognitive complexity in accordance to their interpersonal perception. To take this one step further it is important to define exactly what cognitive complexity is. In this case cognitive complexity is the degree of ability to distinguish between personalities, no matter how obvious the personality difference may be or how minute the personality difference may be. When someone has a high level of cognitive complexity they are able to put themselves in that person's shoes and relate to them on their level, as well as better understanding the events happening around them. Researchers believe that those with more sets of constructs have an advantage of social perception skills compared to those who have only a small amount of constructs to interpret people with (Griffin 99). Delia and Burleson (constructivist theorists) define two types of people: those who think there are two kinds of people in the world and those who don't (Griffin 100). If we use this as our base then those who only view the world made up of one type of person can be coined as lackluster. Those who view more than one type of person in the world are a notch above the rest, elevated human beings able to distinguish the different characteristics amongst those they interact with. It is the degree of differences that are tested upon with the RCQ, revealing how intricate and complicated the person's mind is (Griffin 100).

Person-Centred Messages

The main premise of Constructivism is the ability to construct person-centred messages to accomplish one's goal. Griffin explains a person-centred message is a "tailor-made message for a specific individual and context" (Griffin 101). If one is able to carry through with their person-centred message then they are able to manipulate their original message in mind and adjust it to whatever level the person they are talking to will best understand it.

Problem-based Learning

Problem-based learning follows a constructivist perspective in learning since the role of the instructor is to guide and challenge the learning process. Students learn about a subject through the experience of problem solving.

Learning Theory (Education)

Learning theories are conceptual frameworks that describe how information is absorbed, processed, and retained during learning. Cognitive, emotional, and environmental influences, as well as prior experience, all play a part in how understanding, or a world view, is acquired or changed, and knowledge and skills retained. Behaviourists look at learning as an aspect of conditioning and will advocate a system of rewards and targets in education. Educators who embrace cognitive theory believe that the definition of learning as a change in behaviour is too narrow and prefer to study the learner rather than the environment, and in particular the complexities of human memory. Humanists emphasize the importance of self-knowledge and relationships in the learning process. Those who advocate constructivism believe that a learner's ability to learn relies to a large extent on what he already knows and understands, and that the acquisition of knowledge should be an individually tailored process of construction.

Outside the realm of educational psychology, techniques to directly observe the functioning of the brain during the learning process, such as event-related potential and functional magnetic resonance imaging, are used in educational neuroscience. As of 2012, such studies are beginning to support a theory of multiple intelligences, where learning is seen as the interaction between dozens of different functional areas in the brain, each with their own individual strengths and weaknesses in any particular human learner.

Behaviourism (Philosophy of Education)

Behaviourism, as a perspective in education, is based on a change in knowledge through controlled stimulus/response conditioning. This type of learner is dependent upon an instructor for acquisition of knowledge. The instructor must demonstrate factual knowledge, then observe, measure, and modify behavioural changes in specified direction. This type of learning is a conditioned response or rote memorization of facts, assertions, rules, laws, and terminology. The correct response is achieved through stimulation of senses. The focus of intelligence development is visual/spatial, musical/rhythmic, and bodily/ kinesthetic intelligence. The purpose in education is to help a learner build initial schema by adopting knowledge from an instructor through use of the learner's senses. This learning goal is the lowest order learning: factual knowledge, skill development, and training.

Behaviourists

Etienne Bonnot de Condillac, 1754/1982, 1756 Condillac's works include Essays on the origin of human knowledge (1746), Treatise on the system (1749), Treatise on the senses (1754), and an extensive course of study in 13 volumes [Cours d'études] (1767–1773) that emphasize the importance of using the senses to increase learning. Condillac's work is significant to the field of education because he is among the first to emphasize the importance of manipulating matter as well as ideas to construct behavioural learning. Condillac advocates a sense luscious environment that provides a stimulus response-learning environment consistent with Behaviourism.

Jean Marc Gaspard Itard 1801/1962; Itard, sometimes called the father of special education, believed that anyone could be educated [as evidenced in his work with The Wild Boy of Aveyron published in 1801, 1806/1962]. Itard did not accomplish the goals he set for himself to train the wild boy; however, he did bring about an inclusive philosophy of education that emphasized the use of objects as training tools to develop sensual skills leading to cognitive development. Through his attempts to train the wild boy, Itard learned that positive reinforcement [rather than punishment] was an effective means of obtaining necessary behavioural responses. This stimulus response method is consistent with Behaviourism.

B. F. Skinner, 1954 Skinner's key point is the need of immediate reinforcement to strengthen behaviour. The use of mechanical devices to strengthen behaviour in 1954 foreshadows the use of computers in today's classrooms. According to Skinner, organisms learn by making changes in their environments. Skinner noted, "A significant change in behaviour is often obvious as the result of a single reinforcement." Maintaining behaviour strength requires gradual contingency changes and skillful use of schedules in conjunction with positive reinforcement. Competition has adverse consequences for all but one participant, where as cooperation provides positive reinforcement for many. Cooperation is, therefore, preferable to competition. In addition, cooperation can be set up more easily than competition. The progressive education reform movement sought to use immediate positive consequences to modify or strengthen desired behaviour, rather than relying on adverse events such as the teacher's displeasure, ridicule of classmates, low grades, poor showing in competition, talks from the principal, or the birch rod from caregivers. When instructors use adverse events rather than positive reinforcement, the results are anxieties, boredom, and aggression rather than reinforced learning. A revision of classroom practices is needed. A single teacher cannot devote all of his or her time to providing positive reinforcement to only one child A rough estimate of the contingencies required for successful behaviour in mathematics during the first four years of school is approximately 25,000 contingencies. The responses to be set up far exceed the essential minimum provided by the homework or in class drills used in current classroom practice. Reinforcement devices have been designed that can provide immediate feedback to a pupil at work for an appropriate time each day. Using these devices allows a child to progress at his own rate. Skinner's prophetic defense of mechanical devices states, "A country which annually produces millions of refrigerators, dish-washers, automatic washing-machines, automatic clothes-driers, and automatic garbage disposers can certainly afford the equipment necessary to educate its citizens to high standards of competence in the most effective way". After 50 years, Skinner's argument may still be drawn on to support the use of laptops as educational tools in today's classrooms. Laptops provide the immediate positive reinforcement that Skinner refers to, in addition to linking a learner to the information highway of the new millennium. Typical of the Behaviourist, Skinner uses a sense luscious environment to stimulate learning.

Instructional Theory

An instructional theory is "a theory that offers explicit guidance on how to better help people learn and develop." Instructional theories focus on how to structure material for promoting the education of human beings.

Instructional Theory vs Learning Theory

Instructional theory differs from learning theory in that a learning theory *describes* how learning takes place and an instructional theory *prescribes* how to better help people learn. Learning theories often inform instructional theory. General theoretical stances for learning theories are: behaviourism (learning as response acquisition), cognitivism (learning as knowledge acquisition), humanism (interpersonal and intrapersonal learning), and constructivism (learning as knowledge construction).

Terms Used in Instructional Theory

Andragogy an•dra•go•gy [an-druh-goh-jee, -goj-ee] Originally used by Alexander Kapp (a German educator) in 1833, andragogy was developed into a theory of adult education by the American educator Malcolm Knowles. The word comes from the Greek íäñï (andro-) or "man" [rather than åíÞëéê which means "adult"] and Üãù (ago) to "lead"; so it literally means, "to lead the man." Learning strategies focus on mature learning with a mentor that encourages, enables the mature learner by providing access to appropriate resources, and refrains from obtrusive interference.

Diaskagogy di•as•ka•go•gy [dee-es-kuh-goh-jee, -goj-ee] A neologism developed for preschool education that focuses on schema building: Caregiver demonstrates factual knowledge. Caregiver observes, measures, and modifies behavioural change in specified direction. The teacher/child relationship in this scenario is one of entertainment. The word for entertainer in Greek is äéáóêåäÜæùí (the Latin translation is genius). When combined with the Greek Üãù (ago) to "lead," the construed meaning is "to lead the entertainer" and the transliteration from the Greek leads to the word Diaskagogy di•as•ka•go•gy [dee-es-kuh-goh-jee, -goj-ee] which could be used to describe Preschool education.

Heutagogy heu•ta•go•gy [hyoo-tah-goh-jee, -goj-ee] The term, attributed to Stewart Hase [Southern Cross University] and Chris Kenyon of Australia, is the study of self-determined learning. The word appears to come from an irregular formation of the Greek words åõñåôéêüò (heurista) meaning to "discover," åöåõñåôéêüò (heuretikos) meaning "inventive," åýñçìá (heuriskein) meaning to "find," and Üãù (ago) to "lead"; so it is construed to mean "to lead to invention, discoveries, findings" and consists of learning strategies focused on mature learners where a facilitator enables quested learning to allow for modification of existing knowledge and creation of new knowledge.

Pedagogy [ped-ah-goh-jee, -goj-ee] The word comes from the Greek ðáéäáãùãÝù (pedagogue); in which ðáéäß (ped) means "child" and Üãù (ago) means "lead"; so it literally means "to lead the child" where a teacher develops conceptual knowledge and manages the content of learning activities. Other relevant roots from Greek include ìéêñü ðáéäß or toddler; áãüñé or boy child; êïñéôóéþí or girl child; ìéêñü ðáéäß or young child.

Instructional Theorists

Socrates (circa 470–399 BC) introduces method of "elenchus," where a problem is broken down into a series of questions, the answers to which gradually elicit the sought after answer. This approach is most strongly felt today in the use of the scientific method, where hypothesis is the first stage of problem solving.

Aristotle (circa 384-322 BC) postulates experience is the source of knowledge and believed that knowledge was gained through experiencing the environment. He believed knowledge was associative, meaning one idea will trigger the recall of the other which is a prelude to sequential learning and schema development.

Plato (428/427 BC– 348/347 BC) believed people learn about ideas through reasoning. Plato taught mental discipline. He believed if we exercised our mind, our mind would strengthen; therefore, he touted rigor and mental discipline.

John Locke (29 August 1632 – 28 October 1704) believed that skills and knowledge are acquired through example and practice, not exhaustive drills that require children to memorize rules or principals; also, that desirable behaviours are learned by unconsciously imitating the manners of role models.

Étienne Bonnot de Condillac's (30 September 1715 – 3 August 1780) doctrine reigned in the schools of France for over fifty years. Condillac's works include Essays on the origin of human knowledge (1746), Treatise on the system (1749), Treatise on the senses (1754), and an extensive course of study in 13 volumes, Cours d'études (1767-1773), that emphasize the importance of using the senses to increase learning. Condillac's work is significant to the field of education because he is among the first to emphasize the importance of manipulating matter as well as ideas to construct behavioural learning advocating a sense luscious environment to provide a stimulus response-learning environment.

John Dewey (20 October 1859 – 1 June 1952) argues that in order for education to be most effective, content must be presented in a way that allows the student to relate the information to prior experiences, thus deepening the connection with this new knowledge.

Jean Piaget (9 August 1896 – 17 September 1980) explored changes in internal cognitive structure as well as recognizing the contribution of environment to learning. He identified four stages of mental growth (sensorimotor, preoperational, concrete operational, and formal operational).

B. F. Skinner's (20 March 1904 – 18 August 18, 1990) theories of behaviour were highly influential on many early instructional theorists because their hypotheses can be tested fairly easily with the scientific process.

Benjamin Bloom (21 February 1913 – 13 September 1999), a University of Chicago professor, developed Taxonomy of Education Objectives — one of the first modern codifications of the learning process.

Malcolm S. Knowles (24 August 1913 – 27 November 1997) joined the staff at Boston University in 1959, spending 14 years there, during which time his publications became foundational for adult education discourse in the United States, introducing the instructional theory called andragogy. In 1974 he joined the faculty of North Carolina State University where he developed courses using 'the andragogical model'. He also published a new book on Self Directed Learning.

Jerome Bruner (born 1 October 1915) explored how mental processes could be linked to teaching (emphasizing, among other things, learning through discovery).

Robert M. Gagné (21 August 1916 – 28 April 2002) developed a model that highlighted eight different forms of learning and in 1965 published *Conditions of Learning* for the Florida State University's Department of Educational Research.

Paulo Freire's (19 September 1921 – 2 May 1997) work is significant because of his emphasis on respectful cooperative dialogue involving people working with each other; his concern with praxis, informed action that enhances community and leads us to act in ways that make for justice and human flourishing; his attention to developing consciousness for educating the oppressed; his insistence on situating educational activity in the lived experience of participants; and his ability to transcend the divide between teachers and learners.

9

Instructional Design

Instructional Design (also called Instructional Systems Design (ISD)) is the practice of creating "instructional experiences which make the acquisition of knowledge and skill more efficient, effective, and appealing." The process consists broadly of determining the current state and needs of the learner, defining the end goal of instruction, and creating some "intervention" to assist in the transition. Ideally the process is informed by pedagogically (process of teaching) and andragogically (adult learning) tested theories of learning and may take place in student-only, teacher-led or community-based settings. The outcome of this instruction may be directly observable and scientifically measured or completely hidden and assumed. There are many instructional design models but many are based on the ADDIE model with the five phases: analysis, design, development, implementation, and evaluation. As a field, instructional design is historically and traditionally rooted in cognitive and behavioural psychology, though recently Constructivism (learning theory) has influenced thinking in the field.

History

History of the System Approach to Instructional Design

1940's - The Origins of Instructional Design, World War II

- During the war a considerable amount of training materials for the military were developed based on the principles of instruction, learning, and human behaviour. Tests for assessing a learner's abilities were used to screen candidates for the training programmes. After the success of military training, psychologists began to view training as a system, and developed various analysis, design, and evaluation procedures.

1946 – Edgar Dale's Cone of Experience

- In 1946, Dale outlined a hierarchy of instructional methods and their effectiveness.

Mid-1950s Through mid-1960s - The Programmed Instruction Movement

- In B. F. Skinner's 1954 article "*The Science of Learning and the Art of Teaching*", he stated that effective instructional materials, called programmed instructional materials, should include small steps, frequent questions, immediate feedback, and allow self-pacing.
- The Popularization of Behavioural Objectives - Robert Mager popularized the use of learning objectives with his 1962 article "*Preparing Objectives for Programmed Instruction*". In the article, he describes how to write objectives including desired behaviour, learning condition, and assessment.
- In 1956, a committee led by Benjamin Bloom published an influential taxonomy of what he termed the three domains of learning: Cognitive (what one knows or thinks), Psychomotor (what one does, physically) and Affective (what one feels, or what attitudes one has). These taxonomies still influence the design of instruction.

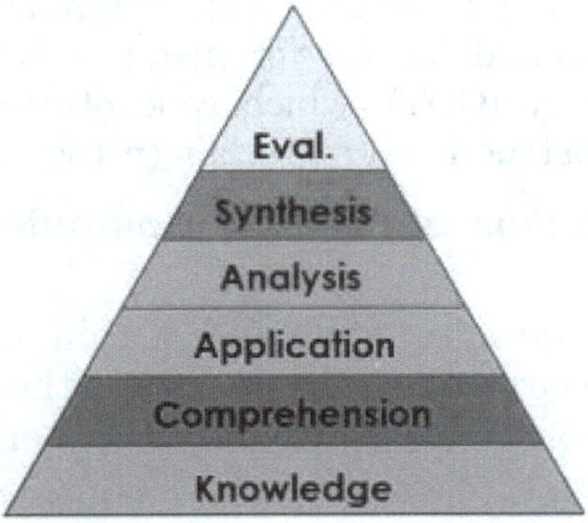

Figure: *Bloom's Taxonomy*

Early 1960s - The Criterion-Referenced Testing Movement

- Robert Glaser first used the term "criterion-referenced measures" in 1962. In contrast to norm-referenced tests in which an individual's performance is compared to group performance, a criterion-referenced test is designed to test an individual's behaviour in relation to an objective standard. It can be used to assess the learners' entry level behaviour, and to what extent learners have developed mastery through an instructional programme.

1965 - Domains of Learning, Events of Instruction, and Hierarchical Analysis

- In 1965, Robert Gagne described five domains of learning outcomes and nine events of instruction in "*The conditions of Learning*", which remain foundations of instructional design practices.
- Gagne's work in learning hierarchies and hierarchical analysis led to an important notion in instruction – to ensure that learners acquire prerequisite skills before attempting superordinate's ones.

1967 - Formative Evaluation

- In 1967, after analyzing the failure of training material, Michael Scriven suggested the need for formative assessment – e.g., to try out instructional materials with learners (and revise accordingly) before declaring them finalized.

The 1970s - Growing of Interest in the Systems Approach

- During 1970s, the number of instructional design models greatly increased and prospered in different sectors in military, academia, and industry. Many instructional design theorists began to adopt an information-processing-based approach to the design of instruction. David Merrill for instance developed Component Display Theory (CDT), which concentrates on the means of presenting instructional materials (presentation techniques).

The 1980s - Introduction of Personal Computers into the Design Process

- During this decade, while interest in instructional design continued to be strong in business and the military, there was little evolution of ID in schools or higher education.
- This was the era, however, where educators and researchers began to consider how the personal computer could be used in an educational environment and efforts began to design instruction that utilized this new tool. PLATO (Programmed Logic for Automatic Teaching Operation) is one example of how computers began to be integrated into instruction. Many of the first uses of computers in the classroom were for "drill

and skill" exercises. Computer-based educational games and simulations also became popular.

- This is also the time where there is a growing interest in how cognitive psychology can be applied to instructional design. In the late 1980s and throughout the 1990s cognitive load theory began to find empirical support for a variety of presentation techniques.

The 1990s - A Growing Interest in Constructivist Theory and the Importance of Performance

- As constructivist theory began to gain traction, its influence on instructional design became more prominent as a counterpoint to the more traditional cognitive learning theory. Constructivists believe that learning experiences should be "authentic" and produce real-world learning environments that allow the learner to construct their own knowledge. This emphasis on the learner was a significant departure away from traditional forms of instructional design.
- Another trend that surfaced during this period was the recognition of performance improvement as being an important outcome of learning that needed to be considered during the design process.
- The World Wide Web is developed and begins to surface as a potential online learning tool with hypertext and hypermedia being recognized as good tools for e-learning.
- As technology advanced and constructivist theory gained popularity, technology's use in the classroom began to evolve from mostly drill and skill exercises to more interactive activities that required more complex thinking on the part of the learner.
- Rapid prototyping was first seen during the 1990s. In this process, an instructional design project is prototyped quickly and then vetted through a series of try and revises cycles. This is a big departure from traditional methods of instructional design that took far longer to complete.

The 2000s - Rise of the Internet and Online Learning

- The Internet, with its social media tools and multitudes of information resources, became a very popular tool for online learning, and instructional designers recognized the need to integrate e-learning into the creation of learning objects and curricula.

- There is a great increase in the number of online courses offered by higher education institutions.
- Technology advanced to the point that sophisticated simulations were now readily available to learners, thus providing more authentic and realistic learning experiences.

2010 and Forward

- The influence of e-tools continues to grow and has seemingly encouraged the growth of informal learning throughout a person's lifetime. The challenge for instructional designers is how to create learning opportunities that now may occur anywhere and anytime.

Instructional Media History

Instructional Media History			
Era	***Media***	***Characteristics***	***Outcome***
1900s	Visual media	School museum as supplementary material (First school museum opened in St. Louis in 1905)	Materials are viewed as supplementary curriculum materials. District-wide media center is the modern equivalent.
1914-1923	Visual media films, Slides, Photographer	Visual Instruction Movement	The impact of visual instruction was limited because of teacher resistance to change, quality of the file and cost etc.
Mid 1920s to 1930s	Radio broadcasting, Sound recordings, Sound motion pictures	Radio Audiovisual Instruction movement	Education in large was not impacted.
World War II	Training films, Overhead projector, Slide projector, Audio equipment, Simulators and training devices	Military and industry at this time had strong demand for training.	Growth of audio-visual instruction movement in school was slow, but audiovisual device were used extensively in military services and industry.
Post World War II	Communication medium	Suggested to consider all aspects of a communication process (influenced by communication theories).	This view point was first ignored, but eventually helped to expand the focus of the audiovisual movement.
1950s to mid-1960s	Television	Growth of Instructional television	Instructional television was not adopted to a greater extent.
1950s-1990s	Computer	Computer-assisted instruction (CAI) research started in the 1950s, became popular in the 1980s a few years after computer s became available to general public.	The impact of CAI was rather small and the use of computer was far from innovative.
1990s-2000s	Internet, Simulation	The internet offered opportunites to train many people long distances. Desktop simulation gave advent to levels of Interactive Multimedia Instruction (IMI).	Online training increased rapidly to the point where entire curriculums were given through web-based training. Simulations are valuable but expensive, with the highest level being used primarily by the military and medical community.
2000s-2010s	Mobile Devices, Social Media	On-demand training moved to people's personal devices; social media allowed for collaborative learning.	The impact from both are too new to be measured.

Cognitive Load Theory and the Design of Instruction

Cognitive load theory developed out of several empirical studies of learners, as they interacted with instructional materials. Sweller and his associates began to measure the effects of working memory load, and found that the format of instructional materials has a direct effect on the performance of the learners using those materials.

While the media debates of the 1990s focused on the influences of media on learning, cognitive load effects were being documented in several journals. Rather than attempting to substantiate the use of media, these cognitive load learning effects provided an empirical basis for the use of instructional strategies. Mayer asked the instructional design community to reassess the media debate, to refocus their attention on what was most important: learning.

By the mid- to late-1990s, Sweller and his associates had discovered several learning effects related to cognitive load and the design of instruction (e.g. the split attention effect, redundancy effect, and the worked-example effect). Later, other researchers like Richard Mayer began to attribute learning effects to cognitive load. Mayer and his associates soon developed a Cognitive Theory of Multimedia Learning.

In the past decade, cognitive load theory has begun to be internationally accepted and begun to revolutionize how practitioners of instructional design view instruction. Recently, human performance experts have even taken notice of cognitive load theory, and have begun to promote this theory base as the science of instruction, with instructional designers as the practitioners of this field. Finally Clark, Nguyen and Sweller published a textbook describing how Instructional Designers can promote efficient learning using evidence-based guidelines of cognitive load theory.

Instructional Designers use various instructional strategies to reduce cognitive load. For example, they think that the onscreen text should not be more than 150 words or the text should be presented in small meaningful chunks. The designers also use auditory and visual methods to communicate information to the learner.

Gagné's Theory of Instruction

Gagné's instructional theory is widely used in the design of instruction by instructional designers in many settings, and its continuing influence in the field of educational technology can be seen in the more than 130 times that Gagné has been cited in prominent journals in the field during the period from 1985 through 1990. Synthesizing ideas from behaviourism and cognitivism, he provides a clear template, which is easy to follow for designing instructional events. Instructional designers who follow Gagné's theory will likely have tightly focused, efficient instruction.

Overview of Gagné's Instructional Theory

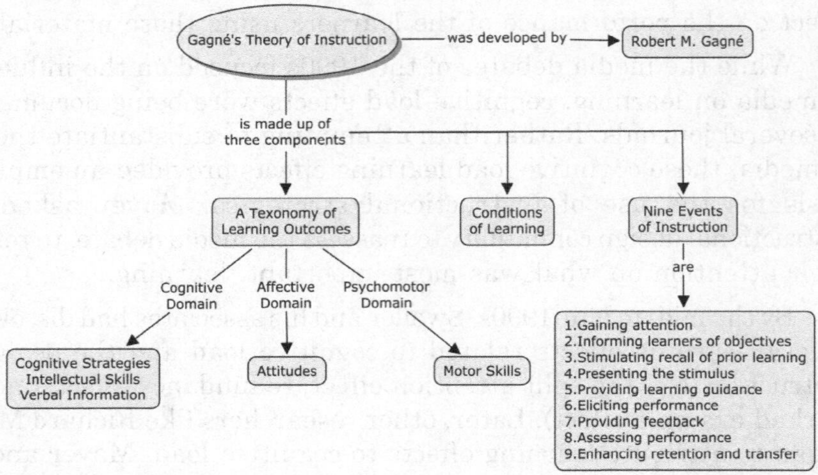

A Taxonomy of Learning Outcomes

Robert Gagné classified the types of learning outcomes. To identify the types of learning, Gagné asked how learning might be demonstrated. These can be related to the domains of learning, as follows:

- Cognitive Domain
  1. Verbal information - is stated
  2. Intellectual skills - label or classify the concepts
  3. Intellectual skills - to apply the rules and principles
  4. Intellectual skills - problem solving allows generating solutions or procedures
  5. Cognitive strategies - are used for learning
- Affective Domain
  1. Attitudes - are demonstrated by preferring options
- Psychomotor Domain
  1. Motor skills - enable physical performance

Types of Learning Outcomes

Gagné, & Driscoll elaborated on the types of learning outcomes with a set of corresponding standard verbs:

- Verbal Information: state, recite, tell, declare
- Intellectual Skills

1. Discrimination: discriminate, distinguish, differentiate
2. Concrete Concept: identify, name, specify, label
3. Defined Concept: classify, categorize, type, sort (by definition)
4. Rule: demonstrate, show, solve (using one rule)
5. Higher Order Rule: generate, develop, solve (using two or more rules)

- Cognitive Strategy: adopt, create, originate
- Attitude: choose, prefer, elect, favour
- Motor Skill: execute, perform, carry out

The Nine Events of Instruction (as Conditions of Learning)

According to Gagné, learning occurs in a series of learning events. Each learning event must be accomplished before the next in order for learning to take place. Similarly, instructional events should mirror the learning events:

1. Gaining attention: To ensure reception of coming instruction, the teacher gives the learners a stimulus. Before the learners can start to process any new information, the instructor must gain the attention of the learners. This might entail using abrupt changes in the instruction.
2. Informing learners of objectives: The teacher tells the learner what they will be able to do because of the instruction. The teacher communicates the desired outcome to the group.
3. Stimulating recall of prior learning: The teacher asks for recall of existing relevant knowledge.
4. Presenting the stimulus: The teacher gives emphasis to distinctive features.
5. Providing learning guidance: The teacher helps the students in understanding (semantic encoding) by providing organization and relevance.
6. Eliciting performance: The teacher asks the learners to respond, demonstrating learning.
7. Providing feedback: The teacher gives informative feedback on the learners' performance.
8. Assessing performance: The teacher requires more learner performance, and gives feedback, to reinforce learning.

9. Enhancing retention and transfer: The teacher provides varied practice to generalize the capability.

Some educators believe that Gagné's taxonomy of learning outcomes and events of instruction oversimplify the learning process by over-prescribing. However, using them as part of a complete instructional package can assist many educators in becoming more organized and staying focused on the instructional goals.

Gagné's Influence on Instructional Design Theorists

Robert Gagné's work has been the foundation of instructional design since the beginning of the 1960s when he conducted research and developed training materials for the military. Among the first to coin the term "instructional design", Gagné developed some of the earliest instructional design models and ideas. These models have laid the groundwork for more present-day instructional design models from theorists like Dick, Carey, and Carey (The Dick and Carey Systems Approach Model), Jerold Kemp's Instructional Design Model, and David Merrill (Merrill's First Principle of Instruction). Each of these models are based on a core set of learning phases that include (1) activation of prior experience, (2) demonstration of skills, (3) application of skills, and (4) integration or these skills into real world activities.

Gagné's main focus for instructional design was how instruction and learning could be systematically connected to the design of instruction. He emphasized the design principles and procedures that need to take place for effective teaching and learning. His initial ideas, along with the ideas of other early instructional designers, can be summed up in *Psychological Principles in Systematic Development* which was written by Roberts B. Miller and edited by Gagné. Gagné believed in internal learning and motivation which paved the way for theorists like Merrill, Li, and Jones who designed the Instructional Transaction Theory, Reigeluth and Stein's Elaboration Theory, and most notably, Keller's ARCS Model of Motivation and Design.

Gagné's Influence on Education Today

Prior to Robert Gagné, learning was often thought of as a single, uniform process. There was little to no distinction between "learning to load a rifle and learning to solve a complex mathematical problem". Gagné offered an alternative view which developed the ideas of different learners required different learning strategies. Understanding and designing instruction based on a learning style defined by the individual brought about new theories and approaches to teaching. Gagné‘s understanding and theories of human learning added significantly to understanding the stages in cognitive processing and instructions. For example, Gagné argued instructional designers must understand the characteristics and functions of short term and long-term memory to facilitate meaningful learning. This idea encouraged instructional designers to include cognitive needs a top-down instructional approach.

Gagné's continuing influence on education has been best developed in The Legacy of Robert M. Gagne.

Gagné (1966) defines curriculum as a sequence of content units arranged in such a way that the learning of each unit may be accomplished as a single act, provided the capabilities described by specified prior units (in the sequence) have already been mastered by the learner.

His definition of curriculum has been the basis of many important initiatives in schools and other educational environments.. In the late 1950s and early 1960s, Gagné had expressed and established an interest in applying theory to practice with particular interest in applications for teaching, training and learning. Increasing the effectiveness and efficiency of practice was of particular concern. His ongoing attention to practice while developing theory continues to have an impact on education and training.

Gagné's work has had a significant influence on American education, military and industrial training. Gagné was one of the early developers of the concept of instructional systems design which suggests the components of a lesson can be analyzed and should be designed to operate together as an integrated plan for instruction. In "Educational Technology and the Learning Process" (Educational Researcher, 1974), Gagné defined instruction as "the set of planned external events which influence the process of learning and thus promote learning.".

Learning Design

The concept of learning design arrived in the literature of technology for education in the late nineties and early 2000s with the idea that "designers and instructors need to choose for themselves the best mixture of behaviourist and constructivist learning experiences for their online courses". But the concept of learning design is probably as old as the concept of teaching. Learning design might be defined as "the description of the teaching-learning process that takes place in a unit of learning (eg, a course, a lesson or any other designed learning event)". As summarized by Britain, learning design may be associated with:

- The concept of learning design
- The implementation of the concept made by learning design specifications like PALO, IMS Learning Design, LDL, SLD 2.0, etc...
- The technical realisations around the implementation of the concept like TELOS, RELOAD LD-Author, etc...

Instructional Design Models

ADDIE Process: Perhaps the most common model used for creating instructional materials is the ADDIE Model. This acronym stands for the 5 phases contained in the model (Analyze, Design, Develop, Implement, and Evaluate).

Brief History of ADDIE's Development – The ADDIE model was initially developed by Florida State University to explain "the processes involved in the formulation of an instructional systems development (ISD) programme for military interservice training that will adequately train individuals to do a particular job and which can also be applied to any interservice curriculum development activity." The model originally contained several steps under its five original phases (Analyze, Design, Develop, Implement, and [Evaluation and] Control), whose completion was expected before movement to the next phase could occur. Over the years, the steps were revised and eventually the model itself became more dynamic and interactive than its original hierarchical rendition, until its most popular version appeared in the mid-80s, as we understand it today.

The five phases are listed and explained below:

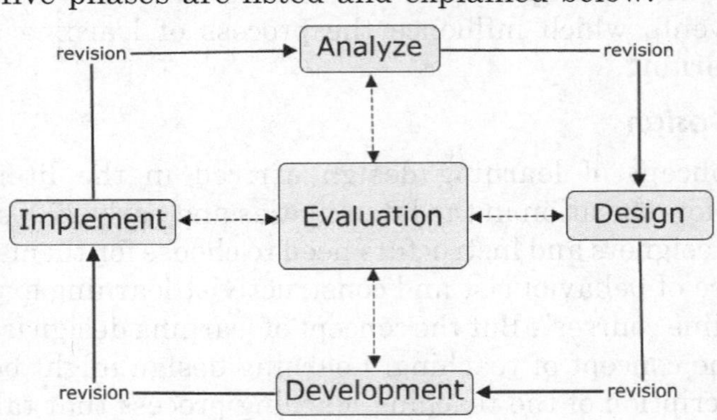

Figure: *ADDIE Model*

Analyze – The first phase of content development begins with Analysis. Analysis refers to the gathering of information about one's audience, the tasks to be completed, and the project's overall goals. The instructional designer then classifies the information to make the content more applicable and successful.

Design – The second phase is the Design phase. In this phase, instructional designers begin to create their project. Information gathered from the analysis phase, in conjunction with the theories and models of instructional design, is meant to explain how the learning will be acquired. For example, the design phase begins with writing a learning objective. Tasks are then identified and broken down to be more manageable for the designer. The final step determines the kind of activities required for the audience in order to meet the goals identified in the Analyze phase.

Develop – The third phase, Development, relates to the creation of the activities being implemented. This stage is where the blueprints in the design phase are assembled.

Implement – After the content is developed, it is then Implemented. This stage allows the instructional designer to test all materials to identify if they are functional and appropriate for the intended audience.

Evaluate – The final phase, Evaluate, ensures the materials achieved the desired goals. The evaluation phase consists of two parts: formative and summative assessment. The ADDIE model is an iterative process of instructional design, meaning at each stage, the designer can assess the project's elements and revise them if necessary. This process incorporates formative assessment, while the summative assessments contain tests or evaluations created for the content being implemented. This final phase is vital for the instructional design team because it provides data used to alter and enhance the design.

Connecting all phases of the model are external and reciprocal revision opportunities. Aside from the internal Evaluation phase, revisions should and can be made throughout the entire process.

Most of the current instructional design models are variations of the ADDIE process.

Rapid Prototyping

Sometimes utilized adaptation to the ADDIE model is in a practice known as rapid prototyping. Proponents suggest that through an iterative process the verification of the design documents saves time and money by catching problems while they are still easy to fix. This approach is not novel to the design of instruction, but appears in many design-related domains including software design, architecture, transportation planning, product development, message design, user experience design, etc. In fact, some proponents of design prototyping assert that a sophisticated understanding of a problem is incomplete without creating and evaluating some type of prototype, regardless of the analysis rigor that may have been applied up front. In other words, up-front analysis is rarely sufficient to allow one to confidently select an instructional model. For this reason many traditional methods of instructional design are beginning to be seen as incomplete, naive, and even counter-productive.

However, some consider rapid prototyping to be a somewhat simplistic type of model. As this argument goes, at the heart of Instructional Design is the analysis phase. After you thoroughly conduct the analysis—you can then choose a model based on your findings. That is the area where most people get snagged—they simply do not do a thorough-enough analysis. (Part of Article By Chris Bressi on LinkedIn)

Dick and Carey

Another well-known instructional design model is The Dick and Carey Systems Approach Model. The model was originally published in 1978 by Walter Dick and Lou Carey in their book entitled *The Systematic Design of Instruction*.

Dick and Carey made a significant contribution to the instructional design field by championing a systems view of instruction as opposed to viewing instruction as a sum of isolated parts. The model addresses instruction as an entire system, focusing on the interrelationship between context, content, learning and instruction. According to Dick and Carey, "Components such as the instructor, learners, materials, instructional activities, delivery system, and learning and performance environments interact with each other and work together to bring about the desired student learning outcomes". The components of the Systems Approach Model, also known as the Dick and Carey Model, are as follows:

- Identify Instructional Goal(s): goal statement describes a skill, knowledge or attitude (SKA) that a learner will be expected to acquire
- Conduct Instructional Analysis: Identify what a learner must recall and identify what learner must be able to do to perform particular task

- Analyze Learners and Contexts: Identify general characteristics of the target audience including prior skills, prior experience, and basic demographics; identify characteristics directly related to the skill to be taught; and perform analysis of the performance and learning settings.
- Write Performance Objectives: Objectives consists of a description of the behaviour, the condition and criteria. The component of an objective that describes the criteria that will be used to judge the learner's performance.
- Develop Assessment Instruments: Purpose of entry behaviour testing, purpose of pretesting, purpose of post-testing, purpose of practive items/practive problems
- Develop Instructional Strategy: Pre-instructional activities, content presentation, Learner participation, assessment
- Develop and Select Instructional Materials
- Design and Conduct Formative Evaluation of Instruction: Designer try to identify areas of the instructional materials that are in need of improvement.
- Revise Instruction: To identify poor test items and to identify poor instruction
- Design and Conduct Summative Evaluation

With this model, components are executed iteratively and in parallel rather than linearly.

Instructional Development Learning System (IDLS)

Another instructional design model is the Instructional Development Learning System (IDLS). The model was originally published in 1970 by Peter J. Esseff, PhD and Mary Sullivan Esseff, PhD in their book entitled *IDLS—Pro Trainer 1: How to Design, Develop, and Validate Instructional Materials.*

Peter (1968) & Mary (1972) Esseff both received their doctorates in Educational Technology from the Catholic University of America under the mentorship of Dr. Gabriel Ofiesh, a Founding Father of the Military Model mentioned above. Esseff and Esseff contributed synthesized existing theories to develop their approach to systematic design, "Instructional Development Learning System" (IDLS).

The components of the IDLS Model are:

- Design a Task Analysis

- Develop Criterion Tests and Performance Measures
- Develop Interactive Instructional Materials
- Validate the Interactive Instructional Materials

Other Instructional Design Models

Other useful instructional design models include: the Smith/Ragan Model, the Morrison/Ross/Kemp Model and the OAR Model of instructional design in higher education, as well as, Wiggins' theory of backward design. Learning theories also play an important role in the design of instructional materials. Theories such as behaviourism, constructivism, social learning and cognitivism help shape and define the outcome of instructional materials.

Motivational Design

Motivation is defined as an internal drive that activates behaviour and gives it direction. The term motivation theory is concerned with the process that describe why and how human behaviour is activated and directed.

Motivation Concepts *Intrinsic and Extrinsic Motivation*

- Instrinsic: defined as the doing of an activity for its inherent satisfactions rather than for some separable consequence. When intrinsically motivated a person is moved to act for the fun or challenge entailed rather than because of external rewards. Intrinsic motivation reflects the desire to do something because it is enjoyable. If we are intrinsically motivated, we would not be worried about external rewards such as praise.

Examples: Writing short stories because you enjoy writing them, reading a book because you are curious about the topic, and playing chess because you enjoy effortful thinking

- Extrinsic: reflects the desire to do something because of external rewards such as awards, money and praise. People who are extrinsically motivated may not enjoy certain activities. They may only wish to engage in certain activities because they wish to receive some external reward.

Examples: The writer who only writes poems to be submitted to poetry contests, a person who dislikes sales but accepts a sales position because he/she desires to earn an above average salary, and a person selecting a major in college based on salary and prestige, rather than personal interest.

John Keller has devoted his career to researching and understanding motivation in instructional systems. These decades of work constitute a major contribution to the instructional design field. First, by applying motivation theories systematically to design theory. Second, in developing a unique problem-solving process he calls the ARCS Motivation.

The ARCS Model of Motivational Design

The ARCS Model of Motivational Design was created by John Keller while he was researching ways to supplement the learning process with motivation. The model is based on Tolman's and Lewin's expectancy-value theory, which presumes that people are motivated to learn if there is value in the knowledge presented (i.e. it fulfills personal needs) and if there is an optimistic expectation for success. The model consists of four main areas: Attention, Relevance, Confidence, and Satisfaction.

Attention and relevance according to John Keller's ARCS motivational theory are essential to learning. The first 2 of 4 key components for motivating learners, attention and relevance can be considered the backbone of the ARCS theory, the latter components relying upon the former.

Attention: The attention mentioned in this theory refers to the interest displayed by learners in taking in the concepts/ideas being taught. This component is split into three categories: perceptual arousal, using surprise or uncertain situations; enquiry arousal, offering challenging questions and/or problems to answer/solve; and variability, using a variety of resources and methods of teaching. Within each of these categories, John Keller has provided further sub-divisions of types of stimuli to grab attention. Grabbing attention is the most important part of the model because it initiates the motivation for the learners. Once learners are interested in a topic, they are willing to invest their time, pay attention, and find out more.

Relevance: Relevance, according to Keller, must be established by using language and examples that the learners are familiar with. The three major strategies John Keller presents are goal oriented, motive matching, and familiarity. Like the Attention category, John Keller divided the three major strategies into subcategories, which provide examples of how to make a lesson plan relevant to the learner. Learners will throw concepts to the wayside if their attention cannot be grabbed and sustained and if relevance is not conveyed.

Confidence: The confidence aspect of the ARCS model focuses on establishing positive expectations for achieving success among learners. The confidence level of learners is often correlated with motivation and the amount of effort put forth in reaching a performance objective. For this reason, it's important that learning design provides students with a method for estimating their probability of success. This can be achieved in the form of a syllabus and grading policy, rubrics, or a time estimate to complete tasks. Additionally, confidence is built when positive reinforcement for personal achievements is given through timely, relevant feedback.

Satisfaction: Finally, learners must obtain some type of satisfaction or reward from a learning experience. This satisfaction can be from a sense of achievement, praise from a higher-up, or mere entertainment. Feedback and reinforcement are important elements and when learners appreciate the results, they will be motivated to learn. Satisfaction is based upon motivation, which can be intrinsic or extrinsic. To keep learners satisfied, instruction should be designed to allow them to use their newly learned skills as soon as possible in as authentic a setting as possible.

Motivating Opportunities Model

Although Keller's ARCS model currently dominates instructional design with respect to learner motivation, in 2006 Hardré and Miller proposed a need for a new design model that includes current research in human motivation, a comprehensive treatment of motivation, integrates various fields of psychology and provides designers the flexibility to be applied to a myriad of situations.

Hardré proposes an alternate model for designers called the Motivating Opportunities Model or MOM. Hardré's model incorporates cognitive, needs, and affective theories as well as social elements of learning to address learner motivation. MOM has seven key components spelling the acronym 'SUCCESS'- Situational, Utilization, Competence, Content, Emotional, Social, and Systemic.

Classical Conditioning

Classical conditioning (also Pavlovian conditioning or respondent conditioning) is a form of learning in which the *conditioned stimulus* or CS, comes to signal the occurrence of a second stimulus, the *unconditioned stimulus* or US. (A stimulus is a factor that causes a response in an organism.) The conditioned response is the learned response to the previously neutral stimulus. The US is usually a biologically significant stimulus such as food or pain that elicits a response from the start; this is called the *unconditioned response* or UR. The CS usually produces no particular response at first, but after conditioning it elicits the *conditioned response* or CR. Classical conditioning differs from *operant* or *instrumental* conditioning, in which behaviour emitted by the subject is strengthened or weakened by its consequences (i.e. reward or punishment).

There are many examples of these innate (unconditioned) reflexes (corneal, coughing, swallowing, withdrawal reflexes etc.) or learned (conditioned) reflexes.

"In any animal, regardless of its prior history, painful stimulation of the foot causes the leg to be withdrawn by bending at all its joints. This *flexor reflex* is an example of an *unconditioned reflex*, an innate response based on fixed connections in the chain of neurons from the receptor (sensor) to the effector. Of still more interest in everyday life are the *acquired* or *conditioned reflexes*, in which the functional connections between the excited sensors and the patterns of activity in effector organs become established by learning process."

Conditioning is usually done by pairing the two stimuli, as in Pavlov's classic experiments. Pavlov presented dogs with a ringing bell followed by food.

The food elicited salivation (UR), and after repeated bell-food pairings the bell also caused the dogs to salivate. In this experiment, the unconditioned stimulus is the dog food as it produces an unconditioned response, saliva. The conditioned stimulus is the ringing bell and it produces a conditioned response of the dogs producing saliva.

It was originally thought that the process underlying classical conditioning was one where the conditioned stimulus becomes associated with, and eventually elicits, the unconditioned response. But many observations do not support this hypothesis. For example, the conditioned response is often quite different from the unconditioned response.

Learning theorists now more commonly suggest that the CS comes to signal or predict the US. In the case of the salivating dogs in Pavlov's experiment, the bell tone signaled and predicted the arrival of the dog food, thus resulting in the dog salivating. Robert A. Rescorla provided a clear summary of this change in thinking, and its consequences, in his 1988 article "Pavlovian conditioning: It's not what you think it is."

Origins

I. P. Pavlov provided the most famous example of classical conditioning, though E. B. Twitmyer published his findings a year earlier (a case of simultaneous discovery). During his research on the physiology of digestion in dogs, Pavlov noticed that, rather than simply salivating in the presence of food, the dogs began to salivate in the presence of the lab technician who normally fed them. Pavlov called this anticipatory salivation *psychic secretion*. From this observation he predicted that, if a particular stimulus in the dog's surroundings was present when the dog was given food, then this stimulus would become associated with food and cause salivation on its own. In his initial experiment, Pavlov used a bell to call the dogs to their food and, after a few repetitions, the dogs started to salivate in response to the bell. Pavlov called the bell the *conditioned* (or *conditional*) *stimulus* (CS) because its effect depended on its association with food. He called the food the *unconditioned stimulus* (US) because its effect did not depend on previous experience. Likewise, the response to the CS was the *conditioned response* (CR) and that to the US was the *unconditioned response* (UR). The timing between the presentation of the CS and US is integral to facilitating the conditioned response. Pavlov found that the shorter the interval between the bell's ring and the appearance of the food, the more quickly the dog learned the conditioned response and the stronger it was.

As noted earlier, it is often thought that the conditioned response is a replica of the unconditioned response, but even Pavlov noted that saliva produced by the CS differs in composition from that produced by the US. In fact, the CR may be any new response to the previously neutral CS that can be clearly linked to experience with the conditional relationship of CS and US. It was also thought that repeated pairings are necessary for conditioning to emerge, however many CRs can be learned with a single trial as in fear conditioning and taste aversion learning.

Classical Conditioning Procedures

Forward Conditioning: Learning is fastest in forward conditioning. During forward conditioning the onset of the CS precedes the onset of the US in order to signal that the US will follow. Two common forms of forward conditioning are delay and trace conditioning.

- Delay conditioning: In delay conditioning the CS is presented and is overlapped by the presentation of the US.

- Trace conditioning: During trace conditioning the CS and US do not overlap. Instead, the CS is presented, a period of time is allowed to elapse during which no stimuli are presented, and then the US is presented. The stimulus-free period is called the *trace interval*. It may also be called the *conditioning interval*.

Simultaneous Conditioning

During simultaneous conditioning, the CS and US are presented and terminated at the same time.

Second-order Conditioning

This form of conditioning follows a two-step procedure. First a neutral stimulus ("CS1") comes to signal a US through forward conditioning.

Then a second neutral stimulus ("CS2") is paired with the first (CS2-CS1) and comes to yield its own conditioned response. For example, a bell (CS1) might be paired with food (US) until the bell elicits salivation. If a light is then paired with the bell the light also may come to elicit salivation.

Backward Conditioning

Backward conditioning occurs when a CS immediately follows a US. Unlike the usual conditioning procedure, in which the CS precedes the US, the conditioned response given to the CS tends to be inhibitory. This presumably happens because the CS serves as a signal that the US has ended, rather than as a signal that the US is about to appear.

Temporal Conditioning

When a US is presented at a number of regularly timed intervals a CR often develops shortly before the US is scheduled to appear. This suggests that animals have a biological clock that can serve as a CS. This method has also been used to study timing ability in animals.

Zero Contingency Procedure

In this procedure, the CS is paired with the US as usual, but the US also occurs at other times, so that the US is just as likely to happen in that absence of the CS as it is following the CS. Here, in other words, the CS does not "predict" the US. In this case, conditioning fails: the CS does not come to elicit a CR. This finding - that *prediction* rather than CS-US pairing is the key to conditioning - greatly influenced subsequent conditioning research and theory.

Extinction

In the extinction procedure, the CS is presented repeatedly in the absence of a US. This is done after a CS has been conditioned by one of the methods above. When this is done the CR frequency eventually returns to pre-training levels. However, spontaneous recovery show that extinction does not completely eliminate the effects of the prior conditioning.

Phenomena Observed in Classical Conditioning

Acquisition: During acquisition the CS and US are paired in one of the ways described above. The extent of conditioning may be tracked by test trials in which the CS is presented alone and the CR is measured. A single CS-US pairing may suffice to yield a CR on test, but usually a number of pairings are necessary, during which the strength and/or frequency of the CR gradually increases. The speed of conditioning depends on a number of factors, including the nature and strength of both the CS and the US, the animal's motivational state, and previous experience Acquisition may occur with a single pairing of the CS and US, but more commonly there is a gradual increase in the conditioned response to the CS which slows as the process nears completion.

Extinction: The process of presenting a CS alone, without the US, that causes the learned behaviour to disappear eventually is called *extinction*. When the presentation of the CS with the US absent is done often enough, the CS ordinarily stops eliciting a CR; that is, it has been *extinguished*.

External Inhibition: External inhibition may be observed if a strong or unfamiliar stimulus is presented just before, or at the same time as, the CS. This causes a reduction in the conditioned response to the CS.

Recovery from Extinction: Several procedures can cause an extinguished CR to recover. The outcomes of these procedures suggest that extinction does not entirely erase the effects of conditioning. Each of the following descriptions assumes that a CS has been conditioned and then the CR extinguished through the procedures described above.

Reacquisition: If the CS is again paired with the US, a CR is again acquired, but this second acquisition usually happens much faster than the first one.

Spontaneous Recovery: If the CS is tested at a later time (for example an hour or a day) after conditioning it will again elicit a CR, a phenomenon called *spontaneous recovery*. This renewed CR is usually much weaker than the CR observed prior to extinction

External Disinhibition: If the CS is tested just after intense but associatively neutral stimulus has occurred, there may be a temporary recovery of the conditioned response to the CS

Reinstatement: If the US used in conditioning is presented to a subject in the same place where conditioning and extinction occurred, but without the CS being present, the CS often elicits a response when it is tested later.

Renewal: If conditioning and extinction are conducted in different contexts (for example, conditioning occurs in one experimental chamber and extinction occurs in a chamber with a different colour and shape), a return to the conditioning context may cause the CS to again elicit a CR.

Stimulus Generalization: *Stimulus generalization* is said to occur if, after a particular CS has come to elicit a CR, another test stimulus elicits the same CR. Usually the more similar are the CS and the test stimulus the stronger is the CR to the test stimulus. The more the test stimulus differs from the CS the more the conditioned response will differ from that previously observed.

Stimulus Discrimination: One observes *stimulus discrimination* when one stimulus ("CS1") elicits one CR and another stimulus ("CS2") elicits either another CR or no CR at all. This can be brought about by, for example, pairing CS1 with an effective US and presenting CS2 in extinction, that is, with no US.

Latent Inhibition: In this procedure, a CS is presented several times before paired CS–US training commences. This slows the rate of CR acquisition relative to that observed without such pre-exposure.

Conditioned Suppression: This is one of the most common ways to measure the strength of learning in classical conditioning. In a typical example of this procedure, a rat first learns to press a lever through operant conditioning. Classical conditioning follows: in a series of trials the rat is exposed to a CS, often a light or a noise. This CS is followed by the US, a mild electric shock. As an association between the CS and US develops, the rat slows or stops its lever pressing when the CS comes on. The rate of pressing during the CS measures the strength of classical conditioning; that is, the slower the rat presses, the stronger is the association of the CS and the US. (Slow pressing indicates a "fear" conditioned response, and it is an example of a conditioned emotional response)

Conditioned Inhibition

Three phases of conditioning are typically used:

Phase 1: A CS (CS+) is paired with a US until asymptotic CR levels are reached.

Phase 2: CS+/US trials are continued, but these are interspersed with trials on which the CS+ is paired with a second CS, (the CS-) but not with the US (i.e. CS+/CS- trials). Typically, organisms show CRs on CS+/US trials, but stop responding on CS+/CS" trials.

Phase 3

- *Summation test for conditioned inhibition:* The CS- from Phase 2 is presented together with a new CS+ that was conditioned as in Phase 1. Conditioned inhibition is found if the response is less to the CS+/CS- pair than it is to the CS+ alone.
- *Retardation test for conditioned inhibition:* The CS- from Phase 2 is paired with the US. If conditioned inhibition has occurred, the rate of acquisition to the previous CS" should be less than the rate of acquisition that would be found without the Phase 2 treatment.

Blocking

This form of classical conditioning involves two phases.

Phase 1: A CS (CS1) is paired with a US.

Phase 2: A compound CS (CS1+CS2) is paired with a US.

Test: A separate test for each CS (CS1 and CS2) is performed. The blocking effect is observed in a lack of conditional response to CS2, suggesting that the first phase of training blocked the acquisition of the second CS.

Theories of Classical Conditioning

Data Sources: Experiments on theoretical issues in conditioning have mostly been done on vertebrates, especially rats and pigeons, but conditioning has also been studied in invertebrates, and very important data on the neural basis of conditioning has come from experiments on the sea slug, *Aplysia*. Most relevant experiments have used a classical conditioning procedure, though instrumental (operant) conditioning experiments have also been used, and the strength of classical conditioning is often measured through its operant effects, as in *conditioned suppression* and autoshaping.

The Rescorla-Wagner Model

The Rescorla-Wagner (R-W) model is a relatively simple yet powerful model of conditioning. The model predicts a number of important phenomena, but it also fails in important ways, thus leading to number modifications and alternative models. However, because much of the theoretical research on conditioning in the past 40 years has been instigated by this model or reactions to it, the R-W model deserves a brief description here.

A key idea behind the R-W model is that a CS *signals* or *predicts* the US. One might also say that before conditioning the subject is "surprised" by the US, but after conditioning the subject is no longer surprised, because the CS predicts the coming of the US. (Note that the model can be described mathematically and that words like "predict", "surprise", and "expect" are only used to help explain the model.) Here the workings of the model are illustrated with brief accounts of acquisition, extinction, and blocking. The model also predicts a number of other phenomena.

R-W Model: Acquisition

The R-W model measures conditioning by assigning an "associative strength" to the CS. Before a CS is conditioned its associative strength is zero. Pairing the CS and the US causes a gradual increase in the associative strength of the CS from zero to a maximum that is determined by the nature of the US (e.g. its intensity).

The amount of learning that happens during any single CS-US pairing depends on the difference between the current associative strength of the CS and the maximum set by the US. On the first pairing of CS and US this difference is large and the associative strength of the CS takes a big step up. As CS-US pairings accumulate, the US becomes more predictable, and the increase in associative strength on each trial becomes smaller and smaller. Finally the difference between the associative strength of the CS and the maximum strength reaches zero. That is, the CS fully predicts the US, the associative strength of the CS stops growing, and conditioning is complete.

R-W Model: Extinction

The associative process described by the R-W model also accounts for extinction. The extinction procedure starts with a CS with a positive associative strength, which means the CS predicts that a US will occur. However, in the extinction procedure, the US fails to occur. As a result of this "surprising" outcome, the associative strength of the CS takes a step down. Extinction is complete when the strength of the CS reaches zero; no US is predicted, and no US occurs.

R-W Model: Blocking

The most important and novel contribution of the R-W model is its assumption that the conditioning of a CS depends not just on that CS alone, and its relationship to the US, but also on all other stimuli present in the conditioning situation. In particular, the model states that the US is predicted by the sum of the associative strengths of all stimuli present in the conditioning situation. Learning is controlled by the difference between this total associative strength and the strength supported by the US. When this sum of strengths reaches a maximum set by the US, conditioning ends as just described.

The R-W explanation of the blocking phenomenon illustrates one consequence of the assumption just stated. In blocking, CS1 is paired with a US until conditioning is complete. Then on additional conditioning trials a second stimulus (CS2) appears together with CS1, and both are followed by US. Finally CS2 is tested and shown to produce no response because learning about CS2 was "blocked" by the initial learning about CS1. The R-W model explains this by saying that after the initial conditioning CS1 fully predicts the US. Because there is no difference between what is predicted and what happens, no new learning occurs on the additional trials with CS1+CS2, hence CS2 later yields no response.

Theoretical Issues and Alternatives to the Rescorla-Wagner Model

One of the main reasons for the importance of the R-W model is that it is relatively simple and makes clear predictions. Tests these predictions have led to a number of important new findings and a considerably increased understanding of conditioning. Some of this new information has supported the theory, but much has not, and it is generally agreed that the theory is, at best, too simple. As yet no single model seems to account for all the phenomena that experiments have produced. Following are brief summaries of some related theoretical issues.

The Content of Learning

The R-W model reduces conditioning to the association of a CS and US, and measures this with a single number, the associative strength of the CS. A number of experimental findings indicate that more is learned than this. Among these are two phenomena described earlier in this article

- Latent inhibition: If a subject is repeatedly exposed to the CS before conditioning starts, then conditioning takes longer. The R-W model cannot explain this because preexposure leaves the strength of the CS unchanged at zero
- Recovery of responding after extinction: It appears that something remains after extinction has reduced associative strength to zero because several procedures cause responding to reappear without further conditioning.

The Role of Attention in Learning

Latent inhibition might happen because a subject stops attending to a CS that is seen frequently before it is paired with a US. In fact, changes in attention to the CS are at the heart of two prominent theories that try to cope with experimental results that give the R-W model difficulty. In one of these, proposed by Nicholas Mackintosh, the speed of conditioning depends on the amount of attention devoted to the CS, and this amount of attention depends in turn on how well the CS predicts the US. A related model based on a different attentional principle was proposed by Pearce and Hall Although neither model explains all conditioning phenomena, the attention idea still has an important place in conditioning theory.

Context

As stated earlier, a key idea in conditioning is that the CS signals or predicts the US. But the room or chamber in which conditioning takes place also "predicts" that the US may occur, although with much less certainty than does the experimental CS itself. The role of such context is illustrated by the fact that the dogs in Pavlov's experiment would sometimes start salivating as they approached the experimental apparatus, before they saw or heard any CS. Such so-called "context" stimuli are always present; they have been found to play an important role in conditioning and they help to account for some otherwise puzzling experimental findings. Context plays an important role in the *comparator* and *computational* theories outlined below.

Comparator Theory

To find out what has been learned, we must somehow measure behaviour ("performance") in a test situation. However, as students know all too well, performance in a test situation is not always a good measure of what has been learned. As for conditioning, there is evidence, for example, that subjects in a blocking experiment do learn something about the "blocked" CS but fail to show this learning because of the way that they are usually tested.

"Comparator" theories of conditioning are "performance based;" that is, they stress what is going on at the time of test. In particular, they look at all the stimuli that are present during testing and at how the associations acquired by these stimuli may interact. To oversimplify somewhat, comparator theories assume that during conditioning the subject acquires both CS-US and context-US associations. At test, these associations are compared, and a response to the CS occurs only if the CS-US association is stronger than the context-US association. After a CS and US are repeatedly paired, as in simple acquisition, the CS-US association is strong and the context-US association is relatively weak, so the CS elicits a strong CR. In "zero contingency", the conditioned response is weak or absent because the context-US association is about as strong as the CS-US association. Blocking and other more subtle phenomena can also be explained by comparator theories, though, again, they cannot explain everything.

Computational Theory

An organism's need to predict future events is central to modern theories of conditioning. Most theories use associations between stimuli to take care of this prediction; for example, in the R-W model, the associative strength of a CS tells us how strongly that CS predicts a US. A different approach to prediction is suggested by models such as that proposed by Gallistel & Gibbon (2000, 2002). Here response is not determined by associative strengths. Instead, the organism records the times of onset and offset of CSs and USs and uses these to calculate the probability that the US will follow the CS. A number of experiments have shown that humans and animals do learn to time events, and the Gallistel & Gibbon model yields very good quantitative fits to a variety of experimental data.

Applications

Neural Basis of Learning and Memory: Pavlov proposed a physiological account of conditioning that involved connections between brain centres for the conditioned and the unconditioned stimuli. Though Pavlov's physiology has been abandoned, classical conditioning is extensively used in modern studies of the neural structures and functions that underlie learning and memory. Forms of classical conditioning that are used for this purpose include, among others, fear conditioning, eyeblink conditioning, and the foot contraction conditioning of *Hermissenda crassicornis*, a sea-slug.

In their textbook on human physiology, Nikolai Agajanyan and V. Tsyrkin list five criteria for demarcation between unconditioned and conditioned reflexes. Unconditioned reflexes are relatively stable; in contrast, conditioned reflexes are unstable and can be modified and extinguished as described above. This distinction is reflected in underlying neural processes; A leading role in the performance of unconditioned reflexes is played by the lower divisions of the higher nervous system, the subcortical nuclei, brain stem and spinal cord. Conditioned reflexes, in contrast, are a function of the cerebral cortex and can involve the most varied stimuli applied to different receptive fields.

Behavioural Therapies

Some therapies associated with classical conditioning are aversion therapy, systematic desensitization and flooding. Aversion therapy attempts to associate an unpleasant CR, such as nausea, with stimuli associated with unwanted behaviour, such as the smell of alcohol. Systematic desensitization attempts to eliminate an unwanted CR, such as anxiety, by gradually exposing the patient to associated CS's (e.g. angry words) in a relaxing situation. Flooding attempts to eliminate an unwanted CR through massive exposure of the associated CS, as in extinction. Such therapies and treatments using classical conditioning differ from those using operant conditioning.

Classical conditioning usually takes less time with therapists and less effort from patients than humanistic therapies.

Conditioned Drug Response

A stimulus that is present when a drug is administered or consumed may eventually evoke a conditioned physiological response that mimics the effect of the drug. This is sometimes the case with caffeine; habitual coffee drinkers may find that the smell of coffee gives them a feeling of alertness. In other cases, the conditioned response is a compensatory reaction that tends to offset the effects of the drug. For example, if a drug causes the body to become less sensitive to pain, the compensatory conditioned reaction may be one that makes the user more sensitive to pain. This compensatory reaction may contribute to drug tolerance. If so, a drug user may increase the amount of drug consumed in order to feel its effects, and end up taking very large amounts of the drug.

In this case a dangerous overdose reaction may occur if the CS happens to be absent, so that the conditioned compensatory effect fails to occur. For example, if the drug has always been administered in the same room, the stimuli provided by that room may produce a conditioned compensatory effect; then an overdose reaction may happen if the drug is administered in a different location where the conditioned stimuli are absent.

Conditioned Hunger

Signals that consistently precede food intake can become conditioned stimuli for a set of bodily responses that prepares the body for food and digestion. These reflexive responses include the secretion of digestive juices into the stomach and the secretion of certain hormones into the blood stream, and they induce a state of hunger. An example of conditioned hunger is the "appetizer effect." Any signal that consistently precedes a meal, such as a clock indicating that it is time for dinner, can cause people to feel hungrier than before the signal. The lateral hypothalamus (LH) is involved in the initiation of eating. The nigrostriatal pathway, which includes the substantia nigra, the lateral hypothalamus, and the basal ganglia have been shown to be involved in hunger motivation.

Conditioned Emotional Response

The influence of classical conditioning can be seen in emotional responses such as phobia, disgust, nausea, anger, and sexual arousal. A familiar example is conditioned nausea, in which the CS is the sight and/or smell of a particular food that in the past has resulted in an unconditioned stomach upset. Similarly, when the CS is the sight of a dog and the US is the pain of being bitten, the result may be a conditioned fear of dogs.

As an adaptive mechanism, emotional conditioning helps shield an individual from harm or prepare it for important biological events such as sexual activity. Thus, a stimulus that has occurred before sexual interaction comes to cause sexual arousal, which prepares the individual for sexual contact. For example, sexual arousal has been conditioned in human subjects by pairing a stimulus like a picture of a jar of pennies with views of an erotic film clip. Similar experiments involving blue gourami fish and domesticated quail have shown that such conditioning can increase the number of offspring. These results suggest that conditioning techniques might help to increase fertility rates in infertile individuals and endangered species.

In Popular Culture

One of the earliest literary references to classical conditioning can be found in the comic novel *The Life and Opinions of Tristram Shandy, Gentleman* (1759) by Laurence Sterne. The narrator Tristram Shandy explains how his mother was conditioned by his father's habit of winding up a clock before having sex with her:

My father [...] was, I believe, one of the most regular men in every thing he did [...] [H]e had made it a rule for many years of his life,—on the first Sunday-night of every month throughout the whole year,—as certain as ever the Sunday-night came,—to wind up a large house-clock, which we had standing on the back-stairs head, with his own hands:—And being somewhere between fifty and sixty years of age at the time I have been speaking of,—he had likewise gradually brought some other little family concernments to the same period, in order, as he would often say to my uncle Toby, to get them all out of the way at one time, and be no more plagued and pestered with them the rest of the month. [...] [F]rom an unhappy association of ideas, which have no connection in nature, it so fell out at length, that my poor mother could never hear the said clock wound up,—but the thoughts of some other things unavoidably popped into her head—& vice versa:—Which strange combination of ideas, the sagacious Locke, who certainly understood the nature of these things better than most men, affirms to have produced more wry actions than all other sources of prejudice whatsoever.

In the 1932 novel *Brave New World*, written by Aldous Huxley, conditioning plays a key role in the maintenance of social peace, especially in maintaining the caste system upon which society is based. Children are conditioned, both in their sleep and in their daily activities, to be happy in their Government-assigned social role as Alphas, Betas, etc., as well as in adopting other "socially acceptable" types of behaviour, including consuming manufactured goods and transport, practicing free sex, etc. For example, early on in the book, the Director of the Central London Hatchery and Conditioning Centre shows his young visitors how a group of toddlers of the Delta caste is conditioned to avoid books and flowers, by using shrill noises to terrorise them and applying "mild electric shocks". Also, in a later explanation by Resident World Controller of Western Europe Mustapha

Mond of how their society really works, he explains how early conditioning is an essential part of how social harmony among the different castes is maintained. Lower-caste members like Epsilons are as happy as upper-caste Alpha-Pluses, in large part due to their conditioning.

Another example is in the dystopian novel, *A Clockwork Orange* in which the novel's anti-hero and protagonist, Alex, undergoes a procedure called the Ludovico technique, where he is fed a solution to cause severe nausea and then forced to watch violent acts. This renders him unable to perform any violent acts without inducing similar nausea. Unintentionally, he also forms an aversion to classical music.

In the science-fiction book *Ender's Shadow*, "Pavlovian mental bans" are also used to prevent crime. In the book, a controversial scientist, Anton, is kept from researching genetic experimentation by associating his work with anxiety. A device is then surgically placed in his head that would increase detected anxiety, sending him into a panic attack. The result is that Anton must remain good humored at all times, can only speak of his work through self-deceptive metaphors, and even after his Pavlovian mental ban is lifted can no longer study science. An abusive father is also mentioned to have received such a ban; he proceeds to become very nice for a time, before eventually committing suicide.

The metal band Rorschach have a song titled "Pavlov's dogs" (the title being an obvious reference to Ivan Pavlov's experiment) whose lyrics also treat about classical conditioning.

One of the most popular singles by American singer-songwriter, Academy Awards and Grammy Award nominee, Aimee Mann's is the song "Pavlov's Bell," the lyrics of which explicitly compare Mann's own actions to those of the dogs in Pavlov's experiments. Aimee Mann performed the song on the television show *Buffy the Vampire Slayer*, during a 2002 episode in which a main cast member is being controlled by a form of classically conditioned trigger.

Rolling Stones reference Pavlov's early experiments in their song "Bitch" with the line "*Yeah when you call my name, I salivate like a Pavlov dog.*"

In the "Phyllis's Wedding" episode of NBC's TV series *The Office*, Jim conditions Dwight to want a breath mint whenever he hears a computer chime.

Operant Conditioning

Operant conditioning (or instrumental conditioning) is a type of learning in which an individual's behaviour is modified by its consequences; the behaviour may change in form, frequency, or strength. Operant conditioning is a term that was coined by B. F. Skinner in 1937. The word operant refers to, "an item of behaviour that is initially spontaneous, rather than a response to a prior stimulus, but whose consequences may reinforce or inhibit recurrence of that behaviour".

Operant conditioning is distinguished from *classical conditioning* (or *respondent conditioning*) in that operant conditioning deals with the modification of "voluntary behaviour" or operant behaviour. Operant behaviour operates on the environment and is maintained by its consequences, while classical conditioning deals with the conditioning of reflexive (reflex) behaviours which are elicited by antecedent conditions. Behaviours conditioned via a classical conditioning procedure are not maintained by consequences.

Historical Notes

Thorndike's Law of Effect: Operant conditioning, sometimes called *instrumental learning*, was first extensively studied by Edward L. Thorndike (1874–1949), who observed the behaviour of cats trying to escape from home-made puzzle boxes. When first constrained in the boxes, the cats took a long time to escape. With experience, ineffective responses occurred less frequently and successful responses occurred more frequently, enabling the cats to escape in less time over successive trials. In his law of effect, Thorndike theorized that behaviours followed by satisfying consequences tend to be repeated and those that produce unpleasant consequences are less likely to be repeated. In short, some consequences *strengthened* behaviour and some consequences *weakened* behaviour. Thorndike produced the first known animal learning curves through this procedure.

Skinner

B.F. Skinner (1904–1990) is the person whose work is most often cited in connection with operant conditioning. His book "The Behaviour of Organisms", published in 1938, initiated his lifelong study of operant conditioning and its application to human and animal behaviour. Following the ideas of Ernst Mach, Skinner rejected Thorndike's reference to unobservable mental states such as satisfaction, building his analysis on observable behaviour and its equally observable consequences.

To implement his empirical approach, Skinner invented the operant conditioning chamber in which subjects such as pigeons and rats were isolated from extraneous stimuli and free to make one or two simple, repeated responses. Another invention, the cumulative recorder, produced a graphical record of these responses from which response rates could be estimated. These records were the primary data that Skinner and his colleagues used to explore the effects on response rate of various reinforcement schedules. A reinforcement schedule may be defined as, "any procedure that delivers a reinforcer to an organism according to some well-defined rule". The effects of schedules became, in turn, the basic experimental data from which Skinner developed his account of operant conditioning. He also drew on many less formal observations of human and animal behaviour.

Many of Skinner's writings are devoted to the application of operant conditioning to human behaviour. In 1957, Skinner published *Verbal Behaviour*, which extended the principles of operant conditioning to language, a form of human behaviour that had previously been analyzed quite differently by linguists and others. Skinner defined new functional relationships such as "mands" and "tacts" to capture the essentials of language, but he introduced no new principles, treating verbal behaviour like any other behaviour controlled by its consequences, which included the reactions of the speaker's audience.

Tools and Procedures of Operant Conditioning

Consequences that shape behaviour: Reinforcement, punishment, and extinction

Reinforcement and punishment, the core tools of operant conditioning, are either positive (delivered following a response), or negative (withdrawn following a response). This creates a total of four basic consequences, with the addition of a fifth procedure known as extinction (i.e. no change in consequences following a response).

- Reinforcement is a consequence that causes a behaviour to occur with greater frequency.
- Punishment is a consequence that causes a behaviour to occur with less frequency.
- Extinction is caused by the lack of any consequence following a behaviour. When a behaviour is inconsequential (i.e.,

producing neither favourable nor unfavourable consequences) it will occur less frequently. When a previously reinforced behaviour is no longer reinforced with either positive or negative reinforcement, it leads to a decline in that behaviour.

It is important to note that actors are not spoken of as being reinforced, punished, or extinguished; it is the actions that are reinforced, punished, or extinguished. Additionally, reinforcement, punishment, and extinction are not terms whose use is restricted to the laboratory. Naturally occurring consequences can also be said to reinforce, punish, or extinguish behaviour and are not always delivered by people.

Five Operant Conditioning Procedures

Five procedures are defined by the presentation or removal of a reinforcement or punishment. Here the terms *positive* and *negative* are not used in their popular sense, but rather: *positive* refers to addition, and *negative* refers to subtraction. The procedures are:

1. Positive reinforcement (Reinforcement): Occurs when a behaviour (response) is followed by a stimulus that is appetitive or rewarding, increasing the frequency of that behaviour. In the Skinner box experiment, a stimulus such as food or a sugar solution can be delivered when the rat engages in a target behaviour, such as pressing a lever. This procedure is usually called simply *reinforcement.*
2. Negative reinforcement (Escape): Occurs when a behaviour (response) is followed by the removal of an aversive stimulus, thereby increasing that behaviour's frequency. In the Skinner box experiment, negative reinforcement can be a loud noise continuously sounding inside the rat's cage until it engages in the target behaviour, such as pressing a lever, upon which the loud noise is removed.
3. Positive punishment (Punishment) (also called "Punishment by contingent stimulation"): Occurs when a behaviour (response) is followed by a stimulus, such as introducing a shock or loud noise, resulting in a decrease in that behaviour. *Positive punishment* is sometimes a confusing term, as it denotes the "addition" of a stimulus or increase in the intensity of a stimulus that is aversive (such as spanking or an electric shock). This procedure is usually called simply *punishment.*

4. Negative punishment (Penalty) (also called "Punishment by contingent withdrawal"): Occurs when a behaviour (response) is followed by the removal of a stimulus, such as taking away a child's toy following an undesired behaviour, resulting in a decrease in that behaviour.
5. Extinction: Occurs when a behaviour (response) that had previously been reinforced is no longer effective. For example, a rat is first given food many times for lever presses. Then, in "extinction", no food is given. Typically the rat continues to press more and more slowly and eventually stops, at which time lever pressing is said to be "extinguished."

Some Other Common Terms and Procedures

- Escape and Avoidance In escape learning, a behaviour terminates an aversive stimulus. For example, shielding one's eyes from sunlight terminates the aversive stimulation of bright light in one's eyes. In avoidance learning, the behaviour precedes and prevents an aversive stimulus, for example putting on sun glasses before going outdoors. Because, in avoidance, the aversive stimulation does not occur, avoidance behaviour seems to have no means of reinforcement. Indeed this non-occurrence of the aversive stimulus has been a problem for reinforcement theory, which has been dealt with in various ways.
- Noncontingent reinforcement refers to delivery of reinforcing stimuli regardless of the organism's behaviour. Noncontingent reinforcement may be used in an attempt to reduce an undesired target behaviour by reinforcing multiple alternative responses while extinguishing the target response. As no measured behaviour is identified as being strengthened, there is controversy surrounding the use of the term noncontingent "reinforcement".
- Schedules of reinforcement Schedules of reinforcement are rules that control the delivery of reinforcement. The rules specify either the time that reinforcement is to be made available, or the number of responses to be made, or both.
  - o Fixed interval schedule: Reinforcement occurs following the first response after a fixed time has elapsed after the previous reinforcement.

- o Variable interval schedule: Reinforcement occurs following the first response after a variable time has elapsed from the previous reinforcement.
- o Fixed ratio schedule: Reinforcement occurs after a fixed number of responses have been emitted since the previous reinforcement.
- o Variable ratio schedule: Reinforcement occurs after a variable number of responses have been emitted since the previous reinforcement.
- o Continuous reinforcement: Reinforcement occurs after each response.

- Discrimination, generalization and context. Most behaviour is under stimulus control. Several aspects of this may be distinguished:
  - o "Discrimination" typically occurs when a response is reinforced only in the presence of a specific stimulus. For example, a pigeon might be fed for pecking at a red light and not at a green light; in consequence, it pecks at red and stops pecking at green. Many complex combinations of stimuli and other conditions have been studied; for example an organism might be reinforced on an interval schedule in the presence of one stimulus and on a ratio schedule in the presence of another.
  - o "Generalization" is the tendency to respond to stimuli that are similar to a previously trained discriminative stimulus. For example, having been trained to peck at "red" a pigeon might also peck at "pink", though usually less strongly.
  - o "Context" refers to stimuli that are continuously present in a situation, like the walls, tables, chairs, etc. in a room, or the interior of an operant conditioning chamber. Context stimuli may come to control behaviour as do discriminative stimuli, though usually more weakly. Behaviours learned in one context may be absent, or altered, in another. This may cause difficulties for behavioural therapy, because behaviours learned in the therapeutic setting may fail to occur elsewhere.

Operant Conditioning to Change Human Behaviour

Researchers have found the following protocol to be effective when they use the tools of operant conditioning to modify human behaviour:

1. State goal (aims for the study) That is, clarify exactly what changes are to be brought about. For example, "reduce weight by 30 pounds."
2. Monitor behaviour (log conditions) Keep track of behaviour so that one can see whether the desired effects are occurring. For example, keep a chart of daily weights.
3. Reinforce desired behaviour (give reward for proper behaviour) For example, congratulate the individual on weight losses. With humans, a record of behaviour may serve as a reinforcement. For example, when a participant sees a pattern of weight loss, this may reinforce continuance in a behavioural weight-loss programme. A more general plan is the token economy, an exchange system in which tokens are given as rewards for desired behaviours. Tokens may later be exchanged for a desired prize or rewards such as power, prestige, goods or services.
4. Reduce incentives to perform undesirable behaviour For example, remove candy and fatty snacks from kitchen shelves.

Factors that Alter the Effectiveness of Consequences

When using consequences to modify a response, the effectiveness of a consequence can be increased or decreased by various factors. These factors can apply to either reinforcing or punishing consequences.

1. Satiation/Deprivation: The effectiveness of a consequence will be reduced if the individual's "appetite" for that source of stimulation has been satisfied. Inversely, the effectiveness of a consequence will increase as the individual becomes deprived of that stimulus. If someone is not hungry, food will not be an effective reinforcer for behaviour. Satiation is generally only a potential problem with primary reinforcers, those that do not need to be learned such as food and water.
2. Immediacy: After a response, how immediately a consequence is then felt determines the effectiveness of the consequence. More immediate feedback will be more effective than less immediate feedback. If someone's license plate is caught by a traffic camera for speeding and they receive a speeding ticket in the mail a week later, this consequence will not be very effective against speeding. But if someone is speeding and is

caught in the act by an officer who pulls them over, then their speeding behaviour is more likely to be affected.

3. Contingency: If a consequence does not contingently (reliably, or consistently) follow the target response, its effectiveness upon the response is reduced. But if a consequence follows the response consistently after successive instances, its ability to modify the response is increased. The schedule of reinforcement, when consistent, leads to faster learning. When the schedule is variable the learning is slower. Extinction is more difficult when learning occurs during intermittent reinforcement and more easily extinguished when learning occurs during a highly consistent schedule.
4. Size: This is a "cost-benefit" determinant of whether a consequence will be effective. If the size, or amount, of the consequence is large enough to be worth the effort, the consequence will be more effective upon the behaviour. An unusually large lottery jackpot, for example, might be enough to get someone to buy a one-dollar lottery ticket (or even buying multiple tickets). But if a lottery jackpot is small, the same person might not feel it to be worth the effort of driving out and finding a place to buy a ticket. In this example, it's also useful to note that "effort" is a punishing consequence. How these opposing expected consequences (reinforcing and punishing) balance out will determine whether the behaviour is performed or not.

Most of these factors exist for biological reasons. The biological purpose of the Principle of Satiation is to maintain the organism's homeostasis. When an organism has been deprived of sugar, for example, the effectiveness of the taste of sugar as a reinforcer is high. However, as the organism reaches or exceeds their optimum blood-sugar levels, the taste of sugar becomes less effective, perhaps even aversive.

The Principles of Immediacy and Contingency exist for neurochemical reasons. When an organism experiences a reinforcing stimulus, dopamine pathways in the brain are activated. This network of pathways "releases a short pulse of dopamine onto many dendrites, thus broadcasting a rather global reinforcement signal to postsynaptic neurons." This results in the plasticity of these synapses allowing recently activated synapses to increase their sensitivity to efferent signals, hence increasing the probability of occurrence for the recent responses preceding the reinforcement. These responses are, statistically, the most likely to have been the behaviour responsible for successfully achieving reinforcement. But when the application of reinforcement is either less immediate or less contingent (less consistent), the ability of dopamine to act upon the appropriate synapses is reduced.

Operant Variability

Operant variability is what allows a response to adapt to new situations. Operant behaviour is distinguished from reflexes in that its response topography (the form of the response) is subject to slight variations from one performance to another. These slight variations can include small differences in the specific motions involved, differences in the amount of force applied, and small changes in the timing of the response.

If a subject's history of reinforcement is consistent, such variations will remain stable because the same successful variations are more likely to be reinforced than less successful variations. However, behavioural variability can also be altered when subjected to certain controlling variables.

Avoidance Learning

In avoidance learning an organism's behaviour is reinforced by the termination or prevention of an aversive stimulus. There are two kinds of commonly used experimental settings: discriminated and free-operant avoidance learning.

Discriminated Avoidance Learning

In discriminated avoidance learning, a novel stimulus such as a light or a tone is followed by an aversive stimulus such as a shock (CS-US, similar to classical conditioning). During the first trials (called escape-trials) the animal usually experiences both the CS (Conditioned Stimulus) and the US (Unconditioned Stimulus), showing the operant response to terminate the aversive US. During later trials, the animal will learn to perform the response already during the presentation of the CS thus preventing the aversive US from occurring. Such trials are called "avoidance trials."

Free-operant Avoidance Learning

In this experimental session, no discrete stimulus is used to signal the occurrence of the aversive stimulus. Rather, the aversive stimulus (mostly shocks) are presented without explicit warning stimuli. There are two crucial time intervals determining the rate of avoidance learning. This first one is called the S-S-interval (shock-shock-interval). This is the amount of time which passes during successive presentations of the shock (unless the operant response is performed). The other one is called the R-S-interval (response-shock-interval) which specifies the length of the time interval following an operant response during which no shocks will be delivered. Note that each time the organism performs the operant response, the R-S-interval without shocks begins anew.

Two-Process Theory of Avoidance

This theory was originally proposed in order to explain discriminated avoidance learning, in which an organism learns to avoid an aversive stimulus by escaping from a signal for that stimulus. The theory assumes that two processes take place:

Classical Conditioning of Fear: During the first trials of the training, the organism experiences the pairing of a CS with an aversive US. The theory assumes that during these trials an association develops between the CS and the US through classical conditioning and, because of the aversive nature of the US, the CS comes to elicit a conditioned emotional reaction (CER) – "fear."

Reinforcement of the Operant Response by Fear-reduction: As a result of the first process, the CS now signals fear; this unpleasant emotional reaction serves to motivate operant responses, and those responses that terminate the CS are reinforced by fear termination. Although, after this training, the organism no longer experiences the aversive US, the term "avoidance" may be something of a misnomer, because the theory does not say that the organism "avoids" the US in the sense of anticipating it, but rather that the organism escapes an aversive internal state that is caused by the CS.

Four Term Contingency

Applied behaviour analysis, which is the name of the discipline directly descended from Skinner's work, holds that behaviour is explained in four terms: conditioned stimulus (S^c), a discriminative stimulus (S^d), a response (R), and a reinforcing stimulus (S^{rein} or S^r for reinforcers, sometimes S^{ave} for aversive stimuli).

Operant Hoarding

Operant hoarding is a referring to the choice made by a rat, on a compound schedule called a multiple schedule, that maximizes its rate of reinforcement in an operant conditioning context. More specifically, rats were shown to have allowed food pellets to accumulate in a food tray by continuing to press a lever on a continuous reinforcement schedule instead of retrieving those pellets.

Retrieval of the pellets always instituted a one-minute period of extinction during which no additional food pellets were available but those that had been accumulated earlier could be consumed. This finding appears to contradict the usual finding that rats behave impulsively in situations in which there is a choice between a smaller food object right away and a larger food object after some delay.

Biological Correlates of Operant Conditioning

The first scientific studies identifying neurons that responded in ways that suggested they encode for conditioned stimuli came from work by Mahlon deLong and by R.T. Richardson. They showed that nucleus basalis neurons, which release acetylcholine broadly throughout the cerebral cortex, are activated shortly after a conditioned stimulus, or after a primary reward if no conditioned stimulus exists.

These neurons are equally active for positive and negative reinforcers, and have been demonstrated to cause plasticity in many cortical regions. Evidence also exists that dopamine is activated at similar times. There is considerable evidence that dopamine participates in both reinforcement and aversive learning.

Dopamine pathways project much more densely onto frontal cortex regions. Cholinergic projections, in contrast, are dense even in the posterior cortical regions like the primary visual cortex. A study of patients with Parkinson's disease, a condition attributed to the insufficient action of dopamine, further illustrates the role of dopamine in positive reinforcement. It showed that while off their medication, patients learned more readily with aversive consequences than with positive reinforcement. Patients who were on their medication showed the opposite to be the case, positive reinforcement proving to be the more effective form of learning when the action of dopamine is high.

Operant Conditioning in Economics

Both psychologists and economists have become interested in applications of operant conditioning concepts and findings to the behaviour of humans in the marketplace. One concept that encompasses both of economics and instrumental conditioning is consumer demand. With consumer demand,the focus is on the price of the commodity and the amount purchased. The degree to which price influences consumption is defined as being the elasticity of demand. Certain commodities are more elastic than others.

Price change in certain foods can affect the amount bought, while gasoline and essentials seem to be less effected by price changes. For these examples, gasoline and essentials would be less elastic than certain foods like cake and candy. On a graph model representation, something less elastic would not be stretched out as far as a commodity that's consumption fluctuates greatly due to the price.

Questions About the Law of Effect

A number of observations seem to show that operant behaviour can be established without reinforcement in the sense defined above. Most cited is the phenomenon of autoshaping (sometimes called "sign tracking"), in which a stimulus is repeatedly followed by reinforcement, and in consequence the animal begins to respond to the stimulus.

For example, a response key is lighted and then food is presented. When this is repeated a few times a pigeon subject begins to peck the key even though food comes whether the bird pecks or not. Similarly, rats begin to handle small objects, such as a lever, when food is presented nearby. Strikingly, pigeons and rats persist in this behaviour even when pecking the key or pressing the lever leads to less food (omission training).

These observations and others appear to contradict the law of effect, and they have prompted some researchers to propose new conceptualizations of operant reinforcement (e.g. A more general view is that autoshaping is an instance of classical conditioning; the autoshaping procedure has, in fact, become one of the most common ways to measure classical conditioning. In this view, many behaviours can be influenced by both classical contingencies (stimulus-reinforcement) and operant contingencies (response-reinforcement), and the experimenter's task is to work out how these interact.

Transformative Learning

At the core of transformative learning theory is the process of "perspective transformation" with three dimensions: psychological (changes in understanding of the self), convictional (revision of belief systems), and behavioural (changes in lifestyle).

"Transformative learning is the expansion of consciousness through the transformation of basic worldview and specific capacities of the self; transformative learning is facilitated through consciously directed processes such as appreciatively accessing and receiving the symbolic contents of the unconscious and critically analyzing underlying premises."

Perspective transformation leading to transformative learning occurs infrequently. Mezirow believes that it usually results from a *disorienting dilemma*, which is triggered by a life crisis or major life transition, although it may also result from an accumulation of transformations in meaning schemes over a period of time. Less dramatic predicaments, such as those created by a teacher, also promote transformation.

An important part of transformative learning is for individuals to change their frames of reference by critically reflecting on their assumptions and beliefs and consciously making and implementing plans that bring about new ways of defining their worlds. This process is fundamentally rational and analytical.

Other Perspectives

There are a number of critical responses to Mezirow's theory of transformative learning have emerged over the years. One criticism of Mezirow's theory is its emphasis upon rationality. Some studies support Mezirow. Others conclude that Mezirow grants rational critical reflection too much importance. Taylor has since suggested neurobiological research as a promising area that may offer some explanation about the role emotions play, closing the gap between rationality and emotion in the transformative learning process. Taylor implies that with available modern technology such as magnetic resonance imaging (MRI) and positron emission topography (PET), these once obscure factors can now be examined through determining which neurological brain systems are at work during disorienting dilemmas and the journey of recovery that follows. This research also stresses the importance of the role of implicit memory, from which emerges habits, attitudes and preferences that are related to unconscious thoughts and actions.

While this learning process is certainly rational on some levels, it is also a profound experience that can be described as a spiritual or emotional transformation as well. The experience of undoing racist, sexist, and other oppressive attitudes can be painful and emotional, as these attitudes have often been developed as ways to cope with and make sense of the world. This type of learning requires taking risks, and a willingness to be vulnerable and have one's attitudes and assumptions challenged.

Other theorists have proposed a view of transformative learning as an intuitive and emotional process. Dirkx, Boyd, Myers and Ruether link Mezirow's rational, cognitive and analytical approach to a more intuitive, creative and holistic view of transformative learning. This view of transformative learning is based primarily on the work of Robert Boyd, who has developed a theory of transformative education based on analytical (or depth) psychology.

For Boyd, transformation is a "fundamental change in one's personality involving [together] the resolution of a personal dilemma and the expansion of consciousness resulting in greater personality integration." This calls upon extrarational sources such as symbols, images, and archetypes to assist in creating a personal vision or meaning of what it means to be human.

First, an individual must be receptive or open to receiving "alternative expressions of meaning," and then recognize that the message is authentic. Grieving, considered by Boyd to be the most critical phase of the discernment process, takes place when an individual realizes that old patterns or ways of perceiving are no longer relevant, moves to adopt or establish new ways, and finally, integrates old and new patterns.

More recent research has specifically explored the process of transformative learning as it occurs in bereaved elders, maintaining that the "disorienting dilemma" deemed necessary by Mezirow is present in the loss of a loved one, with an additional devastating factor being the isolation that the elderly in particular are likely to face. In another study, transformative learning in the context of suicide bereavement; in these cases the dilemma is compounded by the questioning of conceptions or misconceptions that were held about the relationship with the deceased and resolving the meaning of that relationship during the grieving process.

Unlike Mezirow, who sees the ego as playing a central role in the process of perspective transformation, Boyd and Myers use a framework that moves beyond the ego and the emphasis on reason and logic to a definition of transformative learning that is more psychosocial in nature.

Another definition of transformative learning was put forward by O'Sullivan:

Transformative learning involves experiencing a deep, structural shift in the basic premises of thought, feelings, and actions. It is a shift of consciousness that dramatically and irreversibly alters our way of being in the world.

Such a shift involves our understanding of ourselves and our self-locations; our relationships with other humans and with the natural world; our understanding of relations of power in interlocking structures of class, race and gender; our body awarenesses, our visions of alternative approaches to living; and our sense of possibilities for social justice and peace and personal joy.

Positing that understanding transformative learning may have been hindered by perspectives of rational thought and Western traditions, King provides an alternate model grounded in a meta-analysis of research, the *Transformative Learning Opportunities Model.*

Recent considerations of these varying perspectives seem to indicate that one perspective does not need to exclude the other. For example, Mezirow and Dirkx discussed their views on transformative learning at a 2005 International Transformative Learning Conference. This dialogue, facilitated by Cranton, continued via email after the conference and the overview was published in The Journal of Transformative Education. Dirkx focuses on subjectivity, in the power of the inner world in one's shift in view of the outer world. Mezirow emphasizes critical assessment of assumptions. Although their approaches are different, they agree that their perspectives are similar in several aspects. This includes transforming frames of reference that have lost meaning or have become dysfunctional and fostering enhanced awareness and consciousness of one's being in the world. Both perspectives are required to deepen understanding and to incorporate these ways of learning into transformative education.

One of the difficulties in defining transformative learning is that it bleeds into the boundaries of concepts such as "meaning making" or "critical thinking".

The term "meaning making" (i.e., constructing meaning) is found most frequently in constructivist approaches to education, based on the work of educators such as John Dewey, Maria Montessori, Jean Piaget, Jerome Bruner, and Lev Vygotsky. In the constructivist view, meaning is constructed from knowledge.

Mezirow posits that all learning is change but not all change is transformation. There is a difference between transmissional, transactional and transformational education. In the first, knowledge is transmitted from teacher to student.

In transactional education, it is recognized that the student has valuable experiences, and learns best through experience, enquiry, critical thinking and interaction with other learners. It could be argued that some of the research regarding transformative learning has been in the realm of transactional education, and that what is seen as transformative by some authors is in fact still within the realm of transactional learning.

According to Brookfield, learning can only be considered transformative if it involves a fundamental questioning or reordering of how one thinks or acts; a challenge to hegemonic implications. In other words, reflection alone does not result in transformative learning unless the process involves a critical reflection, a recognition and analysis of taken for granted assumptions.

Transformative Learning in Practice

On the surface, the two views of transformative learning presented here are contradictory. One advocates a rational approach that depends primarily on critical reflection whereas the other relies more on intuition and emotion. However, the differences in the two views may best be seen as a matter of emphasis. Both utilize rational processes and incorporate imagination as a part of a creative process. The two different views of transformative learning described here as well as examples of how it occurs in practice suggest that no single model of transformative learning exists.

When transformative learning is the goal of adult education, fostering a learning environment in which it can occur should consider the following:

The Role of the Educator

In order to foster transformative learning, the educator's role is to assist learners in becoming aware and critical of assumptions. This includes their own assumptions that lead to their interpretations, beliefs, habits of mind or points of view as well as the assumptions of others. Educators must provide learners practice in recognizing frames of reference. By doing so, educators encourage practice in redefining problems from different perspectives. The goal is to create a community of learners who are "united in a shared experience of trying to make meaning of their life experience".

Educators need to provide learners with opportunities to effectively participate in discourse. Discourse involves assessing beliefs, feelings, and values. This dialogue has the goal of assessing reasons behind competing interpretations through critical examination of evidence, arguments, and alternate points of view. Learners are able to validate how and what they understand as well as develop well-informed judgements regarding a belief. Educators can encourage critical reflection and experience with discourse through the implementation of methods including metaphor analysis, concept mapping, consciousness raising, life histories, repertory grids, and participation in social action.

The educator must encourage equal participation among students in discourse. One strategy is to encourage procedures that require group members to take on the roles of monitoring the direction of dialogue and ensuring equal participation. Educators can also encourage dialogue from different perspectives through controversial statements or readings from opposing points of view. It is necessary that the educator avoids shaping the discussion.

The role of educators is also to set objectives that include autonomous thinking. By fostering learners' critical reflection and experience in discourse, autonomous thinking is possible. The foundations to thinking autonomously begin in childhood and continue in adulthood. The educator assists adult learners in becoming more critical in assessing assumptions, better at recognizing frames of references and alternate perspectives, as well as effective at collaborating with others to assess and arrive at judgements in regards to beliefs.

It is the role of the educator to promote discovery learning through the implementation of classroom methods such as learning contracts, group projects, role play, case studies, and simulations. These methods facilitate transformative learning by helping learners examine concepts in the context of their lives and analyze the justification of new knowledge.

The educator's role in establishing an environment that builds trust and care and facilitates the development of sensitive relationships among learners is a fundamental principle of fostering transformative learning. The educator also serves as a role model by demonstrating a willingness to learn and change. As a result, professional development is important to assist educators in becoming authentic and critically reflective.

The Role of the Learner

The educator becomes a facilitator when the goal of learning is for learners to construct knowledge about themselves, others, and social norms. As a result, learners play an important role in the learning environment and process.

Learners must create norms within the classroom that include civility, respect, and responsibility for helping one another learn. Learners must welcome diversity within the learning environment and aim for peer collaboration.

Learners must become critical of their own assumptions in order to transform their unquestioned frame of reference. Through communicative learning, learners must work towards critically reflecting assumptions that underlie intentions, values, beliefs, and feelings. Learners are involved in objective reframing of their frames of reference when they critically reflect on the assumptions of others. In contrast, subjective reframing occurs when learners critically assess their own assumptions.

The role of the learner involves actively participating in discourse. Through discourse, learners are able to validate what is being communicated to them. This dialogue provides the opportunity to critically examine evidence, arguments, and alternate points of view which fosters collaborative learning.

The Role of Professional Development for the Educator

Transformative learning about teaching occurs when educators critically examine their practice and develop alternative perspectives of understanding their practice. It is essential that this becomes the role of professional development. With this taken into consideration, the role of professional development is to assist educators in bringing awareness to their habit of minds regarding teaching. When this occurs, educators critically examine the assumptions that underlie their practice, the consequences to their assumptions, and develop alternative perspectives on their practice.

Teachers need education and professional development that will help them to question, challenge and experience critical discussions on school improvement. Transforming teachers so they see themselves as agents of social change can be a challenge within education.

Strategies for transformative professional development include action plans, reflective activities, case studies, curriculum development and critical theory discussions. Action plans and reflective activities provide practice and modelling of critical reflection on the profession of education and provide guidance for the teaching and learning experience. Through the use of real-life examples, case studies provide opportunity to analyze assumptions as well as the consequences of choices and actions.

This provides focus for reflection on practice and the opportunity to be involved in discourse to analyze philosophical and practical aspects of educators' practice. Curriculum development creates the opportunity to connect theory and practice. In addition to introducing new teaching techniques, educators can test and compare these new concepts and practices with previous techniques.

This moves away from uncritically accepting new teaching methods. Critical theory discussions can be implemented to guide educators to question the purpose and meaning of information. This then fosters opportunity for educators to question the selection of information they provide for their students.

Examples of Transformative Learning in Educator Professional Development

Mentoring is another strategy for transformative professional, personal and organizational development. By creating a supportive culture, mentoring can provide the environment for transformative learning to occur. Through this experience mentoring becomes a transformative relationship in which individuals reconstruct possible selves. As a two-way process, mentoring is a learning tool for both the mentor as well as the mentee.

In a recent study, Swanson applied theories of critical reflection, critical incident model and a learning partnership to design a programme for practicing teachers with the purpose of transformative teacher development.

Experiences were created to support teachers in reflecting on their assumptions, ask them to consider alternative perspectives and develop a language for making connections between theory and practice. Over this two year period, teachers were able to develop ownership and transfer this knowledge into their practice. To be effective, transformative teacher development must value what teachers bring from their personal and professional experience and acknowledge that learning is both an individual and social experience. The process involved: transparency through negotiation of curriculum and finding a common language through discussion of individual assumptions, continuous feedback through critical incident questions, and action research through teacher application of the programme within their classrooms.

Autobiography and journaling were additional techniques used to within this learning partnership. Both teachers and faculty participating in the programme were transformed as beliefs were challenged and knowledge was co-constructed through the experience.

New academics often find expectations ambiguous and lack the self-awareness and understanding to navigate the educational environment. A transformative learning framework was used in a Foundations course for participants to build on individual and collective analysis of teaching experiences and help them to reframe their practice.

The author investigated 'transformation narratives' which emerged from written reflection of participants teaching practice. Reflections were based on individual reflection and group discussion.

By using Mezirow's work along with Kegan's constructive developmental theory Constructivism (learning theory), the author found the following themes: a move from non-reflective habitual action to a more conscious practice, a change in perspective to a more sophisticated view of teaching, an increased sense of agency including the concept that academic practice is an object which can be controlled and shaped rather than something externally imposed, increased confidence to take risks and experiment, and a more multifaceted idea of what it means to be an academic.

The conducive environment allowed for transformative experiences to occur. Through creation of a safe social context where 'disorienting dilemmas' can be examined, questioned and explored participants were able to develop a new 'frame of reference'and reintegrate learning into practice.

The author cautions that there are limitations to the framework such as the possibility that participants will conform to expectations in their reflections. The author notes that the 'transformation narratives' examined are not a single, final narrative of the self but a snapshot for further exploration. Similar to Fletcher's findings, transformative learning helps to make sense of a complex and often ambiguous work environment which requires multiple selves.

Benefits of Transformative Learning—

When learning is contextualized in a community, connected to one's social identities, and when it asks a group of learners to be better as a people, it is not generally forgotten, because it holds tremendous importance for the learner. As a result, transformative learning develops autonomous thinking that is transferable to other learning contexts.

Challenges of Transformative Learning Environments

While supporting engagement of the entire class, often the most self-efficacious students will voice their suggestions, ideas and concerns. Those with lower self-efficacy can become spectators if not given equal encouragement to participate. Transformative learning inherently requires taking risks and a willingness to be vulnerable and have ones attitude and assumptions challenged.

Acknowledging the Role of Self-Efficacy in Transformative Learning

Psychologist Albert Bandura has defined self-efficacy as one's belief in one's ability to succeed in specific situations. One's sense of self-efficacy can play a major role in how one approaches goals, tasks, and challenges. The theory of self-efficacy lies at the centre of Bandura's social cognitive theory, which emphasizes the role of observational learning and social experience in the development of personality. The main concept in social cognitive theory is that an individual's actions and reactions, including social behaviours and cognitive processes, in almost every situation are influenced by the actions that individual has observed in others. Because self-efficacy is developed from external experiences and self-perception and is influential in determining the outcome of many events, it is an important aspect of social cognitive theory. Self-efficacy represents the personal perception of external social factors. According to Bandura's theory, people with high self-efficacy—that is, those who believe they can perform well—are more likely to view difficult tasks as something to be mastered rather than something to be avoided.

In a transformative learning environment, consideration of one's current level of self-efficacy can assist both the Educator and student in preparing for engagement in discourse. As frames of reference play a critical role in shaping one's past and present assumptions or beliefs, so to do they influence the self-efficacy of an individual participating in adult learning activities.

Academic Self-efficacy

In a study, the majority of a group of students questioned felt they had a difficulty with listening in class situations. Instructors then helped strengthen their listening skills by making them aware about how the use of different strategies could produce better outcomes.

This way, their levels of self-efficacy were improved as they continued to figure out what strategies worked for them. Understanding how to foster the development of self-efficacy is important for educators, and others in leadership positions, and to anyone seeking to build happier, more productive, and highly efficacious students.

Through transformative learning, the Educator plays a similar role in facilitating the development of trust, care and sensitivity, so that students feel empowered to discuss their assumptions and beliefs in a way that works best for them, while incorporating strategies that best accommodate their current level of self-efficacy.

The Destiny Idea Further information: Locus of Control

Bandura also showed that difference in self-efficacy correlates to fundamentally different world views. People with high self-efficacy generally believe that they are in control of their own lives, that their own actions and decisions shape their lives, while people with low self-efficacy may see their lives as outside their control.

Such evidence speaks directly to the outcomes of transformative learning, in that the assumptions, beliefs and values of individuals (as a result of their level of self-efficacy), can potentially shape the direction of the critical discourse taking place in the classroom, based on their feelings of either being in control or not in control of their destiny.

Social Learning Theory

Social learning theory describes the acquisition of skills that are developed exclusively or primarily within a social group. Social learning depends on how individuals either succeed or fail at dynamic interactions within groups, and promotes the development of individual emotional and practical skills as well as accurate perception of self and acceptance of others. According to this theory, people learn from one another through observation, imitation, and modelling. Self-efficacy reflects an individual's understanding of what skills he/she can offer in a group setting.

Transformative learning ideally promotes equal participation among members of a group, as they work towards establishing a consensus in exploring the depths of subject matter. Should an individual feel they can either offer a lot, in comparison with one who feels they can offer little, the equal participation in transformative learning may become more difficult to attain.

The Role of the Rational and the Affective

Transformative learning has two components that at times seem to be in conflict: the cognitive, rational, and objective and the intuitive, imaginative, and subjective. Both the rational and the affective play a role in transformative learning. Although the emphasis has been on transformative learning as a rational process, teachers need to consider how they can help students use feelings and emotions both in critical reflection and as a means of reflection.

There are a number of educational and research institutions that are based on the principles of transformative learning. Some examples include the Transformative Studies Institute and The Transformative Learning Centre at the Ontario Institute for Studies on Education (OISE) of the University of Toronto.

Evidences are emerging on the applicability of transformative theory in new educational programmes. Some examples include in business and industry education, health professional education, community education such as courses offered by YMCA, and informal settings such as self-help groups. Describes how students in a service-learning section experienced perspective transformation and shifts of their world-view when their training was derived in part by the principles of transformative learning theory.

Bibliography

Allen, G. : *New Education: American Opinion*, May issue, 1971.

Banach, Banach, and Cassidy: *The Abc Complete Book Of School Marketing*, Ray Township, MI: Author, 1996.

Boud. D. and Miller, N. : *Working with Experience: Animating Learning*, London, Routledge, 1997.

Bransford, J., Brown, A. L., & Cocking, R. R.: *How People Learn: Brain, Mind, Experience, and School*, National Academies Press, Washington, 2000.

Cenkner, William : *A Tradition of Teachers: Sankara and the Jagadgurus Today*, Delhi, Motilal Banarsidass, 1983.

Chaklader, Snehamoy : *Sociolinguistics: A Guide to Language Problems in India*, New Delhi, Mittal, 1990.

Clark, R. C. and Zuckerman, P.: *Handbook of Human Performance Technology*, Pfeiffer, San Francisco, 1999.

Clark, R.C., Nguyen, F., and Sweller, J.: *Efficiency in Learning: Evidence-Based Guidelines to Manage Cognitive Load*, Pfeiffer, San Francisco, 2006.

de Jong, T.: *Cambridge Handbook of Multimedia Learning,* Cambridge University Press, Cambridge, UK, 2005.

DeVries: *Developing Constructivist Early Childhood Curriculum: Practical Principles and Activities*, Teachers College Press, New York, 2002.

Duckworth, E. R.: *"The having of Wonderful Ideas" and other Essays on Teaching and Learning,* Teachers College Press, New York, 2006.

Duffy, T.M. & Jonassen, D.: *Constructivism and the Technology of Instruction: A conversation*, Lawrence Erlbaum Associates, Hillsdale NJ, 1992.

Fordham, P., Holland, D. and Millican, J. : *Adult Literacy, A Handbook for Development Workers*, Oxford, Oxfam, 1995.

Galbraith, M.W. : *Education Through Community Organizations*, San Francisco, Jossey-Bass, 1990.

Jonassen, D., Mayes, T., & McAleese, R.: *Designing Environments for Constructive Learning,* Springer-Verlag, Heidelberg, 2002.

Kincheloe, Joe L. Toil and Trouble: *Good Work, Smart Workers, and the Integration of Academic and Vocational Education*, Peter Lang Publishing, New York, 1995.

Kincheloe, Joe L.: *How Do We Tell the Workers? The Socio-Economic Foundations of Work and Vocational Education,* Westview Press, Boulder, CO, 1999.

Kolb, D. A. & Fry, R.: *Theories of Group Process*, John Wiley, London, 1975.

Mayo, M. : *Communities and Caring: The mixed economy of welfare*, London, Macmillan, 1994.

Piaget, Jean: *The Psychology of Intelligence*, Routledge, New York, 1950.

Premi, M.K. : *Educational Planning in India*, New Delhi, Sterling, 1972.

Reeves, Diane Lindsey: *Career Academy Toolkit*, Bright Futures Press, Raleigh, North Carolina, 2006.

Ries, A., and Trout, J.: *The 22 Immutable Laws Of Marketing*, HarperCollins Publishers, New York, 1993.

Rogers, A. : *Adults Learning for Development*, London, Cassell, 1992.

Scott, C. : *Social Education*, Boston, Ginn and Co., 1908.

Sewell, Robert : *A Forgotten Empire: Vijayanagar*, London, Sonnenschein, 1900.

Sweller, J.: *Instructional Design in Technical Areas*, ACER Press, Camberwell, Australia, 1999.

Sweller, J.: *The Psychology of Learning and Motivation*, Academic Press, San Diego, 2003.

Vygotskii, L.S.: *Mind in Society: The Development of Higher Mental Processes*, Harvard University Press, Cambridge, MA, 1978.

Wolf, A.: *Does Education Matter? Myths about Education and Economic Growth,* Penguin, London, 2002.

Wood, D.: *How Children Think and Learn,* Blackwell Publishers Ltd., Oxford, 1998.

Index

□□□